LOOKING FOR YOUR SELF IN ALL THE WRONG PLACES

How To Recognize Your
Authentic Self
To Live On Your Terms

Stephen R. Van Schoyck, Ph.D.

To My Patients . . .

CONTENTS

ACKNOWLEDGEMENTS

This book would never have been written without the help of two key people. It began with my desire to create a framework to understand the patterns that I observed with my patients over 35 years of practice. I sent several hundred pages of my thoughts to my editor, Nellie Sabin and asked for her feedback. In her inimitable style, Nellie said there was great stuff in those pages but "it read like it fell off the top of my car". She spent nearly a year digesting and organizing the material before we met in her home. She outlined four books for me from the material I had sent; one about the self, a second about marriage, a third about the family and a fourth about the nation. This is the first book she envisioned.

Nellie painstakingly edited the chapters I sent her. The organization of this book demonstrates the clarity of her mind and her emotional investment in the material. I thank her for the personal effort she made to make this book possible.

This book could not have happened without the help of my wife Diane. Her struggles in her life helped shape my framework and knowledge about how a scapegoat survives in a family. I learned much from her about the right to be angry and the tenacity required to survive against difficult circumstances.

I will always be grateful for the privilege of treating the people who trusted me to share their emotions and lives with me as my patients. I believe the patterns that I saw in their lives are universal patterns. I hope that the readers of this book will see those same patterns in their lives and that this book will enrich the lives of all who read it.

INTRODUCTION...65,000 Hours

After one particularly long day, I calculated that over the past 35 years I have spent at least 65,000 hours sitting in an office chair talking to people about their lives. I'm not complaining. To me there is nothing more interesting than figuring out other people's problems, and nothing more gratifying than watching my patient learn to live a more satisfying life.

I wrote *LOOKING FOR YOUR SELF IN ALL THE WRONG PLACES* because I wanted others to put into practice what I have learned from witnessing the suffering and joys of my patients. I studied a lot about psychology in school for many years, but I've learned even more from listening to them. I have had the rare privilege of being exposed to the most intimate emotions that people experience. I get to see what others do not see. I thank my patients every day for the trust that they place in me. As a result of that trust, I have gained invaluable insights into what makes people tick. I see the enormous significance of small things, and the emotional patterns that people unknowingly retrace again and again.

I see people who are in pain, relationships in jeopardy, and patients who are mystified by their own behavior. I also see awareness awakened, lives turned around, and relationships restored. My patients have shown me the answers that will change your way of life. Now I want to share that information with you.

Come sit in my chair and you will learn a whole new psychology that finally fits the American way of life. I realized that the essential skill we must learn in order to untangle our complicated lives is how to recognize our authentic emotions. After years of studying, self-examination, clinical experience, and reflection, I created the New American Psychology to provide my patients with a completely different way of viewing their inner emotional lives.

Reading this book is like picking up a new pair of glasses and being able to see yourself and others in a completely different way.

You will learn how to avoid the automatic, unthinking reactions that create problems in your life, and how to make thoughtful decisions with positive consequences. Once you start being true to your emotions, you'll have more satisfying relationships with other people and the world becomes a warmer and friendlier place.

This book is designed to help you by providing a new approach to everyday well-being. It will meet you where you are, whether things are basically OK, or your life has gone seriously off the rails.

In *LOOKING FOR YOUR SELF IN ALL THE WRONG PLACES*, I illustrate how The New American Psychology works in real life by including case histories of real people dealing with genuine problems. You will hear men, women, and children of different backgrounds tell their stories. You will hear what they have to say about love, hate, anger, fear, sex, and pain. You will overhear parents despairing about their kids, and kids fuming about their parents. You will learn about other people's successes and defeats; about their problems with family, fidelity, and work; about the relationships they hold dear and the ones they lost. And you will discover that, despite outward differences, these people are a lot like you. They will change your life forever.

Dr. "Van"

*I have changed all the names and identifying information in case histories to protect the privacy of my patients.

"No man can, for any considerable time, wear one face to himself and another to the multitude, without getting bewildered as to which is the true one"

Nathaniel Hawthorn

"The individual has always had to struggle to keep from being overwhelmed by the tribe. If you try it, you will be lonely often, and sometimes frightened. But no price is too high to pay for the privilege of owning yourself."

– Friedrich Nietzsche

What No One Has Ever Taught You
And What . . .
My Patients Have Taught Me

LOOKING FOR YOUR SELF IN ALL THE WRONG PLACES will provide a new way for you to understand why people behave the way they do, and why they say the things they say. This includes you. Even counterintuitive or self-destructive behaviors have their logic and can be explained using the concepts in this book.

Lisa's Story: The Good Girl Goes Bad

When Lisa first stepped into my office, I was confused about why she was there. She had left me a vague message about its being time to "talk to someone," but I did not know what she wanted to talk about. Lisa was cheerful, out-going, nicely dressed, and seemed like the kind of loving mother who would listen to your problems and give you good advice. Why was she coming to me for help?

In fact, Lisa was all these things. She made everyone else feel comfortable and seemed very content. But I am no longer surprised when the words and pictures don't match that is when a patient comes to me looking fine but feeling distressed inside, or looking fragile and haunted but being very self-aware. I soon learned that Lisa had a secret. I asked my usual opening question: "So, how can I help you today?" After several false starts and the sudden appearance of tears,

Lisa told me she felt frantic inside Sometimes she thought about just getting into her car and driving and driving…but then she would remember her two children and keep steering her car toward the mall, the grocery store, the toy store, or her lover's house.

Nothing surprises me anymore. Although Lisa considered herself happily married, she had taken up with a younger man she described as "completely inappropriate." She couldn't even explain what she saw in him.

But neither could she stop sneaking off to see him. She knew she was risking her marriage and entire family life, and worried incessantly about being found out…but she couldn't stop.

It did not take long to find out that Lisa had always been The Good Girl in her family. Being good became even more important when Lisa's older brother starting talking back to their parents and getting into trouble – crashing the car, selling drugs, staying out all night, and upsetting their parents so much that their father yelled constantly and their mother spent much of her time crying. She did not have any emotional energy left for Lisa, who felt she should give her parents as few problems as possible to make up for her brother's behavior.

Lisa's brother continued to be ornery and destructive, getting into scrapes with the police and taking risks with behavior that would land him in jail if he got caught. Lisa's parents lived in fear for him, but no amount of yelling or crying persuaded him to change.

Lisa was the angel in the family. She turned into a lovely teenager who behaved politely, soothed her mother, never upset her father, went to church, got good grades, became a cheerleader, and volunteered at the food pantry on weekends. After graduating from high school, she went to a nearby college so she could come home and visit her mother – where she performed well and got a reputation as a "goody-goody." Having learned from her brother's example, she would not go near drugs or alcohol, and developed a small circle of goody-goody friends, one of whom, Kent, she married after graduation.

Lisa's parents were ecstatic. Lisa had a beautiful wedding – except for her brother, who drank too much, gave a profane toast, was rude to the guests, and threw up on the dance floor. Although Lisa's parents were beyond mortified, they both felt this was not the place to have a family scene. They soldiered on as if nothing was wrong until Lisa's brother passed out, which was a huge relief for everyone.

After getting married, Lisa followed a well-worn path. She had two beautiful children, went to all their recitals and games, became a PTA president, was active in her church, sent cards and gifts to her in-laws, and was polite and supportive to everyone. She maintained a spotless home, where she did the laundry on Mondays, ironed on Tuesdays, changed the sheets on Wednesdays, washed the blinds on Thursdays, and vacuumed on Fridays. That is until she met TJ.

Lisa was at a birthday dinner for a PTA board member when she saw TJ sitting alone at the bar. Her own reaction amazed her. It was if her body had been dormant for 38 years and it suddenly woke up. It was clear that TJ, unlike Lisa's husband, was not a goody-goody. He was probably ten years younger than Lisa and had long, wavy hair to below his collar. He was wearing a sweatshirt with the sleeves cut off which carelessly revealed his muscles and broad chest. His boots and jeans did not indicate what kind of work he did, and Lisa thought he had an air of mystery around him. She kept glancing at him surreptitiously, trying not to let the other PTA mothers see what she was doing. Finally, her cheeks burning, she boldly walked past him, pretending she had to go to the bathroom. After hyperventilating in the bathroom for a few minutes, she walked past him the other way. He glanced up from his beer and looked at her narrowly. Lisa smiled brightly and returned to her table, astonished at what she had just done.

After lunch was over, Lisa dawdled at the table looking in her purse for her keys, certain that TJ was watching her. Her heart was beating as fast as a rabbit's. She left the restaurant as casually as she could, and walked to her car.

"Ma'am, if you'd excuse me, I wonder if I could trouble you for a ride to the auto body shop?" said a deep voice behind her. It was TJ, and that was the moment Lisa lost her mind. She answered politely that it would be no trouble at all, and they ended up driving directly to TJ's house.

Lisa returned home an hour later than usual, and no one noticed. She was self-aware enough to realize this incident was completely disconnected from her normal suburban life, but she has no clue why she had just done what she did – and why she wanted to do it again. Her own behavior made absolutely no sense to her. Where was it coming from?

Lisa had been secretly meeting TJ for several weeks before she scared herself into coming to see me. I began Lisa's treatment the same way I do with any new patient - I ask them to write their autobiography. From it, I can tell a great deal about the emotional patterns and pressures in a person's life. After reading her autobiography, I suspected what Lisa's problem was, but knew that she had to come to understand it herself. My job was to guide her through the process.

When we reviewed her history, Lisa at first talked about how loving her parents and husband were and how lucky she felt. After a few weeks of setting the groundwork, Lisa came to her fourth session with a completely different demeanor. She was furious. I had never seen her angry before, so to me, this was a good sign. To Lisa, being angry was very upsetting. How could she be so ungrateful, selfish and weak? What was her problem, anyway? She had a great life. How could she want anything more? It turned out that the new Lisa wanted to go see an R-rated sexy movie and Kent was adamantly opposed. He could not understand why his wife was acting so out of character. Lisa had married Kent specifically because he was mild-mannered, conservative, and devoted to her. All of a sudden, she was enraged with him for the same qualities. It was if a dam had broken. Stories poured out in treatment about how meek, annoying, predictable, and unexciting Kent was. And of course, TJ was everything that Kent was not.

Together we reviewed Lisa's family history as The Good Girl, how she had always done everything expected of her, and how her brother had gotten all the attention because he was a pain. Being The Good Girl was not everything it was cracked up to be. Finally, Lisa realized that, when she was honest with herself and allowed herself to feel her real emotions, she was hopping mad and tired of the self-denial that came from being good all the time. TJ had ignited feelings inside her she had not even known she had. There was an explanation for her bizarre, potentially dangerous behavior.

4

My goal was to continue working with Lisa so she could learn to use her anger more productively. Her relationship to TJ was not due to some character flaw or immorality. It had to do with hiding her real emotions from herself all these years and finally being unable to shove them down any longer. She was angrier with her family than she realized, had learned to suppress her emotions to make up for her brother and please her parents, and had continued the same pattern in her marriage to Kent. Lisa now needed to restructure how she connected to all the people in her life. I hoped that she could learn to be more emotionally honest with her family and her husband, learn to solve problems more constructively, and that, before too long, Lisa would no longer need TJ as an outlet for her hidden emotions.

Improve Your Life

My patients come to me when their lives are falling apart, and they don't know what to do or where else to turn. Some blame themselves for having a flawed character or negative personality traits. They say they are "forgetful" or "weak," or "lazy," or "selfish," labeling themselves in negative ways rather than examining the emotions behind their actions. Some become so alienated from their authentic feelings that they develop chronic rage, depression, or anxiety, and don't know how to get better. Some feel nothing at all – or try not to feel anything by getting into bad habits, like drinking too much. Others find themselves acting in bizarre, even frightening ways, like having sex with strangers, shopping or gambling excessively, or destroying important relationships. Many wonder if they are crazy or self-destructive. They aren't crazy, and most often they do not even need medication. They are cracking under the strain of denying their true feelings.

If you keep doing the same thing, you will keep getting the same results. Similarly, you can't fix something if you don't know what is broken. I know what is broken and how to fix it. It's not that I am some genius or something. It's far simpler: my patients tell me what needs to be done. What the thousands of patients confirmed over and over again is that their usual approach to life does not work anymore. Fortunately, there is an approach that does.

This Book Will Help You To:

- Recognize the power of your family, the role you play, and how you carry that role into your marriage, your parenting, and your everyday life.
- Create a strong sense of self by overcoming ingrained, outdated behavior.
- Understand what motivates others, including members of your own family.
- Overcome your fears – including the fear of your deepest emotions
- Be alone but not lonely.
- Learn the value of distance in a relationship, and how to let it breathe.
- Recognize your authentic feelings, and use them to power your way to a more satisfying life.
- Discover that anger is your best friend, and learn how to use it to solve life's problems.
- Discover that emotional dynamics rather than a flawed personality are responsible for why you do what you do.
- See how authentic emotional exchanges are the basis of satisfying, long-term relationships.
- Learn from your mistakes, and discover how to earn forgiveness with sincere regret and reparation.
- Anticipate and avoid unthinking reactions that get you into trouble.
- Connect with others in new, healthy ways that are based on emotional honesty and mutual respect.
- Learn how to be a better partner and, if you have children, a better parent.

Most importantly, you will learn to set yourself free from the ties that bind you. It is possible – more than possible: necessary – to free yourself from early learned behavior and to release the shame and guilt that keep you stuck in dependent relationships based on obligation or subservience. Later in this book, you will use a simple but powerful process, The Delphi Process, that will enable you to break free, to become independent, to operate from authentic feelings, and to be loved for the person you truly are.

Our Default Setting Is Emotional Dependence

The New American Psychology that I have developed with the aid of my patient's experiences is about relationships – specifically, how to have loving but independent relationships that allow you to be your Authentic Self. I advocate a new way to relate to others through what I call independent connections. I view relationships on a spectrum from childish and dependent (less healthy) to adult and independent (more healthy). Relationships are not static, so they can improve or regress, or even sway back and forth depending on the situation.

I find that people often misunderstand the concept of "independence," and see it as something negative. They associate it with being aloof, cold, or even selfish. Independent connections are more loving than dependent connections because they are based on authentic feelings and freedom of choice.

THE RELATIONSHIP SPECTRUM

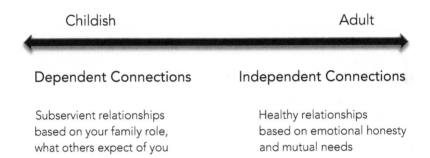

Childish

Adult

Dependent Connections

Independent Connections

Subservient relationships
based on your family role,
what others expect of you

Healthy relationships
based on emotional honesty
and mutual needs

Our Family Roles

Some people think personal independence is at odds with the common good. Others are afraid of independence because they think personal freedom only comes with a high price. I believe all these false impressions of independence exist because being independent does not come easy. The default position of all human beings is dependency. Babies are born helpless – dependent upon others to meet their most basic needs. Then our dependency is reinforced at an early age because it suits the adults around us. It is imprinted upon us while we are most vulnerable. We learn to read the emotions and actions of our parents, and to do what it takes to please them and not make them mad. As we get older, we get our marching orders from them. The more we do as we are told, the more we are rewarded.

No wonder we become focused on pleasing our parents. We need them to survive. They have all the power. To stay alive, we learn to see ourselves through their eyes. Everyone does it. It's as essential as food and water. We are dependent on our family and must learn what they want and how to please them to get what we need as well as reduce our own stress. Our parents create a family role for us, and we stick to it. If siblings are in the mix, we learn certain ways to accommodate them, too.

Compliance Has Many Rewards

- The first and most basic benefit is safety. When we behave correctly, we feel connected to our parents and protected by them.
- A second benefit is love. The more acceptances we gain for our good behavior, the more we feel loved and included.
- A third benefit is feeling less doubt and anxiety about making decisions. When we live up to the expectations our parents have for us, we are more certain about what to do. The more we fulfill our role, the less fear we feel. The world makes more sense when we do as our parents say.

The imprint of our family role is never completely erased from our psyche. Even when we grow older, we still experience less fear when we stick to the script. Some people spend their entire lives believing that "father knows best." In truth, all parents are "some good and some bad." Even parents with the very best intentions will do some damage in the process of bringing up their children. How many parents want to help their children grow up to be independent adults with their own values and dreams? How many parents know how to do so?

The family role we develop in childhood is based on obligations and expectations rather than authentic emotional exchanges. A family is not a democracy, and children's roles are designed to benefit the parents. Kids are told not to be fresh, not to talk back, not to disagree, and not to question their elders and other authority figures. There is a price to pay for this compliance, just as there is a price to pay for rebelling.

The Price Of Independence And The Risk Of Independence

Dependency is our default state, but independence is our natural state. We want both at the same time. Children have an innate drive for independence. Think of the two-year-old who says, "Me do it!" He can't explain why it is so important to him, but he knows he wants to do it by himself. At the same time, he is terrified of being isolated and alone. He will lock into his family role and do whatever is required to win acceptance and approval from the parents he loves and depends upon.

Years later, that same two-year-old will keep doing what he was told to do, rather than shedding the role he was given to play and doing what he senses is right for him. He does that because he is controlled by his past. The past is always present in our memories, even if we don't want it to be. The patterns that shaped us at ages five and ten and sixteen years old are still being reinforced by our family when we are thirty, forty, and fifty years old. By that point our role feels so natural we may not even be aware of it.

Some of us are so indoctrinated by our families to behave in a certain way that we never learn how to act independently. It doesn't matter if we live at home, or 3,000 miles away, or even if our parents are dead; we remain stuck in outdated, dependent patterns of behavior. We subconsciously keep trying to please our parents instead of understanding our own needs. I have counseled thousands of patients who sacrificed their independence to maintain the family status quo forever, even though they were personally unhappy.

Even though it is a universal phenomenon, there is a steep price to be paid for roles. The role that is created for us by our parents is crafted to hide the fault lines in the relationship between the two of them. All marriages involve some degree of denial, and some are based on completely ignoring obvious issues.

Peace is maintained by overlooking the flaws of each partner – flaws that create unresolved problems that threaten the marriage. Family roles simply cover them up, like painting over old wallpaper. When circumstances put us in the position of exposing the flaws and fault lines in the relationship between our parents, we are asked to reinforce the denial that protects their marriage. So we go along with what our parents want, even though we know that it is not the right thing to do and that it is in their best interests, not ours. What our parents want for us, and what we want for ourselves, is not the same thing.

As we get older, the discrepancy between what we see is true and what we are told is true becomes more and more apparent. We face a difficult choice: either ignore what we see, stay quiet and do what our parents want, or speak out about our observations and risk the disappointment and isolation that may result. The more we stand up for ourselves, the more we are punished and shunned by parents and siblings alike.

We may find ourselves in the position of being the messenger for a message that nobody wants to hear. Siblings in the same household may turn a blind eye, which makes us the lone troublemaker. Other family members may be annoyed, and say things like, "These kinds of arguments only happen when you are around." The pressure to maintain the status quo is so great that we may be shamed into submission. When children are honest, parents may accuse them of being fresh, big-mouthed, disobedient, disrespectful, ungrateful, selfish, spoiled, and so on.

When we give in to family pressure, bad things happen internally. We quickly learn to bury our observations and to fear our innate emotions. Unfortunately, when we bury our natural reactions to survive, we lose the connection with who we really are. We feel what I call The Split. We feel torn in two, feeling like there are two sides of us. We develop an Authentic Self, which is based on our genuine, honest observations and reactions, and a Self for Others, which acts to perpetuate family roles and myths.

This is where things get tough. It is human nature to feel authentic anger over being asked to maintain a family role that doesn't feel right. But it is also human nature to avoid what feels bad and to seek out what feels good. Even the tiniest infant can make that distinction. It feels good to behave in a way that is rewarded with love and acceptance. So a huge problem appears when what makes us feel bad is our own mother or father. Something has to be stuffed away: either our authentic emotional reactions, such as anger, which disrupt our connection to our parents, or our understandable desire to go along with what our parents want, which blesses us with their continued acceptance and protection. One half of the split will cancel out the other.

Independence has a price, but it can change your life, and it can change the world. The birthplace of freedom is in your mind. You must first embrace your real self and free yourself from the ties that bind you. For many of my patients, the ties that need to be broken are unhealthy ties to their families. They need to be replaced with healthier connections based on emotional honesty and shared experiences.

The New American Psychology

Traditionally psychiatrists, psychologists, and teachers have focused on a child's intelligence quotient (IQ). The concept was actually developed to identify children with a low IQ in case they needed extra help. Soon IQ was turned on its head and used to identify children with a high IQ, who were thought to have an advantage because of innate intelligence. But two things happened. First, intelligence turned out to be not an unchanging genetic gift, but a trait that can be developed. Second, it became clear that a high IQ does not necessarily correlate with life success or contentment. In the last thirty years or so, people have finally realized the importance of emotional intelligence (EQ). In reality, emotions are the power behind the throne. We are feeling beings who think, not thinking beings who feel.

What has surprised me the most in my practice is how little people know about their deepest emotions. Many of them know what they think. They often can't see the emotional root behind their thoughts. They operate with their thoughts at the wheel and their emotions in the trunk. In fact, they too often use their thoughts to mask their feelings. Often they have thought a lot about their situation, and they offer me a conceptual reason they have worked out to explain their problems. The emotions behind their actions or thoughts are often absent. But emotions are our source of power and significance.

Early in my career, I realized that old-school European psychiatry has its place in history, but that today it inhibits us from developing the emotional awareness we need for independent thought and action. After listening to my patients for many years, I came to reject Freud's assertion that people are motivated only by sexuality and aggression. In that framework, emotions are treated as scary instinctual reactions that cause bad things to happen. I agree that we do hide our emotions from ourselves, but not for deep, dark, or mysterious reasons. We are not selfish at heart, nor do normal people have a secret death wish, or want to kill one parent to have sex with the other. We hide our emotions for a good reason – we are afraid that they will damage the relationships that we need to survive.

There is another important difference that sets this new framework apart from the old psychology. Experts who espouse the traditional psychology point to character flaws and personality traits to explain why people do what they do. I find this approach blames the person for the problem. My years of needing to explain human behavior in all its varied forms has led me to believe that we can understand ourselves and others better if we understand the emotions behind the actions. We act to relieve the pressures from our emotions that build up over time.

I believe these emotional dynamics provide a more accurate explanation for people's behavior than character traits. If you look for an explanation based on the emotions behind the actions, people's choices make perfect sense. We are innately capable of making good choices. Sometimes what appears to be a bad choice is better understood when it is viewed in a different light. Our internal logic may be well hidden, but that does not mean it is either nonexistent or destructive. We cannot fathom our deepest logic without understanding our deepest feelings.

I called my approach, The New American Psychology because it is grounded in the same philosophy of man that our Founding Fathers adopted. The Founding Fathers created a political system based on the belief that people could govern themselves because they, individually and collectively, could decide what was in their best interests. They didn't need a higher authority to tell them what was good for them.

This New American Psychology is a psychology that complements this core belief. Like the Founding Fathers, it too rests on the idea that people are rational creatures whose choices make sense to them. People are not self-destructive. The emotions that drive them can be used for constructive purposes; to forge deep and meaningful relationships and to further the causes that support life. If they can find and listen to their authentic emotions, human beings can be trusted to make healthy decisions for themselves.

The more experience I got, the clearer my convictions became. As I continued to work at being a good therapist and a good husband, father, son, son-in-law, brother and friend, the New American Psychology took shape in my mind. The concepts are not hard to describe but are difficult to put into practice.

Some core principles that apply to everyone are:

- The answers to life's dilemmas lie within each individual. We are born with the capacity to know what is good for us.
- Emotions are the engine. Our mind is the steering wheel. You need both to drive a car effectively, but the power is in the engine.
- The past is always present. What we feel at any given moment is the emotions of our past mixed with the reactions of the present.
- When faced with doubt or internal conflict, we instinctively can find the right path by listening to our authentic emotions.
- Loving relationships are built on emotional listening – the kind of listening that you cannot rush through to make a quick fix.
- A satisfying life is based on a balance of work, love, and play. Too much attention to any one aspect, to the exclusion of the others, is unhealthy.
- Achievements and material success are not the gold standards for being a healthy human being.
- All parents are "some good, some bad." Unfortunately, it is impossible to be a perfect parent. It is the job nobody can get right. You can learn to get it less wrong by listening to your partner and your children, especially when they are telling you the same thing.
- A family should be a school where independence, the pursuit of self-knowledge, and the understanding of emotions are taught and practiced. All family members take turns being the student and the teacher, and all learn to forge emotionally honest, independent relationships with each other and the world.

There is much more to the New American Psychology, which you will read in the following chapters. Simply stated, recognizing authentic feelings is vital to everyone. You need your authentic emotions to create healthy relationships. You are born with authentic emotions and quickly learn to hide them. Children are very rarely taught how to recognize and deal with the array of conflicting emotions they feel as they grow up. The opposite is often the case. Children are taught to squash their feelings, become afraid of reacting naturally, and learn to fear their own emotions. This is why people fall back on their family roles, even though doing so inhibits emotional honesty, and promotes dependence on authority.

Learned Emotions

Following our family role, doing what our parents want us to do, creates learned emotions. We learn to feel guilty or ashamed about certain activities or even thoughts. We learn to feel afraid if we go astray. These learned emotions govern our behavior and are laid on top of our innate emotions. Because of the way we were raised, our authentic emotions – such as anger – may be almost completely hidden, and our learned emotions may be much more obvious. The quietest whisper in your head may be an important inner warning trying to be heard, while the loudest voice may be an oft-repeated reprimand from your mother or father. Which one is most likely going to get your attention?

Until you are aware of them, you cannot use your authentic emotions to free yourself from your family role. I wrote *LOOKING FOR YOUR SELF IN ALL THE WRONG PLACES* to help you learn how to recognize and feel your authentic emotions, instead of denying them to play a part that has become outdated and self-defeating. This book will help you unleash the power of your emotions and help you develop independent connections with others. You will learn to face the fear of embracing the truth and earn the freedom that comes from living a self-aware and psychologically responsible life.

Rage, Anxiety, Depression

While dependency may seem like a safe place, the act of giving up our authentic reactions – the essence of who we are – creates trouble. We cannot react naturally because that is not acceptable, so we retreat into the learned behavior and emotions associated with our family role. We hope this will put an end to our distress. But it doesn't. Our authentic emotions and observations are honest and true, and they do not simply disappear. When we try to deny them and cover them up, this is when the split opens between our Authentic Self and our Self for Others.

The first result of this split is anger. To keep the peace in our family, we may have to hide our angry feelings quickly. But stuffing anger away does not make it vanish. If we do not pay attention to it, our anger will go underground and later manifest itself as destructive rage – against others, or against ourselves, and often in ways that are not obvious. Also, ignoring our authentic anger creates a vicious cycle. We try to hide our anger, but eventually, it boils over into a rage, which simply confirms our worst fears about the danger of our authentic emotions, which in turn makes us want to hide our anger even more.

Although our parents told us otherwise, we have the right to embrace our authentic emotions, particularly our gut anger. I believe anger is our best friend. Whether it lasts for a long period of seething, or for one hot second, it is our ally. It exists because there is a problem. It is trying to tell us that something is wrong. *LOOKING FOR YOUR SELF IN ALL THE WRONG PLACES* will show you how to recognize your authentic anger and use it to fuel constructive behavior and change.

A second predictable result of denying our authentic feelings is anxiety. Although anxiety can manifest itself in strange ways, it is really very logical. Anxiety is a type of fear that lets us know that if we follow our anger, we are in danger of violating the rules we must follow to stay connected to our parents. We fear that we will be alone and cut off emotionally. When we are afraid of acknowledging our authentic feelings, we are afraid of ourselves. What could create more anxiety than that?

A third response to burying our genuine feelings is depression. When we cannot acknowledge our anger, or believe in our Authentic Self, we may become hopeless and helpless. Instead of directing our anger at our family, we make ourselves the target of our anger, which creates depression. As we get older, we continue this pattern of burying our genuine feelings, and this becomes a habit in all situations. Instead of holding others accountable for our troubles– our boss, co-workers, partner, or even circumstances beyond our control – we blame ourselves, and this makes us depressed.

Hiding our anger protects our family and others from our wrath and prevents us from risking alienation – but the problem that made us angry in the first place is not solved. Moreover, because we did not speak up, the fact that the problem is ongoing is now our fault. This is a no-win situation: we are raised to behave a certain way, but when we behave correctly, it makes us depressed.

There is nothing to fear from simply acknowledging our inner anger. This will not turn us into impulsive hotheads. On the contrary, it is the split created by ignoring our initial anger that creates rage reactions and out-of-control behavior.

Growing Up

It takes courage to be your Authentic Self and to have a voice. To unlearn the emotions and messages that you've been taught for so long, you must face fear. You must not listen to your Self for Others when it says, "This is how you are supposed to do it." Instead of being who you've been taught to be, you must listen to your Authentic Self and honor who you really are. When you reclaim your independence in this way, you become an adult. To have a content and fulfilling life, it is critical to establish emotional independence – that is, to rely on your own sense of what is good for you, and good for your community. To have satisfying adult relationships, you need to be able to distinguish between your authentic feelings and your learned emotions. Your Self for Others makes this difficult. It has been in control for years, probably decades. Some of my patients have even completely fused with it and see it as their real self. As a result, millions of people are walking around as semi-adults – not entirely independent, not entirely self-aware, and not entirely grown up.

Using this book, you will learn to put your emotions at the wheel, and your thoughts in the trunk. You will learn to be emotionally honest, and your relationships will improve. You will develop independent connections that are not based on subservience. You will no longer have to play a role or be an imposter. You will be able to negotiate and resolve differences through compromise. You won't need to deny yourself to maintain a relationship. You will be able to share your real self-more openly. You will connect through the emotions that are revealed rather than hidden. Getting past your past will open up a future that is rooted in the rich soil of your Authentic Self, not a life struggling to survive in the shallow surface of your learned behavior.

Fixing Our Relationships With Family

Historically, our relationship with our family has never been right. Americans have never known how to live according to the principles that were handed to us during the birth of our nation. We have never had a clear idea about how to embrace independence in ourselves, create marriages based on independent connections, or raise children who know both what freedom means and its price.

I believe this is the new world that our Founding Fathers envisioned. We tried to make it happen once but failed. The essence of the social revolution of the sixties was an attempt to break free of traditional family roles and to experience self and relationships in a different way. If you're a Baby Boomer, you remember peace, love, happiness, and flower power. Unfortunately, the Baby Boomers could not comprehend at that time the depth of the social change they were trying to achieve. They went for a walk in the woods without an emotional compass to guide them. Hippies had no path to follow, and it turned out sex, booze, drugs, and "love the one you're with" did not help them feel good about themselves, or sustain relationships, or raise healthy children, or change the country. When money and greed came back into vogue, the Baby Boomers were distracted from what really matters for the next fifty years. This book will reveal how we can take up and renew the best ideas of the sixties, and move from "father knows best" to an honest version of "people know best."

Independence brings great rewards, but it must be deliberately nurtured. This book will help you learn to recognize the role you played in your family of origin, and how it restricts your ability to be self-fulfilled today. You'll learn to be alert for that little flash of anger that lets you know when there is a conflict between what you truly want to do or say, and what you think you ought to do or say. My promise to you is that this book will enable you to grow yourself up so you can be a happier, more successful, and better person.

To get started, I'm going to tell you my own story. I was, by all conventional measurements, a successful kid. I was blessed with athleticism and intelligence, and my parents expected me to be the Golden Child. I worked my butt off to get into Princeton University. Everything was going along great, I thought... until I woke up one day completely unable to function. That was my introduction to the importance of hidden feelings, so that's where I'll begin now.

2

The Boy In The Velvet Suit

My Story . . .

Forrest Gump and I were born on the same day: September 9, 1952. I was a product of the same times as Forrest. The cultural events that occurred in his story happened to me at the same age. My teenage years included an unpopular war, protests, and riots in the streets of America. The 1960s brought years of social revolution and change. What I saw and felt had such an impact on me that I am only now beginning to understand its significance at my current age.

Even as a teenager, I knew that something was seriously wrong with the world around me. I felt this truth inside of me and could see the evidence outside of me. And my friends confirmed it. We felt that our spirits were being crushed, and we were fighting for our lives. It was not just the disappointment of losing our heroes like John Kennedy or Martin Luther King. It was not just the chaos and fear created by the images of Watts burning during a race riot in Los Angeles. It was not only about seeing our friends get killed in Vietnam on the news every night. It wasn't just the rage in evidence at the 1968 Democratic National Convention in Chicago, or even the unarmed students killed by the National Guard at Kent State University – an unprecedented event at that time.

Those events were the result of a significant and profound dynamic. We felt it and lived it moment-to-moment within our own families. Every day in a different way, there was a simmering rage that separated kids from parents, friends from friends, and brothers from sisters. The rage was everywhere and ready to boil over at the slightest provocation. In my family, many nights around the dining room table erupted into political arguments. They would end with my father telling me that I was a "pinko" liberal from Princeton and that my professors were former Communists.

My Dad was not Archie Bunker. He just didn't like my beliefs. Others didn't take kindly to my ideas either, including my co-workers at my summer job in construction. One union member threatened to push me off the 13th floor where we worked because I told him that unions were socialist systems and the closest thing to communism that existed in our country.

The divisiveness even invaded simple get-togethers, like a visit to a family friend's beach home in Southampton, New York, back in 1968. I remember the Saturday night with friends of my parents whose political views could best be summed up as: "America: Love It or Leave It." During a dinner discussion about Vietnam and hippies, the father told me to leave the table and give my food to the Vietnamese. To him, I was one of those rebel hippies who needed to be put in their place. My crazy hippie hair and I took him up on that offer, and I left.

Needless to say, I was never invited to return anytime soon to his home. I couldn't have cared less. His vision of America was not the America that I loved. To me, he represented everything that was wrong at that time: money, power, and greed. He was one of the first CEO's to be paid a seven-figure salary, and every year he gave his latest yacht to charity to get a tax deduction. For several reasons, that just didn't sit well with me at all.

Looking back, I now realize that those discussions were really not about politics. We, the crazy hippies, recognized that our most prized possession - our independence - was being threatened. The 1950s way of life did not work for us. America had become a nation of followers. We were supposed to do as we were told. Playing the correct role and meeting the expected obligations were prized over seeking individual truths. This is why so many of us felt compelled to "find ourselves." The arguments were about fighting to keep alive our right to speak our minds and to follow our hearts.

Unfortunately, our words were falling on deaf ears. Free speech and the right to dissent were a thing of the past. The country had lost its spirit of independence, and we didn't know what to do to get it back.

I will use my own experiences to illustrate the nature of the psychological problems that we faced in the social revolution in the 60s, that we continue to face today. To begin my story, let me first give you a little history about my parents.

My parents were the classic example of chasing the American dream. They were both born in the Midwest, the heartland of America. My father was from Waterloo, Iowa, and my mother was from Cincinnati, Ohio. My father was descended from Dutch dairy farmers. My paternal grandfather was the local milkman who delivered milk directly to your home. My mother's family was German and owned a millinery business in Cincinnati. They were financially well off for a period of time but lost the business when my mother was a child, which made a large impression on her.

Born in 1920, my mother was a local Cincinnati beauty queen during her teen years in the late 1930s. She met my father at the University of Cincinnati, where they both were students. My mother was the Homecoming Queen, and my father was the President of his fraternity. They told me that they were the "big ticket" as a couple on the campus.

In her junior year, my mother was offered a job with the prestigious Ford Modeling Agency In New York City. She took the job and abandoned her studies. It was a huge step for a girl from the Midwest to enter the world of international fashion in the Big Apple. Within a year, my father followed her to New York. He was hoping to enlist in the Navy as a helicopter pilot, but he received orders to report to the Army before he heard from the Navy. In the meantime, he had received an offer for Officer Training School from the Coast Guard, which had offered him a commission as a first lieutenant. His options were infantry or officer in the Coast Guard. He chose the Coast Guard.

His offer from the Navy arrived a day later. He was devastated. Rather than go off to war like his buddies, he was left behind to guard the home front. He remained in New York City during the war, overseeing the loading of bombs onto ships. He was an officer but in the least important branch of the armed services. My mother believed that his stress over this perceived shortcoming caused his bleeding ulcers that required hospitalization and extended rehabilitation.

Even though it was not his fault, my Dad was ashamed of his war service. He never got the opportunity to "prove himself" or do what he thought was his part to protect his country. He did remain in the Coast Guard reserves and reached the rank of Commodore before his death – but he did that less out of patriotism and more out of a desire to take advantage of the military benefits, which served my parents well in the last years of their lives. He was proud that he got to coach the Coast Guard basketball team in Madison Square Garden. Other than that, he didn't talk much about it.

My parents were married shortly after the end of the war and lived together in an apartment on Fifth Avenue overlooking Central Park. Over the next 50 years, they went on to become one of the leading fashion design teams in the country. Basing their company in New York under the name of "Roger Van S," they designed and produced one of the first fully integrated lines of handbags, belts, jewelry, and clothing in the fashion industry. Their business empire all began with my father hand-stitching leather purses for my mother, who wore them to her fashion shoots. My father came up with the bright idea of making a handbag out of a wooden bucket. They invested their life savings in this idea, and it paid off handsomely. They bought a factory in Paterson, New Jersey, opened a showroom in New York, and did extremely well for the next 15 years.

Unfortunately - and not unlike the experience of my mother's parents, who lost their millinery operation in Cincinnati – my parents discovered that small business was risky business. They tried to expand into clothing and lost a great deal of money. They were forced to close the factory and liquidate the company. True to their resilience, they were hired by JC Penny Co. as a design team and toured the world for the next ten years establishing factory productions of their designs in Europe and Japan.

My parents never quite got over the loss of their business although they were better off financially. They longed to recover the glow of their past. They were ashamed that decisions had been made that put the company at risk. In their late sixties, they foolishly tried revive the old business. They took out a second mortgage on their home and rented a factory in Paterson to manufacture their designs. While I was busy with my own career, my younger brother and eldest sister came to work for them. They seemed to believe they were creating a business to leave as a family legacy. In retrospect, I think they were lying to themselves. They really were driven by the need to make up for past mistakes and to undo the shame of their prior failures.

My opinion was reinforced by the family dynamics that surfaced over decisions regarding the "family" business. Both of my siblings attempted to influence the direction of the business but to no avail. My father and mother believed that they knew the formula for success and did not listen to their ideas. After several years, the business failed, requiring my parents to sell their house and a portion of their land.

Wounded by the conflicts with my parents, my eldest sister fled to California to live life on her own terms. My brother transitioned into his own small construction company that he still owns and operates to this day. They are both better off pursuing their own independent lives.

To my parents' credit, they never gave in to adversity, even when confronted with another dose of shame. The very independence that led them to a build and rebuild a business and lose it twice now worked in their favor. They still owned an acre of land with a rebuilt garage that included a large apartment. It had originally been built for my grandmother. My parents moved into that apartment and began to rebuild their lives. Now in their seventies, they decided to train as real estate agents and to help their friends moving into retirement to sell their homes. The idea worked well, and they continued to build their real estate business over the next 10 years.

Father Knows Best

Even though they worked together, my parents did not have an equal relationship. In those days Dad was the man of the house, and he was no exception. If he told us to jump, we jumped.

If my father saw a parking space on the opposite side of the street - parking spots in New York City were hard to come by, even in the 1950s - he would tell my older sister to stand in the space to save it while he drove around the block. She would have to tell people to move on, and that the space was reserved for her father. People yelled at her and even tried to back into the space, despite her standing there. Still, she stood her ground did as she was told. It didn't matter to my father that she was only four years old!

My mother died in 2010. After the funeral, I was going through some of her belongings, and I found a letter she wrote to her mother in 1946 when she was 26 years old and newly married to my father. She was writing about the pressure she felt from her new husband to enter another beauty pageant.

My mother already had excelled as a model and had been a cover girl on many fashion magazines, including Vogue and Harper's Bazaar. To promote her career, she was asked to enter the 1946 Miss Rheingold of New York beauty contest. If she won, it would give her great exposure. There was one drawback. The pageant required the contestants to appear both in a gown and in a bathing suit.

As I read her letter, my mother described her insecurities about her body, specifically her short legs. She felt that her legs would be emphasized in a bathing suit and she did not want to expose herself to the potential humiliation. Her modeling had involved being fully clothed in skirts and dresses that were below the knee, hiding what she felt was her deformity. She now had to face the shame of exposing her physical flaw to the world.

In the letter, she told my grandmother about the pressure she felt from my father to participate in the contest. Apparently, my father had said to her that if she did not enroll in the pageant, she should not bother coming home. Knowing their relationship, I am sure he thought she was the greatest thing on earth, and he could not understand how she had any insecurity. She wrote to her mother about how afraid she was, and how guilty it would make her feel if she let my father down. Nowhere did she mention that she was mad at my father for pushing her or not understanding her fears. Both my parents thought this behavior was perfectly normal.

My mother succumbed to my father's tactics, and she ended up winning the contest, short legs and all. In the end, she was grateful for the push from my Dad. She showed no anger for his shaming her or threatening to leave her. The end justified the means. After all, she won the contest. To both my parents, the outcome was all that mattered. There was no such thing as too much pressure. They did not dwell on what might have happened if she had lost, or what the contest might have revealed about their relationship. Neither one of them stopped to realize the emotional impact of what had happened.

Perfection Poison

My parents were united about the importance of achievement, and the need to push yourself to overcome your fears. This was why my father was ashamed of his weak military service. It was why my mother felt obligated to restore the family pride through her accomplishments as a model. It was why both my Mom and Dad had to be the "big thing " in college. Their ambition is what drove them to take risks necessary to set up their fashion business. The achievement was their fuel. It was all they knew and valued. They passed this message onto their children. We did as we were told and were expected to march to their orders at all costs.

Interestingly, they were never pushy parents. If they had screamed or yelled, it would have been easier to see how unhealthy their focus was. Their standards for me were more assumed than demanded. It would have been easier to rebel if they had been more obvious, but the message was not sent in a loud way. Our failures were met with silence. Maybe they just did not know what to say. Perhaps they received the same treatment from their own parents. The bottom line was that they did not know how to nurture children, and did not want to take the time to learn. So whenever we failed, there was only silence. We received the message that failure was such a bad thing that nobody could even talk about it. If you failed, you were breaking the unwritten rules of the family, and that was not acceptable.

Years later I would realize that weaknesses can actually be strengths on steroids. Our perceived shortcomings can motivate us even more than our perceived gifts. Compensating for their "failures," my parents were driven to succeed. Their ambition and entrepreneurial spirit grew too large, and it got the better of them when they tried to expand their first business. It happened again with their second business when they did not listen to my siblings. I can't say for sure that the second business would have succeeded if they had listened better, but I believe that my siblings made sense, and I wish that my parents had been able to learn from them. They just weren't built that way. For them, authority radiated from the top down.

Eventually, I also realized that my parents never knew themselves. They were not able to critically evaluate their own actions or reactions, nor could they discern the influence of their past on their present behavior. They connected through shared strengths but avoided understanding their respective weaknesses. They were emotionally blind to the avoidance of shame that drove them. They did not see, admit, or manage this basis for their bad decisions. My father never stopped to realize his shame about his childhood without money, and my mother never realized her need to succeed had unhealthy roots.

My parents' marriage was based on their accomplishments - working together and raising a family together. They did not stop to look at the emotional ties that bound them, or to sort through what was healthy or unhealthy about their relationship. Their total focus on performance and achievement was like a poisoned apple. They ate it themselves, and they fed it to me.

My parents saw no problem with their obsession with achievement. They saw it as a good thing, a drive that made people successful and significant. They believed it was the secret to success. They surrounded themselves with successful people and pushed each other to achieve to the highest degree.

At the very end, their shame did reveal itself. My parents were so driven to succeed that they made little time to spend with their grandchildren. Business always came first. It wasn't their interest in the business that drove them; it was their need to avoid their own shame.

Despite their internal struggles, my parents were not "bad" people. They did the best they could, but emotionally they were too limited to understand themselves, their children, or their grandchildren. My kids were shielded from their obsession with accomplishment, and have fond memories of the times we got together. Alzheimer's and dementia finally brought their active years to a halt, and they both died at 90 years old.

The Boy In The Velvet Suit

I was born to these ambitious and entrepreneurial parents smack in the middle of the post-World War II Baby Boom. I had two older sisters. One was seven years older than I, and the other was and five and a half years older. Sad to say, they did not matter to my father. All he wanted was a boy.

The day I was born, my father went to Neiman Marcus - one of the most prestigious department stores of the day - and bought me an expensive black velvet suit. I don't think it fit me until I was two years old. It felt more like a suit of armor than regular clothing. It came with a hefty price tag, not just financially but also emotionally. The wearer of that suit was required to fulfill the hopes and dreams of many generations. The price was steep, the suit was heavy, and nobody ever asked me if I wanted to wear it.

This simple black velvet suit symbolized all of my father's ambitions for me. My accomplishments were to be great. I was to be a shining star, like royalty above ordinary people. My wife never lets me forget it, and will refer to me as "the boy in the velvet suit" whenever I get too pushy and demanding.

I was fortunate to be born with many talents, so I fit into the suit only too well. I was blessed with both intelligence and athletic ability. I was at the top of my class starting in elementary school and was groomed by my parents to attend a prep school in New England. To study Latin and qualify for prep school, I was pulled from my elementary school to attend Saddle River Country Day School for seventh and eighth grade. At the 8th grade graduation, I was first in my class and received the Best Athlete Award as well.

When I did well in sports or school, there was a lot of attention paid to me. My parents would tell their friends about my accomplishments. To me, it seemed reasonable for them to be interested in my achievements. In fact, it felt very loving because I got so much attention for what I did. There was no apparent reason for me to believe that the pressure was excessive. I could not tell that the pressure was unreasonable. I never thought about the price I paid to excel, and everyone else was too caught up in my success as a student and an athlete to think about my feelings.

Everything went according to plan, and I applied to the Canterbury School, a Catholic boarding school in New Milford, Connecticut. I was admitted as a freshman in the fall of 1966, a week shy of my 14th birthday. I lived there for the next four years until graduation in the spring of 1970.

The natural reaction of most children to being forced to change schools is anger. In my situation, many kids would have thrown a fit and told their parents to leave them alone. Most thirteen-year-olds would have at least have felt scared about leaving behind all their friends and going away to live at a new school. I was oblivious to how scared and angry I really was. It should have been obvious even to me, but it never clicked. My life seemed reasonable to me. I took my cues from my parents. If they thought it was good for me, it must be good for me. Why would I think otherwise? I trusted that my Mom and Dad loved me so I could not fathom that they would lead me down the wrong road. As I later realized, they could not warn me since they were walking down the same unhealthy road. They were merely taking me to the same place they were going.

I had been raised to be the hero, and I was not going to let anything get in the way of my mission in life. Even the thought of failure made me feel guilt and shame. I continued to uphold my standards in prep school, being the first in my class in every marking period for the full four years. I could not slack off at any time, even during the last marking period when most students get "senioritis." The velvet suit legacy would not allow it. Needless to say, I graduated as valedictorian of my high school class.

My athletic career took a similar path. In elementary school, I had taken up tennis at age seven and quickly started beating kids who were years older than me. Frank Brennan, the coach for Billie Jean King, known by her maiden name of Billie Jean Moffit back then, was also my coach. I went on to play in the junior tennis circuit and earned the right to play in the nationals in the "under twelve" division. I lost in the first round and was not happy about how I played. It's tough to play in the hot sun wearing a velvet suit when everybody else gets to wear tennis whites.

I played baseball too. I remember pitching two complete baseball games on the same day, one for the school team and one for my club team. I knew it could hurt my arm, but I wanted to pitch. I had to excel for both teams. I never told either coach that I was scheduled to pitch for both of them on the same day. I just did it. That's what boys who wore velvet suits did.

When I look back, I see signs of trouble that nobody noticed. On the tennis court, I had a terrible temper. Whenever I missed several shots, I would break my racket. My parents would calmly reprimand me and go buy me another racket, time and time again. I got the message: no matter how I felt, I had to keep succeeding to please them.

My anger did not go away. I would try to calm down, but it never worked. I became scared of my own anger. I felt like I was going to explode inside, so I just tried even harder to be the son my parents wanted me to be as if that would solve my problem. I didn't realize until much later that the emotions inside of me needed to be managed, or they would begin to manage me.

In prep school, I had the chance to continue my sports career at a higher level of competition. In addition to tennis and baseball, I loved football. In my sophomore year, I jumped from being the quarterback on the freshman team to starting as a safety on the Varsity team. In tennis, I immediately earned a berth on the team in both singles and doubles. Fortunately, there was another freshman on the team who was my equal. We played Varsity doubles for four years, and I believe we lost only two matches in our high school career. I don't remember freaking out when we lost and probably thought we just didn't play well that day. It was easier to share the blame, so it didn't affect me as much. I shared with him the Most Outstanding Athlete award at my high school graduation, having earned nine Varsity letters in tennis, football, and ice hockey.

All this and you'd think I'd be happy. Not a chance. The pressures were incredible. I felt fear when I was threatened with failure, and relief when I experienced success. I rarely felt joy over my success. I felt a release of the pressure temporarily, but it lasted only until the next challenge presented itself to me. I would gladly have traded my velvet suit for some regular clothes.

At one point, I almost got the chance. When my parents lost their first business, I was just finishing my freshman year at Canterbury. My parents could no longer afford to pay the tuition. I had done well by the velvet suit. I was at the top of my class and had already earned a Varsity letter playing on the tennis team. I was prepared to go to the local high school and was looking forward to reconnecting with my old friends from elementary school. Mostly, I was hoping to blend in and be less visible than I was in boarding school.

However, that was not to be. When the Headmaster learned of my family's financial situation, the school offered me a full scholarship for the next three years. My parents were thrilled and expected me to stay. I don't remember anybody asking me if I wanted to stay. It was what everyone else wanted. I didn't feel I had much choice. I had already switched schools and given up my hometown friends. There was too much invested in my performance for me to turn back now. Now I was really stuck. I had to wear the velvet suit not only for my parents but also for the Headmaster.

The pressure was building up inside of me, but I was not aware of it, and no one else cared. In 1968, the fall of my junior year, there was much revolution and protest throughout the country. Not to be outdone by the rest of the world, the seniors in my school decided to stage a protest over the food served in the dining hall. They passed the word to the entire student body that they were going to stage a boycott at lunch over the mediocre food. Every student was told not to eat and to leave when the food was served. When the entire student body walked out, my stomach was in knots. I was being asked to protest food that I was being given for free. I just couldn't do it. I watched as all my fellow students and football team members walked by me, and I refused to budge. Only two other scholarships students and I were left in the dining hall. We were terrified.

By now the rest of the student body was out on the lawn chanting slogans and railing against the school administration. Sitting in the dining hall was less terrifying than having to leave it and walk in front of the angry mob. Eventually, two of us managed to slip by, and we went to our third-floor room overlooking the protest. My buddy, being a wise guy, started throwing some donuts to the hungry mob below. This enraged some of the seniors, a dozen of whom came storming up to our floor to beat us to a pulp.

I remember grabbing a heavy metal fire extinguisher off the wall and getting into a corner to defend myself. I was going to plant that copper cylinder in the face of the first person who came close enough to threaten me, and I let them know it. I guess the real respect I had earned on the football field came in handy as no one came any closer. They screamed at me and spat at me, but that was it, and they left.

That afternoon, there was an eerie silence between the other students and myself. In the locker room before football practice, I was ignored. That day, I hit people harder than I had ever hit anybody in my life. I wanted to send a message that there would be a price to pay if you messed with me.

It worked. I was never threatened again by any of the seniors, and I don't remember ever talking about the protest to anybody, certainly not my parents. I just tucked the story away as part of the price I had to pay to do what I had to do. That was what you did when you wore the velvet suit.

All that mattered was that my parents were proud of me, so I did everything I could to maintain that pride. My success at Canterbury led to admission to Princeton University in 1970. I felt rewarded for my efforts and started to buy into the idea that maybe there was some value to wearing the velvet suit.

Princeton And A Big Surprise

My first two years at Princeton were uneventful. I was in awe of the people and professors around me, but I knew I had earned the right to be there. I was playing on the tennis team and doing well in my pre-med courses. I was on the treadmill of life and doing what was expected of me. I knew I was under some pressure, but so was everyone who went to that kind of school. I had no real idea of my true feelings or their strength. The truth was that I did not trust that I was exceptionally smart, and I believed that I needed to work harder than everybody else to succeed. I was the kind of student who completed every assignment and studied for every exam as if my life depended on it. I did get some B's but could rationalize that a B at Princeton was like an A anywhere else. While getting a B was rare, the velvet suit did protect me from feeling dumb or inadequate, but the cost was overwhelming.

In the fall of 1972, during my third year at Princeton - when I was only nineteen - my life turned upside down. I was in the middle of midterm exams. In the blink of an eye, I went from hero to zero. I remember waking up feeling like I didn't know what hit me. As I lay in my bed in my college dorm room, my mind was racing. Behind my thoughts, my own voice kept repeating the name of an old girlfriend in my head. My thoughts were utterly jumbled, and the more I tried to stop, the more they raced. I tried to distract myself from my mental confusion, but that didn't work. The harder I tried, the more I seemed to be losing the battle. And the name kept repeating over and over again. I felt numb, and it was hard to breathe. I felt like I was losing my mind.

There was no warning that this was going to happen. I was a biology major and doing well in all my courses. While I knew there were plenty of people smarter than me at Princeton, I felt comfortable that I could keep up with anybody in any subject. I felt good about myself and what I was able to accomplish. In another year, I would be applying to medical school to become the doctor that everybody expected me to be.

That fall, my girlfriend, Diane, had enrolled in a college in Philadelphia that was 45 minutes away. This was a welcome change, as we had been dating long distance for a year. I lived in northern New Jersey, and she lived in San Juan, Puerto Rico. Previously I'd seen her only in the summer, or whenever her parents would vacation at their home in Coral Gables, Florida. Her coming to Philly for college was a dream come true.

Everything seemed to be going my way. The school was good, and I had somebody who loved me. Who would have thought that I was a ticking time bomb about to explode?

I remember the fateful day when I had to study for a physics exam. I opened the book, and I heard the girl's name in my mind over and over again. I tried to read but kept being distracted by the record that was playing in my head. Now I was worried. I couldn't think straight and had to take the exam the next day.

I tried to calm down by going for a run. Nothing stopped the thoughts. I remember staring at the physics book all night long, feverishly turning the pages and remembering nothing of what I read. All I could hear was that same damn name, over and over again. I began to wonder if I was hearing voices. This is what it must feel like to go crazy, I thought to myself. I really must be losing my mind.

I never went to sleep that night and tried to study right up until the time of the exam. As a ritual that helped me deal with the anxiety of exams, I always took my books with me to the exam room. This was just magical thinking. I believed that if I had my books near me, I would remember what was in each one. I knew it was a crazy idea, but it worked for me, and I was not about to give it up.

Nothing helped me that day. I remember the exam contained a riddle – a joke question to give one point of extra credit. I spent two hours trying to figure out the riddle. I barely looked at the other questions. I just couldn't get my mind to focus on anything other than the riddle. The professor didn't even notice when I handed in the blank book.

After the exam, I walked back to my dorm and lay down in my bed. I knew I was in serious trouble, but all I could think about was my voice in my head repeating the name of my old girlfriend. I started to wonder why I was thinking this way, and that only led to more questions and more obsessional thinking. Was this happening because I really loved the other girl and not Diane? Was I kidding myself? Did I actually need to get back together with her? I knew this girl did not mean much to me, but I could not answer why I kept repeating her name over and over again. I was dazed, confused, and terrified, for myself and for my future.

My Introduction To Psychotherapy

I left Princeton for a semester. Since I couldn't think straight, it seemed like the right thing to do. At the urging of my parents, I went to our family doctor to tell him what was going on with me. He was an old family friend, and I trusted him. He never told me what he thought, but I could tell by his face that he was worried. He referred me to a psychiatrist for an evaluation. I later learned that he told my parents that I was hearing voices and that I could have a severe mental health problem, possibly schizophrenia.

I was petrified. I didn't know what was going inside of me and I thought I had lost the ability to think straight. I think my father was more afraid of my condition than I was. He wanted nothing to do with my treatment. Even before my first consult, he told me, "Don't get stuck on that psychiatrist's couch." He thought therapy was a sign of weakness and wanted my problem to be fixed promptly, like a broken arm. He never asked me what went on in the sessions, nor did he or my Mom want to get involved. They had no idea how to help and handed me over to the doctors to fix. The message was clear: Get this kid back in the velvet suit. It looks good on him.

It didn't take a big-time shrink to understand the message that my parents had sent to me. Performance is the most essential thing in life, and your job is to make us proud. I had been getting that message from the day I was born. I was supposed to be the trophy that would cement their climb from the middle-class world of the Midwest to their appointment in the upper class in New York. Singlehandedly, I could make up for my grandparents losing their business, my father's war career, and any other events that had created family shame.

I scheduled my first appointment with the therapist and entered the world of the mind and the effects of human emotion. I remain in that profession to this day. I never did go on to become the doctor everybody expected me to be. I ended up becoming the doctor that I wanted to be.

Fortunately for me, I was referred to a non-traditional psychiatrist who was educated in England. Unlike my family physician, this doctor knew the difference between hearing your own voice in your head and hearing the voices of others. He diagnosed me with panic attacks and obsessional thinking. I was not schizophrenic. I had severe anxiety, and he could help me. He realized that I took life way too seriously and that my acute fear was not a mental disorder.

As I told my life story to my therapist, I began to understand just how intense my parents' pressure on me had been, and what an enormous burden it was in my life to excel at everything, always. I started to connect the dots, and saw that there were several events in my childhood that should have been danger signs - but at the time I had no awareness of my emotions, and neither did my parents, so my life in the velvet suit had continued.

I remembered that in second or third grade I'd had a fight with my teacher, who happened to be a nun. For God's sake – what kind of eight-year-old tries to take on a nun? The topic was subtraction with multiple integers. The Sister wanted us to learn the process of carrying the "1" by adding it to the top number. I did it by subtracting it from the bottom number and was getting all the problems right. She didn't discover that I was doing it differently until one day she had me do a problem on the blackboard in front of the whole class. I did the problem and got the right answer, but in the process exposed my different method to her. She told me to do it over her way. I told her that I was not going to do that. She did not realize the level of fear that she had encountered. She was playing with my psychological survival. Her response was to put ten more problems on the board, each one harder than the next. No child looks forward to doing a series of difficult math problems in front of the whole class, but I took one look at her and thought to myself, I will show her. I did them all and got every single one right. I remember her saying, "OK, you can go back to your seat." In retrospect, who gets that intense over subtraction? Only one very distressed child who is so bent on pleasing others that he will go head to head with God's representative on earth. The nun never did call my parents. It was just another one of those little battles in life that you handled alone because you were supposed to.

I did have one thing going for me. You get to go to heaven if you wear the velvet suit. Salvation was to be my reward, in another eighty years or so.

I also remembered that in fourth grade, I began to experience a problem with urinary frequency. I had to go to the bathroom every five minutes and didn't feel I could hold it. I was embarrassed about my problem and supremely uncomfortable. Once I even caught my penis in my zipper as I hurried to return to class. I hid it from the teacher and bled profusely throughout the rest of the day. I certainly was not going to have somebody check out my private parts. I never told anyone, and just let it heal on its own. I was probably only ten years old, but I already knew by that age that I had to handle my problems on my own. I didn't want to risk being vulnerable or human. It might make me unlovable.

I couldn't hide my urinary problem forever. Eventually, I was taken to different doctors, who could not figure out what was wrong with me. They scheduled an exploratory surgery to determine if there was some physical problem inside. I remember going to the hospital with a cold, and being sent home to recover before they could put me under anesthesia for the operation. The urinary frequency went away after the cold got better. In retrospect, I think it was scared right out of me. I was terrified of surgery but had to push my fears even deeper in my psyche. I had to find a way to put the velvet suit back on.

I did not realize it at the time, but I became even more obsessive about getting straight A's. If I couldn't get angry and let people know the pressure that I felt, I might as well give them everything they wanted and then some. If I had to wear the suit, I might as well be proud of it.

I soon had a major incident that even worried my parents. We had a large amount of property at my house, so my younger brother and I used to hit golf balls back and forth to each other from about 150 yards away. One day when I was about age ten – he was three years younger – we went out to hit some balls. He yelled to me that he had to go to the bathroom and ran back into the house. I continued to hit more balls. At the end of the follow-through from one swing, I felt a "thwack." I turned to see my brother lying on the ground with his face split open from his eyes to his nose. He had tried to sneak up on me to scare me, and had jumped at me just as I finished my swing. I had hit him square and flayed open his face.

I don't have any memory of what happened next. As a matter of fact, I have no memory of the next day, either, until they brought him back from the hospital. His whole face was covered in bandages with only his eyes visible. He looked terrifying.

My parents told me that they found out about the accident only because they discovered me pounding my head against the house saying I had killed my brother. They later told me that they were as worried about my mental state as they were about my brother's face. They should have been. I was experiencing my worst nightmare. The golden child had not only made a mistake but a gigantic one. I was afraid I'd killed my brother. I felt it was because of my own negligence. How could I not have heard him behind me? My mind blacked out for 24 hours.

My velvet suit was now stained with the blood of my brother. In psychological terms, blacking out is a dissociative response to overwhelming fear; a response to profound psychological trauma. An experience can be so distressing that we hide the emotion deep within our minds. We literally cease to associate with it mentally. We can't even integrate the memories into our everyday lives. The emotion behind a dissociative reaction is so overwhelming we have to bury it to survive. Although I had blacked out, the psychological impact that I carried forward from that incident was the burial of my own reactions way down inside of me. I was now even more afraid of my own potential to do harm. Any strong emotional reaction would cause me to shut down. I did not understand this. I knew I was more intense than other kids, but I thought that was just my personality. Since I was highly rewarded for my ability to ignore my emotions, I did not see the harm in it. I just kept doing it until I ran into myself during that junior year at Princeton.

I had been ignoring my natural feelings for years. Without a roadmap for my emotional world, I was overly vulnerable to the influence and opinions of others. All I recognized were the things I should be doing. These constant demands drowned out the small cries from my authentic emotions. Heeding my true feelings would have enabled me to do what I really wanted to do, and I would have had the energy and enthusiasm to continue. Instead, I fell to pieces.

After talking these things through with the psychiatrist, I was treated with relaxation training for a brief six-week period and responded instantly. True to my desire to please my parents, I did not remain on that couch very long. The restoration of control that the training gave me was enough to reduce my anxiety and return me to my old self - or so I thought. I had gained a new respect for the strength of human emotion. Still, although I no longer discounted the importance of emotions, I had a lot to learn about managing them.

The Power Of Emotions

My journey into the world of anxiety and panic changed my life. I experienced firsthand the raw power of emotion strong enough to disable a human being. I personally experienced a fight between myself and my emotions, and my emotions won.

Before that time, I firmly believed in the power of the intellect. I believed that thinking controlled feeling. I now knew that was not true. I became a convert to the belief that human beings are feeling beings who happen to think, not thinking beings who happen to feel. I now knew better and recognized I could no longer hide from my own emotions. I was forced to realize that emotions are extremely powerful. I had never realized that strong emotions had caused my temper tantrums, urinary frequency, panic attacks, obsessive thoughts, and blacking out. The focus on achievement and performance hindered my ability to recognize and feel my emotions.

I have learned as an adult to recognize the presence of emotional pressures, even when they are disguised. This awareness has made me a better therapist and better person. I know my own fears have caused me to listen poorly at times, to avoid feeling, and to be limited in my ability to nurture the people that I love. Listening and caring require us to feel. Even as a therapist, I am required to both teach and listen. The teaching part is easier than the emotional listening part. Telling somebody what to do makes us feel better, but often makes the recipient feel worse. We feel better because we are relieved. If we offer a quick fix to the other person, we don't have to feel their emotional pain. Helping other people heal requires that we recognize and embrace the emotions in any human story without judgment, and manage our own distress without trying to wish it away.

Today I realize how narrowly I avoided the stigma that can accompany any mental health problem. In the hands of a different doctor, I could have easily been misdiagnosed as having a biological illness like schizophrenia. I could have been put on medications to sedate me and suppress my emotions. I could have been told that I had a chronic mental illness and that I would have to remain on powerful medications for the rest of my life. I could have had my self-esteem permanently damaged by the idea that I was simply a flawed person and my illness originated in my personality, forever limiting my ability to cope with life. The fact that I was acting like a crazy person but did not need medications or a psychiatrist's label to get better made a deep impression on me. Today, as a practicing therapist, I still believe that pills are not always necessary, even in the presence of extreme behavioral changes.

We all struggle to manage our emotions. This is not mental illness. Emotional distress exists because of the imperfections in the way we are raised, and the conflict between what we honestly feel and what we are taught to feel - or not feel. Real mental illness is characterized by biological factors. Conditions such as schizophrenia, developmental disorders, and bipolar disorders have biological roots. These illnesses are common, but not normal. On the other hand, having our hidden fears exposed by life experiences is normal. All people - including those with true biological disorders - are raised by imperfect parents, and grow up with internal emotional conflicts. The symptoms of our distress can vary from the obsessional thinking that I experienced to problems like substance abuse, eating disorders, self-harm, or lack of motivation. These symptoms are not indicative of a chronic mental illness. They are simply indirect expressions of our internal emotional conflicts.

Because of my experience, I developed a deep respect for the ancient adage "Know Thyself." It was inscribed on the Oracle of Delphi by the Greeks thousands of years ago. This statement has been recognized and repeated throughout the ages, but I never appreciated its depth until I fell to pieces during college. At the time I thought I was "losing it." In retrospect, I realize I was "finding it." I now know what the Greeks meant. The journey to self-knowledge is often confusing and full of fear, but I was strengthened by the insights this experience gave me. In the next year, I would make some life-changing decisions that included marriage, career, and starting a family. My new self-knowledge gave me the ability to make these important decisions with confidence because my choices were grounded in an understanding of my own emotions.

Crucial Decisions

I felt better after seeing the psychiatrist, but my life was now more complicated. Should I return to college? Did I still want to become a doctor? How committed was I to Diane? Did I want to live with her for the rest of my life?

Based on my new self-knowledge, my choices became surprisingly simple. I knew I wanted to follow my heart more than my head. I wanted to return to college to study human emotion. I no longer wanted to be a physician. I loved Diane and wanted to live the rest of my life with her. I was going to return to college, and I was going to marry Diane. Going through what I had experienced gave me the ability to make important decisions with an assurance I never could have had previously.

After completing her fall semester, Diane returned for the spring semester in Philadelphia, but she no longer felt motivated to pursue her studies. She dropped out of college in the middle of the winter semester, and we decided to get married.

My stress level increased when this did not go over very well with Diane's parents. She was 19, and I was 20 so I could understand their concerns. This was not the traditional path, and the statistics for the long-term success of our marriage were not in our favor. However, we did not expect their resistance to be so absolute.

Diane's parents forbade her from seeing me again. She was in a terrible position, stuck between pleasing her parents and being with me. In September of 1973, we decided to get married against her parents' will. It was a huge step for each of us to believe in each other against all odds. Despite our ages, we knew what felt right to us, and believed in how we felt.

My parents were surprisingly supportive. My mother once said that I was forty the day I was born. She believed in whatever I did and trusted my judgment. Threatening to cut off my tuition was never mentioned. It wouldn't have worked. I would have changed schools than change my plans. In fact, the dean requested an appointment with me to review my plans to return to school. When I told him that I was married and planning to live off campus, he told me that I needed to get his permission. I told him that I didn't need anybody's permission, and would be happy to transfer if that was the case. He told me he liked my attitude. I had at least earned some respect by wearing the velvet suit.

I returned to Princeton in the fall with a household to manage and the need to generate some income. I had stopped playing intercollegiate tennis and now focused on becoming a tennis coach. I made enough money the first summer as a teaching tennis professional for us to live on for the remaining nine months of the year. I also continued to teach tennis part-time during school.

It was a lot to manage, but now that I was married I had a more balanced life, a soul mate to talk to, and a different reason to want to succeed. I had someone in my life who could hold up a mirror to my behavior and encourage me to do what was best for my emotional well-being. However, listening emotionally to my wife required me to stop focusing on the next achievement, and to control my fears. I had a hard time doing that, and this made my wife feel alone much too often. I had spent so long pleasing my parents that I had to learn an entirely new way of reacting and of organizing my emotional life.

My stress level jumped up another notch six months later when we suspected that Diane was pregnant, even though she was on The Pill. I took her urine sample into the college infirmary, and we anxiously awaited the results for several days. A nurse called to tell us that the results were positive - Diane was pregnant! I asked if she should stop taking the Pill, and was advised that she should discontinue it immediately.

We were referred to a doctor in New York City and were told he was an expert gynecologist who could help us. After examining Diane, he sat us down and told us that she was only a few weeks pregnant and that he could not perform an abortion. We had no idea that we had been referred to an abortion doctor. We were both outraged, since terminating the pregnancy was never our intention.

We were also confused about the dates he was using. We explained that the positive pregnancy result had been more than six weeks before. He asked if we had stopped using birth control at that point. It was then that I realized the initial positive test was a false positive, and that in fact, Diane had gotten pregnant after she stopped taking the Pill.

Diane gave birth to a beautiful baby girl five months before my expected graduation from Princeton. We did not run out and buy her a velvet dress. I now had a wife and daughter to support, and I still needed to continue my studies. Fortunately, we did fine with my tennis income, and I was the only member of the Class of 1975 to have a child at graduation.

After Princeton

Having a "mental breakdown" during my junior year turned out to be one of those extremely difficult events that actually end up leading to a better outcome. Emotional distress feels terrible, but it can be a learning experience that helps us come to understand ourselves. I had been exposed to the world of human emotion and was in awe of its power. When I graduated, I still did not completely understand what had happened to me. I knew that I was not psychotic and that I could now handle stress. But I felt a strong need to learn more about this deep human experience, and I wanted to share what I learned with the world.

In the fall of 1976, I started graduate school at the University of Cincinnati (ironically, the same school my parents had attended), having been admitted to a class of 12 from over 1,000 applicants. Helping people was popular with the Baby Boomers, so it was incredibly hard to get into a graduate program in Clinical Psychology. I felt fortunate to be admitted. As it turned out, my pre-med qualifications came in handy. With only one psychology course to my credit at Princeton, I was a unique candidate. It helped me stand out from the crowd of thousands of Psych majors.

Eight years later, in 1984, I finished my academic, research, and clinical training, and received my Doctorate in Clinical Psychology. True to my roots, my research for my dissertation and master's thesis was on the mind of the athlete. I knew the demands of a competitive environment, so I studied what I knew.

In addition to my schoolwork and professional training, I also embarked on another journey. To better learn my job, to explore my limitations as a father and a husband, to better understand what had happened to me at Princeton, and to learn more about my emotional reactions, I returned to therapy. I began several years after starting my private practice and continued for seven years. This process was something like peeling off the layers of an onion. The more I learned, the more there was to understand.

I knew that years before I had experienced a panic attack with obsessional thinking, and that my escalating emotional stress had suddenly made me non-functional. Still, I did not understand what had scared me to the point of temporarily disabling me. Why had the record kept playing over and over in my mind? Why had I been unable to turn it off? What had triggered the obsessive thinking?

I learned that relentless, uncontrollable internal thoughts are a mental defense mechanism. They distract us from overwhelming emotions that are brewing due to life events. In my case, even a passing thought about an old girlfriend was a cause for incapacitating shame. I was supposed to be so honorable that I wouldn't even think like that, especially since I had professed my love to Diane and was seriously considering being with her for the rest of my life. It is actually completely normal to have passing thoughts about an old girlfriend, and these should not have been anything other than random noise in my head – but not for me. My passing thoughts about a previous girlfriend fed my sense of shame, which made me even more anxious, which led to more obsessive thinking, which created more thoughts about the old girlfriend. I was caught in a self-perpetuating spiral.

My "shameful" thinking added to the shame that I had been storing away for my entire life. And it was not just my shame, but also the family shame that had accumulated throughout generations. I was the one who had been anointed to reverse all that shame. What would happen to me, and to my family, if I made a false step? I was literally scared out of my mind. I had overwhelming anxiety from just the idea that I might experience the unforgivable shame of failure. What if I dishonored the velvet suit?

I finally recognized the impact that family expectations had on my emotional world. I had never thought that my parents affected me much, especially as I got older. I was so wrong. The imprint of parents is huge and forever. I had learned from my parents that performance is everything and emotions are nothing. I never realized how scared I was of my own emotions, nor did I recognize the symptoms of my fears. I always had other explanations for what I did, and I never realized the depth of the impact of my parents' beliefs upon me. Ironically, the role I played as the "golden boy" in my family set the stage for my eventual breakdown.

In the process of learning about myself, I learned that we need to comprehend how emotions work to understand ourselves and others. If we interpret human behavior only according to character traits or temperament – for example, "Oh, Steve is just a perfectionist" - we miss the important role of human emotion in dictating what we say and do. Why is Steve a perfectionist? Why does he fear making mistakes so much? Why is Steve trying to control his own thoughts and feelings? What are the emotions behind the behavior?

Armed with my academic and professional training, what I had learned from my extensive therapy, and my personal experiences as a husband, father, son, and brother with three siblings, I started my professional career as a clinical psychologist in private practice. And I enjoy it to this day. Each patient is like a puzzle for me to figure out, and helping people find their way back to a satisfying life is rewarding work. My Velvet Suit became stained with baby vomit and, for the most part, was locked away.

Today, Diane and I are the parents of four children who are all grown and established on their own. At this writing, we are the proud grandparents of four grandchildren, two boys, and two girls. I have spent over forty years trying to raise my kids right, so this book is not just an academic exercise. It is time tested and based on emotional truths that I have learned through many sources. The first must be my parents, who started shaping my future before I could even speak. The next is my wife, who has taught me about the impact of my family on myself and on our marriage. The third is my four children – and now grandchildren – who are encouraged to speak the truth, even when it is hard to hear what they have to say. The fourth is my three siblings, whose collective experiences within my family of origin either validate or challenge my own emotional reactions. The fifth is my close friends who care enough to speak honestly with me. When all those sources point in the same direction, the truth is very obvious and cannot be denied.

3

Understanding Family Roles

Why The Part You Played Is Outdated

Your life experiences within your family can interfere with the development of emotionally honest relationships. They can be your biggest threat to learning to listen to your authentic emotions. Family ties bind you together with loved ones, yet may prevent you from being who you want to be.

The process begins the moment you are born. As a young child, you see the world first through the eyes of your parents. Through your connections to them and to the rest of your family, you come to know who you are and what you are allowed to be. These experiences are encoded in your emotions that guide your choices throughout your life. You also are born with innate characteristics such as temperament, cognitive style, and so on, but how you are raised affects how comfortably you use those skills to deal with people and solve problems. As a child, you think of your family as the source of all things good. You idealize your parents because, for you to survive, they must be good and loving people. Because you don't know any better, you assume your family is the best. It is comforting to assume your family is made up of good people because, if the family you came from is good, then you must be good as well.

The problem is that families can't be classified as "good" or "bad." They are as imperfect as the people within them. Families are "some good and some bad." Every family and every family member does some things right and some things wrong. That means even well-meaning Wanting parents will do some harm to their children, even if they don't want to. to do the right thing is no guarantee that you will do the right thing. As the popular saying states, "The road to hell is paved with good intentions."

This phrase is especially true when you are talking about raising children. Parents also have fears, and those fears often dictate what a parent does in any given situation. Rather than serving the child's best interests, what a parent does may simply reduce the parent's own anxieties. When parents do not see their own fears, they can easily justify their choices as doing what is right for the child.

Sarah's Story: The Overprotective Father

Sarah's father, Art, was a very anxious man. He had to be at the airport hours ahead of time. Nobody in his family was ever allowed to go anywhere risky. His wife was not allowed to drive a car. He had four daughters and lived in fear of harm coming to any one of them. As a result, he was very overprotective. As a teenager, Sarah was required to be home by 10 PM. Her friends were allowed to stay out to 11 PM and some until 12 midnight. When she would get upset about her father's strict rules, Art would say that the world is a dangerous place and that he was only watching out for her best interests. He would try to make her feel guilty for complaining.

The truth was, Art liked to go to bed early, and he could not sleep if one of his daughters were out of the house. He would fret and worry, and his fears would get the best of him. He would not admit that this was a weakness of his. Instead, his fears gave rise to anger at Sarah and accused her of being "selfish" for wanting to stay out as late as her friends. Sarah told me that she was never clear if she had the right to challenge her father or not. Was she a really bad child, being selfish and demanding?

Family experiences can create lasting scars even if they are not obviously abusive. An incident may be small, but be part of a continuing pattern. Pushing back at her curfew was just one of many experiences Sarah had with Art where she felt misunderstood and unfairly blamed. Because her own father was always mad at her for something, Sarah never felt that she could trust anyone, and never felt that anybody would have her back. Just as bad, she never created basic trust in her bonds with her parents. The lesson she learned was that people took care of themselves and there was little room for her needs.

This is true for Sarah even today. Because of her insecurity, Sarah often comes across as aloof or cranky. What she really wants is affection and validation. Some people incorrectly believe that Sarah causes her own problems by pushing people away. That is the farthest thing from the truth. Sarah is scared and fears that the history of being blamed in her family is going to repeat with others. Her fears make her retreat without explanation.

Sarah's fears show up in her everyday life. Suppose Sarah is making dinner, and somebody else enters the kitchen. She might snap and say, "Why are you standing there? Please get out until I'm ready." The person might have come in to offer help, but Sarah will never assume that anyone will actually help her. She assumes the person is there to put pressure on her to get the meal on the table faster. Similarly, Sarah can't tell the difference between an opinion and a demand. She starts to fight back if you state an opinion. If you say, "I'd like to go to the movies," she might say, "It's always what you want." She doesn't understand that she has a right to express her needs in response to a statement of another's needs. She doesn't know how to engage in "give and take" to resolve differences.

If Sarah isn't included when plans are being made, she withdraws, often leading people to incorrectly believe she is not interested in participating. To Sarah, others never really want her in the first place. Her withdrawal is a plea for help that is easily misread. It is actually a sign of trauma.

Sarah's history gives her a high degree of sensitivity to criticism. A problem could be small like accidentally breaking a dish or not being able to find something that was misplaced. Sarah responds with a yelp: "I didn't do it." She is more concerned with fixing the blame than fixing the problem because she anticipates being blamed, just like in her family. The root problem of Sarah's fears originates in her family and repeats in all her relationships. The same pattern used to repeat over and over again between father and daughter. Sarah would naturally react to her father's demands. Art's denial of his extreme anxiety would make Sarah the problem. Rather than admit his fear, Art chose to make Sarah feel bad for questioning his authority and reasoning.

This created stress in the family because Sarah and her father were not the only players on this stage. Her mother and sisters to would watch this drama playing out and were forced to take sides. "Staying out of it" was not a good option. If they said nothing, they chose to not be part of the solution, enabled the father's denial of his anxiety to go unchallenged, and failed to back up Sarah. This way, they received continued affection from Art. If they sided with Sarah, they ran the risk of antagonizing Art. There was no good choice here. The other family members all risked either the connection to the father or the bond with their sister.

Mom is a very important player here. Should she side with the truth and challenge her husband to face his fears, this would undoubtedly infuriate him and would chastise her for being disloyal to him. He would say, "Whose side are you on anyway?" or "So much for the united front!" He would accuse her of embarrassing him in front of his children. Then he would withdraw emotionally or even threaten to leave her if she persisted in defending Sarah and making him the problem.

Sarah's Mom usually believed she had no choice but to go along with her husband. She had been raised to believe that you are supposed to support your partner in raising children and that disagreeing in front of children undermined her husband's authority. She felt incorrect that she had to choose between her husband and her daughter. She never realized that she could stand up for the truth, rather than take a side. Unfortunately, when Sarah's mother backed up her husband, she unknowingly reinforced the family rule that all family members should blindly worship their father and do as he said regardless of whether it was right or wrong.

This story shows how denial is used theoretically to protect parents and marriage from harm. Even the smallest of family issues, like setting a curfew for adolescent kids, can have a psychological impact on the entire family because somewhere beneath the decision lurks a parent's denial and a child's truth. In the long run, perpetuating the parent's denial actually harms both the marriage and the emotional well -being of the children.

The Power Of A Parent

The way you were raised has a profound impact on how you think and feel, bigger than you realize or can possibly imagine. As a small impressionable child, you depend on your parents to interpret the world around you. It does not matter to the child whether your mother and father are traditional parents, same-sex parents, or parents of adopted children. Your parents' reactions become the basis for how you decide what is good and what is bad. If they react strongly, then there is something important for you to remember. You store their reactions in your memory in the form of feelings, thoughts, and images, but it is your feelings that tag these experiences based on the significance of your parents' emotional reactions.

Unfortunately, what your parents may be teaching you is to absorb their fears, both rational and irrational. Your parents are human and therefore imperfect. They have fears that are unreasonable. What you learn from your parents is as imperfect as they are. Their lessons are both good and bad, irrational and rational, reasonable and unreasonable. You, too, are imperfect because your parents pass on their imperfections and fears, very often without their knowledge.

Human Yelps

My wife and I adopted a dog named, Jenny, a Newfoundland mix. She was taken from her original owner because she was severely abused. The prior owner would tie her to a tree and kick her repeatedly in the head with his boots. You would never know it, as she was one of the sweetest dogs we have ever had. But you saw the effects of her past abuse whenever my feet came close to her. If I stepped anywhere near her, she would let out a yelp and jump up. To this day, after living with us for 13 years, she still jumps at the sight of my feet. The reaction has lessened over time; she doesn't' jump as far or yelp as loud as she once did, but there is still a significant reaction. It is hard to believe that 13 years of loving her has not eliminated the effect of her early abuse. Sadly, it is a permanent scar that affects her to this day.

While this story does illustrate the lasting damage of abuse, there is an important difference between dogs and humans. As they grow up, humans are more dependent on their parents than any other living creature. Children stay with their parents for two decades before they are released into the world to live on their own. It takes that long to teach them how to survive in the world alone and how to relate to other people.

This dependency can be a curse as well as a blessing. Human beings are blessed because they have the safety of their parents and family to shield them from the world for years. Yet they are cursed because they have an equally long time to absorb the bad habits and fears of the parents, or if they are truly unlucky actual abuse.

Hiding Your Emotions

The impact of family experiences is first encoded in your memory at a time when the vulnerability and dependency of infancy make it impossible for you to critically evaluate what you are learning. Your memories are laid down without your awareness or your ability to discriminate the good from the bad.

As you get older, you begin to form your own opinions. You may realize your parents are in error, but it is safer to accept what you are told rather than challenge it. Challenging Mom or Dad is scary and can lead to a distance from loved ones, isolation, rejection, or abandonment. You do have your own natural reactions to family experiences, but the pressure of survival makes you lean toward accepting your parents' point of view over your own. In the face of strong disapproval from a parent, you learn to surrender your own natural reaction and put your faith in the truth according to Mom and Dad. The fear of your parents' rejection quickly overrides any doubts you have. You suppress your emotions to reduce your fears and stay in Mom and Dad's good graces.

You didn't always suppress your emotions. Infants spontaneously express emotion. If it feels good, they are content. If it feels wrong, they let you know it. They make faces or kick and scream. They are not shy. They do not wait to react. As children grow older, they become more aware of their attachment to their parents and the need for their parents' approval to ensure basic survival -food, clothing, and shelter. Once children are capable of having their own personal reactions, the stakes get very high. Testing a limit leads to parental disapproval, which in turn evokes the deepest fears of all children, the loss of connection to the parent. With each incident of parental disapproval, children's authentic responses become infused with fear, and they learn to hide their natural reactions.

So as a child, you learn to hide your honest emotions and natural reactions and do as you are told. But as an adult, you need to find your authentic feelings again to be true to yourself. Your growth and independence as an adult depend on your ability to see any emotions you have hidden away, and to use them to forge independent connections, relationships that are close but don't rely on seeking approval by acting a certain way.

Some people don't wait until adulthood to honor their emotions. Due to temperament, personality, birth order, or a combination of these, some children never surrender but challenge their parents right from the beginning. They seem to emerge willing to risk the rejection of their parents. For some of these children, their temperament is so strong that they can't hide or calm their own reactions. In other cases, parents may be so unhealthy that they blame the children for anything and everything. Whatever happens, the children get in trouble. Why bother to hide their true feelings when the result will be the same? These children have nothing to lose by speaking up, so they do and are seen as defiant.

Some children are so oppressed by the need to please that they forego the usual adolescent rebellion. This keeps things calm…until they find a long-term partner or get married. When partners rip the scab off the shared delusion of a family that is not their own, parent pleasers are forced to decide where the truth lies. Do they side with their parents and say nothing, or side with their partner and rebel for the first time? If the first hint of rebellion occurs after marriage, the in-law is typically blamed and becomes the new scapegoat in the family.

In most cases, parents with good intentions bond with children who are compliant most of the time. Most children will be obedient to get what they want. Most wait until adolescence arrives to begin to actively fight back. Parents roll their eyes about the Terrible Two's, but rip out their hair about their early teens, when children become experts at defiance but are not yet old enough to make good choices. Eventually, life experiences enable them to honor their authentic reactions while simultaneously listening to their parents. This is the process of adult growth: to form independent attachments in which self-aware people learn to share their own reactions and negotiate a compromise, which is simply a blend of reactions.

Family Role Mapping

You have no doubt heard phrases like: "She's the pretty one," or, "He's the smart one," or, "He's the athlete in the family," or, "She's the funny one." These appear to be innocent references to traits or abilities that set apart each child in a family. Equally common are labels that are not complimentary, like, "She's a Daddy's girl," or, "He's the Golden Boy," or, "He's the problem child in the family," or, "She's difficult." One of my patients told me that she was referred to as "the big mouth in the family." I've also had parents refer to their child as "the sick one," "the martyr," and "the super sensitive one." Whether they are flattering or insulting, all these references reveal a deep problem in the relationship between the children and the parents. These phrases lock in the role that the child plays within the family, and a negative label indicates the extent to which the child experiences rejection.

Children's roles set their internal rules for living. It is a universal phenomenon. Your family role is the permanent imprint of your expected childhood behavior and beliefs; what you were allowed to do and to be, how you were supposed to treat others, what were considered reasonable beliefs in your home, what was expected of you, etc. Each child develops a different role in the family based on factors like birth order, sex, temperament, and the state of the family at any given time. Although it is largely created by default, based on the view of your parents, it is impossible to over-estimate the importance of your established family role. It's like carrying your entire childhood experience forward or holding on to the family within.

Your family role is held in place by strong emotions like fear, guilt, and shame that tell you when you are thinking about doing something, or have already done something that violates your role. You know you are breaking the rules when you feel those feelings. They are the result of your parents' early disapproval, the emotional imprint of the way you were raised. This internal alarm system is always present, triggered by situations or thoughts without your awareness. Like a smoke alarm, it is on autopilot, ready to be activated at a moment's notice. You don't even have time to think about it and is so strong that it lasts a lifetime. The role that you play in the family is not always obvious. Role mapping is what I call the process of seeking to discover your lifelong imprint. You can map the rules of your role by observing yourself and your family.

The best way to increase your awareness of your family role is to compare your family experience with that of your siblings. Although they are raised at different times and under different circumstances, children in the same family share the common experience of their parents. They all have to cope with the good and bad in Mom and Dad. In a healthy family, siblings will share these experiences with each other. This sharing helps to validate the observations of each other and offset any parental denial about the bad. In unhealthy families, the siblings will clash. Some will support the parent's denial while others will challenge it.

Another way to determine your family role is to watch or even consult your extended family. Uncles, aunts, and cousins can often see more clearly than family members what is going on, although they may downplay the significance of the patterns they notice. Close family friends also can provide perspective on the behavior of parents, unless the patterns are very subtle. Disapproval is easy to hide.

Even with the help of your siblings, the extended family members, and good friends, your role may be difficult to pin down. Only the immediate family members truly know what goes on. Usually, parents don't have to say anything to get their point across. Their actions speak louder than their words. This means outsiders may completely miss what is happening in your house. One of my patients was floored when a neighbor told her, "There's a lot of love in your home." Her parents' campaign to look like the perfect family to outsiders worked perfectly well.

When parents have conflicting or vague reactions that don't make sense, you are left to draw your own conclusions. I experienced this confusion as a child with my own father. One of his favorite sayings was, "Don't do as I do. Do as I say." This remark would usually come immediately after I pointed out to him that he had just done something that he had told me was against the rules. The inconsistency between his words and actions baffled me. Since he was telling me that he didn't have to follow the rules, I could never tell what the rules really were, and when I might be permitted to break them too. I wanted to please him and was exasperated when I could not figure out how to do that.

Youth Sports

Families that emphasize achievement reward children who excel in sports with praise and privileges. There is nothing wrong with encouraging achievement or wanting your children to be the best that they can be, as long as you are emotionally honest with yourself as a parent. The issue is whether the achievement and the recognition that it brings serves the children's needs or the parents' needs. Is it important because it makes the parents' look good or because it helps the children? If it is for the parents' needs, the children will feel excessive pressure and anxiety because the motivation is coming from the outside. If it is for themselves, they will play their sport enthusiastically without undue anxiety.

You have no doubt seen parents misbehaving badly at the baseball or soccer field, hockey rink, or basketball game. Some get into fights with the referees or other parents. They are clearly over-invested in the game. Other parents are quiet but still can place a great deal of unseen pressure on their children. Young athletes can respond to this pressure in one of two ways. First, they may take on the role. They embrace it wholeheartedly and try to manage the high-performance anxiety that accompanies it. They are trying to be the best that they can be for others rather than themselves. The sport now means too much. It is a means to please their parents and play the sport with the weight of their parents on their back. What started as a fun game to play with their friends has turned into a pressure cooker involving family relationships.

The second way to handle the pressure from Mom and Dad is to push back and refuse to play the role. These young athletes rebel. They may stop playing the sport or stop practicing because it is no longer is enjoyable to them. I have treated numerous young athletes who were referred to me because they didn't want to practice or had temper tantrums on the field or in the locker room. They were often labeled as "problem athletes" who lacked the self-discipline to push themselves. Sometimes, they were seen as "quitters" who were too lazy to put in the necessary practice time to be all they could be. Competition is the nature of sports, so a player who won't compete will receive a lot of negative attention.

In every case, I could trace the behavior of "problem athletes" back to the pressures that had been placed on them by parents, peers, or coaches. Because these children had been imprinted with the importance of performance, they were susceptible to peer pressure and a coach's anger as much as parent disapproval. They were typically angry and had lost the love of their sport. I was able to help some who went on to have fun again. Others were too resentful and needed to stop. Some switched sports and had fun again. Others turned to other pursuits and never looked back. In all cases, the goal was to find the authentic feelings and validate them so the children could make decisions about what was good for them.

Matt's Story: The Frozen Athlete

I remember one case that so clearly illustrates the core issues of youth sports. Matt, the third baseman for a high school baseball team, had always been called the "athletic one" in his family. After being offered a full scholarship to his first-choice college in the fall of his senior year, Matt suddenly could not throw the ball. His arm would begin the motion, but the ball would not leave his hand. It was as if his body had a mind of its own that he couldn't control. While he certainly had the desire and motor memory to execute the throw, he simply could not release the ball.

There was nothing physically wrong with Matt, but being unable to play softball was a catastrophe. When he was referred to me, I recognized that severe anxiety overrode his mind's ability to control his muscles. My job was to find out where the anxiety was coming from, thereby restoring his ability to throw, and his college scholarship.

As it turned out, Matt was under tremendous pressure at home. His divorced mother had recently fallen in love with a new boyfriend and was constantly relying on him to play with and babysit his younger brothers. Mom was so thrilled about her new love life that she did not realize she was spending most nights away from the house. Without a father around, Matt and his mother had been through a lot together, and he liked to see his mother finally happy. However, as the amount of time spent relying on Matt grew, Matt's resentment also grew. He got madder and madder by the day, but he also wanted to help. Matt knew he was mad but didn't recognize how furious he really was or know what to do about it. More importantly, neither Matt nor his mother ever realized that the relationship between the mother and new boyfriend was the core problem causing Matt's inability to throw.

Matt's mother was all he had, so Matt did not let himself feel the full extent of his anger. His problem with his Mom became internalized and then interfered with the fluidity of his neuromuscular movements. The tensions he had in his life translated into tense muscles that did not respond to his motor memory.

In therapy, Matt learned to find his authentic emotions and trust his anger. He realized that simply having feelings would not harm his mother or their relationship. He asked his mother to spend less time with the boyfriend. Fortunately, Mom responded well to this challenge and spent more time taking care of her own responsibilities at home. While it took over a year to restore Matt's ability to throw, he was able to earn his college scholarship and play collegiate baseball.

This problem occurs more frequently in sports than people realize. Steve Blass, a professional baseball player for the Pittsburgh Pirates, experienced a similar problem back in the 1970's. After being one of the premier pitchers in baseball for many years, he lost the ability to throw the ball. Suddenly, he could not find the plate, with each throw sailing to the backstop. This syndrome was named after him and is called the "Steve Blass Disease."

Family Roles Serve The Parents

The family roles of the children actually serve the parents' needs and are not in the children's best interests. In an ideal world without hidden feelings and denial, there would be no need for them. Parents would react to each other authentically, fully aware of their own emotions, and find solutions to problems through negotiation and compromise.

Unfortunately, we don't live in an ideal world. Unresolved problems are a fact of all human marriages. There are three ways to deal with them; hiding them, simply agreeing to disagree, or actively trying to resolve them. Solving problems takes time and effort. Many couples avoid doing this work. It is difficult, can be painful, and may even bring the marriage to the brink of breaking up before it is healed. Even relatively healthy families may avoid this work if it can be ignored. As one of my patients once said to me, "I have my wife on a need-to-know basis." This saves confrontations but is not an honest marriage.

The addition of a child ramps up the need to do this work. Children bring several problems a day for a couple to resolve. Children are careful observers, need emotional honesty, and as they grow up, they challenge parents to resolve their differences. They see right through denial and unhealthy compromises. Differences that were covered over in the absence of children can no longer be hidden. Unless their life experiences cause them to avoid their true feelings, children are emotionally honest and need the same from their parents to feel secure. When the words and pictures don't match, parents say one thing and do another, or present a fake veneer of feeling a certain way, they challenge their parents to find out what the authentic feelings are beneath the parents' behavior. I have heard parents say that children ruined their marriage, but the truth is that the problems brought out by the children most likely pre-dated the kids and remained hidden by both partners.

Exposing the hidden feelings and fault lines in a marriage may threaten a carefully constructed but nonetheless shaky peace. Often, one partner wants to expose an emotional truth the other wants to deny. This causes conflict, erodes trust, and damages the relationship. Resolving differences requires self-knowledge that has to be developed and tested over time. As a result, you are in varying states of denial of your emotions throughout your life. If you deny what your partner sees, the problem cannot be solved. You can't fix it until you admit it.

When both partners deny their weaknesses, this dynamic protects the marriage at the expense of the children. When kids react to a problem, they observe in a parent or between the parents, and the child is blamed or told they are disrespectful; the marital problem is transferred to them. They become the problem. Denial protects the denier but kills the messenger. Instead of being emotionally honest and admitting the problem, parents act as if the problem lies with the children.

When this kind of denial occurs between parents and children, the damage is even worse than it is in a relationship between adults. Children naturally blame themselves for anything that goes wrong in their world. They lack the life experience to understand problems in any other way. Children rely on their parents to understand and interpret for them what is going on. When a parent shifts the blame for a discrepancy or difficulty onto the children, the kids become confused, scared and unable to defend themselves. The harm is now double-barreled. The parents blame the children when the children are already blaming themselves.

It is far easier to silence the children than to face the fears of challenging your partner. Based on what I have seen, this process of "killing the messenger" occurs to different degrees in all families, including my own. This process protects the marriage but forces children to make a choice, either go along with the denial or challenge it.

Parents typically reward children who do not challenge the truth. These kids receive more acceptance and approval. This feels nice but is a problem because the deceit is infused with love, which all children crave. The opposite is true for the children who do not go along with the family script. Their role is imprinted by rejection and repeated abandonment. Their natural reactions cause tension in the parents, which makes the parents defensive and angry. Basic trust between parents and children is never established. For these kids, human contact becomes fraught with fear of the expected rejection. They do not trust easily. Even if they are able to trust, their faith is easily lost.

Being a "good" child can mean different things in different families. In one family, it is defined by academic and/or athletic achievement. For another, it is kind and considerate of other human beings. For still another, the definition of the good child is taking care of the parent's emotional needs by avoiding conflict. Good behavior can sometimes be based on preventing fights between Mom and Dad, even though this makes the child complicit in a big lie. One of my patients asked his parents, in all innocence, why his father always worked late at the office. In truth, the father was having an affair – which the mother did not want to think about. Both parents reacted angrily, and my patient learned at a young age not to ask questions.

When being the good child depends on supporting the weaknesses in the relationship between the parents, an unhealthy role reversal has occurred. The good child is rewarded for parenting the parent rather than the other way around. This role reversal happens anytime parents try to avoid conflict with each other and cannot acknowledge their own emotions. Children are not fooled. They see emotions clearly. When the parents require developing children to deny what they see, the kids become little caretakers for the marriage, a terrible burden to bear.

As long as the parents are not emotionally honest with each other, there is no good outcome for the children. If the kids fight back, they become "bad" for threatening to expose the parents' emotions. Even worse, the parents may turn on the children and attack their character. They may regard the children's failure to comply as a personality flaw of the child and label them selfish, stubborn, or spoiled. The parents may view the children as needing discipline, so they punish them or withhold their affection. The "good" children go along with the subterfuge of the parents, but lose the connection to their own natural emotions. They are terrified of being punished again in the future. Even though the parents shower these children with approval, they are cultivating profound self-doubt and anxiety in them at the same time.

No parent is perfect. No adult can be completely aware of all their emotions all of the time. All parents are capable of denying their emotions at any given moment. As a result, there is always some degree of pressure on the children in any family to play a role.

The Non-Traditional Family

Roles exist because denial exists. This is true regardless of whether the family unit is an intact couple, divorced, or single parent. Separate households do not make either house immune to denial. However, divorce can serve a positive purpose by buffering role creation. The children clearly see that Mom or Dad or both have a psychological problem that breaks them apart. The divorce begins to expose emotional truths about the couple.

In the single parent family, the denial that exists in everyone at any time can cause roles to form. The difference in divorce is that the roles that each child plays with their mother or father can be different and confusing. They must also juggle the incompatible views of their parents and feel compelled to be the messenger of the truth. Issues such as weight control, grades, immunizations, participation in extra-curricular activities may create excessive worry in one or both parents. In the single parent household, the child does not have a parent to buffer them at the moment. The non-custodial parent can buffer the denial, but the custodial parent may block access. Even worse, it can become the basis for yet another round of fighting between the ex's, causing the child to feel caught in the middle and blamed for the fighting.

The support system of the single parent can impact the level of damage done to the children. The opinions of grandparents, aunts, and uncles, even close friends can serve to validate the child's perceptions of the truth and limit how much children blame themselves for their parent's problems. Needless to say, the ability to speak up and defend the child against the parent requires a strong relationship with a high degree of trust. If done healthily, the validation from the support system can greatly minimize the potential harm from any denial that the children may experience in either home.

Impairments in the parent can add to the strength of a family role. If one parent is an alcoholic, drug addict, or mentally impaired, the family role of the children becomes distorted. The children learn to tiptoe around their parent's problem. Most likely, they also take on caregiving responsibilities, either for themselves, other children, the parent, or everybody in the family. If the parent's condition is undiagnosed or a family secret, there is the added confusion for the children of seeing a problem every day that everyone else denies. To stay in the family, they are forced to pretend they don't see what their eyes clearly tell them. They also are obliged to keep up the family charade and make excuses for the parent's behavior. These experiences are unhealthy for children and only serve to strengthen the family role and suppress their authentic reactions.

Family Roles Create A Blueprint For All Relationships

The most important purpose of the family role is to define what you must do to sustain relationships with people. Your emotions hold your role in place. Step out of line, and you experience fear, guilt, and shame. Stay on the path, and you feel calm. Your role is etched into these emotional reactions for the rest of your life – unless you consciously challenge it. Your emotions get triggered over and over again throughout your life and become the blueprint for all future attachments.

In essence, you are programmed to repeat in all relationships what you have learned from your parents. The message is stored in strong emotionally loaded memories that create anxiety if you don't follow the rules. Fear triggered by the experiences that you had with your parents and family becomes the signal that you might risk disapproval and create distance in your current relationships. You relieve the fear by staying in line.

Many people I treat come into my office with the belief that they have outgrown their parent's influence. As one of them recently told me, "I live

3000 miles away from my parents. They have no effect on me." Sadly, this can't be farther from the truth. What she doesn't see is the enormous influence of her emotional blueprint. It is like a bell that is rung in every exchange in every relationship every day. Many people are aware of the thoughts that are in their heads, but they don't know the emotional root cause of those thoughts. They don't see the assumptions behind the fears that cause them to jump to conclusions. Even if they know how they feel, they don't know how to sort through the competing feelings.

Paul's Story: My Family Doesn't Bother Me Anymore

Paul, a 42-year-old insurance broker, had come to me on his physician's insistence. Paul did not believe in psychotherapy and only agreed to come to get his doctor off his back. Paul had recently been diagnosed with Irritable Bowel Syndrome and was completely at a loss about how to cope with his symptoms. At times, his abdominal pain would be so bad that he was unable to go to work. Even if he made it work, he was not able to focus or concentrate due to the pain.

Paul was confused about the origin of his pain. He knew that his work was stressful, but refused to acknowledge that there could be any connection between his work stress and his pain level. In Paul's case, the two did not appear to be linked. When his work stress was high, he did not have the pain. It only appeared in the calm times. There did not appear to be a pattern to the pain episodes, and Paul was baffled about what to do next. He agreed to come to see me because he was out of options and afraid that he would lose his job.

Personal history is the best diagnostic tool I can use to understand any patient. Paul was the eldest of three brothers and a sister raised in a strict Irish Catholic family. Paul's father was very "old school" and did not tolerate any backtalk from any of his children. He believed in the "spare the rod, spoil the child" approach to child-rearing. He saw nothing wrong with using physical punishment to teach his children about life's lessons. Paul's mother didn't agree with his father's methods but felt it was the woman's place to follow her husband. She believed that a united front was in the best interests of the children. She never spoke out against anything that Paul's father did.

Paul was as strong-willed as his father and did not like his father's methods at all. He felt that his father could be mean, arbitrary and controlling. His father did what he wanted when he wanted, without care or concern for the opinion of anyone else, especially that of a child. Paul would challenge his father and would pay a steep price for having a voice. Paul remembers being beaten with a belt over and over, including with the buckle if his father was particularly mad.

To avoid the physical abuse, Paul learned to hide whatever he did from his parents. If he went out with his friends, he would sneak out late at night. He gave up trying to get permission to go out, knowing his father's answer would be negative. Whenever he had asked, his request had been denied, and he'd been given another chore to do to fill up his free time. Interestingly, Paul did not blame his father for being arbitrary and unreasonable. Instead, he blamed himself for being a bad kid.

Whenever the subject of his father came up, Paul would make excuses for his father. His favorite line was, "My Dad always meant well. He did the best he could. His father beat him too so he didn't know any better." If I challenged Paul about the right of a parent to hit a child, Paul would become highly agitated. He would make statements like, "You shrinks always blame the parents. I don't see how talking about my childhood helps my IBS. I am 42 years old. I don't live with my parents any longer and rarely see them. They don't bother me anymore and don't see the purpose of dwelling on my past."

Paul did not see that he had been branded for life by the emotional patterns caused by his abuse. Paul blamed himself for his abuse even as an adult. He could not understand it any other way because he was programmed from birth to believe his father was blameless. This meant he must be the problem, even without apparent cause. He accepted that getting beaten with a belt was his fault.

Paul was used to being unfairly blamed for everything, which made him very touchy. He believed I was blaming him for his IBS pain. He thought I was telling him that his pain was in his head and that he was making it up. To Paul, that made perfect sense.

PAUL: "Why do you keep focusing on my parents every time we talk? The past is the past, and I want to focus on my future."
ME: "Your past is not your past. It is very present. Because you were arbitrarily beaten as a child, you have trouble trusting other people today. Notice how you have trouble trusting me. You don't trust that I have a good reason to keep talking about your parents. In fact, it's because I want you to get better and have less pain."
PAUL: "You are right. I don't trust you. I get tense whenever you bring up my past. I don't want to think about it."
ME: "I can understand that. These are not pleasant memories. It must have terrified you as a child to be beaten like that. I don't mean to upset you, but I think I need to help you to understand the fears left over from your past, so they don't drive you anymore."
PAUL: "What do you mean by driving me? I am an adult now. I don't get beaten by anybody anymore. I can make my own choices now as an adult. I am not a kid anymore."
ME: "We are all human time machines. We are 5, 15 and 42 years old at the same time. Our memories store our emotions from the past and dump them out on us when something in the present cues them. If we believe everything that we feel, we will keep running from the same emotions and repeating our history over and over."
PAUL: "What does all this have to do with my father? I still, don't see it."
ME: "You suppressed your emotions to survive the beatings. You blamed yourself and could not validate your own anger. You still react the same way. When somebody mistreats you now, you know how to silently survive it. You assume the blame even when you

don't deserve it. The pattern is alive and well in all of your relationships."

Although he was highly resistant, Paul did learn to trust me. He learned to listen to his body because it was listening to him. He came to see the link between his suppressed emotion and the spasms in his colon. He saw more and more clearly the emotional avoidance that dominated all his relationships. Eventually, he started to take the risk of giving voice to his emotions. By using this natural path of expression, he no longer needed to store his natural feelings of frustration or resentment in his body. While changing how Paul handled his emotions did not eliminate the IBS pain completely, the frequency, intensity, and duration of his episodes dropped significantly.

The Past Is Always Present

Like Paul, your family role, the emotional program written for you by your parents, is always present to keep the past alive. Understanding this psychological truth is critical, yet is not an easy concept to grasp. You react to the present and the past at the same time. As an emotional being, you are all ages at the same time. You recognize an event because it reminds you of a previous experience. It is rare for a human being to experience a moment that is truly novel. You put most experiences in a certain context because they remind you of something important, something stored in your mind based on the emotional significance of the event. The emotion of the present sets off a cascade of emotions triggered by memories of past events. This flooding of emotion happens quite frequently, even if it occurs at low levels. The past has flooded into the present whenever you rush to judgment. The past makes you prematurely jump to a conclusion before verifying your perceptions. The past has shown up again when you over-react because you are overwhelmed with emotion. It is there when you are quick to blame yourself or others before knowing what happened.

People tend to repeat the same problems in relationships over and over again because emotionally they are on automatic pilot. They follow the path defined by their emotional blueprint and make choices to reduce the tension produced by fear, guilt or shame. They make the mistake of believing that there is truth in these emotions when in fact their usefulness is long gone.

The psychological effects of emotional flooding are both bad and good. The bad is that you treat all people as if they have the same relationship requirements as your parents. Those assumptions confuse people, as they do not have the same blueprint or make the same assumptions. They also confuse yourself. You are listening to your learned emotions, letting them be your guide, and do not realize in the moment what you are doing. You do not see the faulty programming in these emotional reactions, nor the connection to your parents. Understandably, you think these emotions are your authentic emotions because you are feeling them. You do not realize they were instilled in you long ago. Yes, you do feel them, but they may not be relevant to your present experience.

The good news is that your emotions can also become the basis for change. Once you are able to make a distinction between these learned emotions and your authentic, current reactions, you can learn to ignore the learned ones, follow the authentic ones, and consciously make different choices in your relationships. Knowing which feelings to heed takes some practice so I will talk more about this process later.

Family Roles and Fear

Fear of abandonment created your family role and, without your conscious awareness, continues to sustain it even after your role ceases to be beneficial. Your most basic fear comes from being disconnected from the people that you need for survival. When you act in a way that pleases them, your parents love you, and you feel close. When you do something "bad," and they retreat from you, you become detached and afraid. You quickly learn to hide the authentic reaction that is causing the problem. You learn that there is great safety by staying within your family role. Living life within that role protects you from your fears.

As a child, this fear becomes your master. If your reactions please your parents, your level of fear is low, and you feel good. You store your behavior for safekeeping in your memory because it reduces your fear and keeps your love connection with your parents intact. These memories help you stay comfortable and help to maintain your family role. When you do something that results in disapproval, your fear rises. You log those experiences in your memory because they signal that the connection to your parents may be broken and lost, possibly forever. These essential memories are laid down before you can even speak, and are reinforced for years afterward.

The level of healthiness of your family determines the level of fear that you face as a child and the indelibility of your family role. As an adult, the level of fear that you experience is largely due to the level of fear that you faced as a child. In healthy families, children face reasonable levels of fear.

For example, parents get mad because they are scared when you run into traffic. They are fearful and upset because they don't want you to be hurt. You learn not to run into traffic, but you still feel close to your parents. In unhealthy families, children face heightened emotions from parental responses that don't make sense. The safest thing for kids to do is to retreat from the behavior that provoked a scary response, deny their feelings, and turn to the role that relieves the fear. Your fears and the strength of your need to hold on to your role for protection are the result of your family experiences.

The Good, The Bad And The Ugly

There are three levels of fear that a child experiences, depending on how healthy the family is. I call them the Good, the Bad, and the Ugly. When the level of fear is Good or Bad, parental mistakes can be healed with contrition and reparation. Reassurances can repair hurt feelings. In contrast, Ugly levels of fear cause major damage.

Good experiences predominate in a healthy family. You have experiences that feel good for the majority of your time spent with your family, and you experience low levels of confusion, denial, and fear. The family rules make sense, and you feel safe expressing your feelings. You generally feel good because what you are being asked to do what makes sense to you. You are allowed to learn and to have a voice. This leads to a sense of internal calm and joy.

Bad levels of fear result when your parents consistently disapprove of your behavior. You are pressured to honor the family role and to do as you are told, even if it doesn't make sense to you. Furthermore, you are confused because your parents are in denial about the deceit in their marriage. Even if you don't understand the problem, you can tell it exists based on how it makes you feel. You learn that "bad" behavior will separate you from your parents. You feel an elevated level of fear in these instances and a strong pressure to play the role. Retreating to your role ends the confusion and enables you to remain in good graces in the family.

Ugly levels of fear are created in family situations that are unhealthy at their best and abusive at their worst. Fear climbs to intolerable levels and relationships implode. Every interaction with your parents involves confusion, denial, and deceit. You are exposed continuously to rebuke from one parent or another. When your parents insist on an alternate reality, you become confused and deeply afraid that the conflict you are causing will break up the marriage and it will be your fault. Parents scream and yell at the child for no good reason, or worse, beat you for what they did or are doing wrong. You experience a level of fear that is overwhelming. You can't make sense of it and don't know how to behave the "right" way to make the punishment stop. You literally stop functioning in that moment. You shut down internally to survive. The only memory of the event is overwhelming fear.

What matters most is how long you spend in the Ugly zone. Even well-meaning parents have these Ugly moments with their children. Despite their best intentions, every parent can get overwhelmed and respond irrationally to questioning or defiant children. No parent can ever be perfect. Parents are people too, with insecurities and fears that cause them to overreact to situations, say things that they wish they had never said, or do things that harm their children. Because parents are imperfect, everyone is exposed to Ugly episodes of fear as a child.

The higher the number of Ugly experiences you have, the more you hold onto your family role for dear life. You become frozen in fear. Stepping outside of the blueprint set down by your parents gives you an electric shock of emotion. It is designed to keep you in your role no matter what the circumstances. Stay within, and you feel safe. Don't do as you were told and you feel a rush of fear, guilt, and shame.

Even as an adult, after you have learned that what you were taught is wrong, an experience may remind you of the Ugly interactions with your parents. You will not be able to avoid the rush of emotion that comes from acting differently from the way you were programmed. When you are this afraid, you are most likely unable to think and function. These feelings are so awful and overwhelming that you fall back on your family role regardless of the cost to your marriage, children, or job. You are incapable of anything else. You were scared out of your mind as a child, and the memories are so powerful that they incapacitate you years later.

Family Roles Are The Enemy Within

You form your sense of who you are by following your family role. When your role is continuously reinforced, it becomes you. It is your automatic response that gets triggered so fast that you don't even realize what is going on inside of you. Because your responses to any given situation are always consistent, you assume they reflect the real you. It takes work to see that they are learned emotions reinforced constantly by your parents to cope with their own fears.

Hopefully, your Ugly experiences in your family are infrequent and occur over passing matters. For others less fortunate, Ugly events are common, and their emotional impact is huge. This can happen when there is a high level of denial in a marriage or when there is sexual and/or physical abuse occurring. Adults with these backgrounds may encounter triggers that set off the overwhelming fear of the Ugly experience. It is a very powerful force.

Adults who had too many Ugly experiences as children "go numb" under certain conditions. They probably cannot recognize the connection to their emotions and may try to medicate their pain with alcohol, drugs, sex, and other obsessions. They may have physical disorders, episodes of rage, or even dissociative reactions in which they can't remember what happened to them at all. Ingrained fear can hijack any part of the mind or body.

Your family role is the enemy within. If you can learn to recognize that enemy, you can learn to fight it. Unfortunately, you cannot get rid of your blueprint completely. It was set down during your formative years and is permanently embedded in your memories. When you grow up, your internal bell is rung by the fears that are caused by everyday life events.

You can learn to overcome this fear. It is like learning to ride a wave. Fear has a way of lessening if you give it enough time. While you calm down, you look for the competing emotions inside you that are beneath the wave. Understanding your family role will help you to find and use your antidote emotions, the authentic emotions, which in turn will enable you to represent yourself more accurately in all your relationships. Identifying your role will help you to free yourself from the ties that bind you to your family history, and will enable you to create loving but independent relationships based on honest emotional exchanges.

Family Harmony

Even though family roles limit authentic reactions, roles are a reality of every family. Even healthy families create roles as a psychological shield for the parents and the marriage. The difference in the healthy family is the parents teach the children that denial is damaging and emotional honesty needs to rule. They must first practice what they preach and model solving problems in their marriage. Parents disagree with each other in front of the children, but remove themselves from the children if the disagreement escalates. They accept the need to buffer each other's family history and enable authentic reactions to drive the interactions.

In the healthy family, parents and children play by rules of reason to solve problems. Parental mistakes are admitted to the children. If favoritism exists, it is acknowledged and explained to reduce harm. If a parent overreacts, they admit responsibility and repair the damage through contrition and reparation. As long as there is little anxiety in the parent, family rules will make sense to the children. Their sense of self is consistent with what Mom and Dad want for them. Even if they must learn to delay their gratification and get upset when they don't get their way, the experience of learning from a parent who remains calm enables children to appreciate the reasonableness in their parents' reactions. The rules make sense, roles are minimized, and the whole family feels psychologically safe.

In some families, things are not always what they seem. Family interactions appear healthy, but the harmony may be a false front. Children can be obedient for the wrong reasons. They have learned never to honor their authentic reactions. The denial of the parent is so strong, and his or her authority is so powerful, that no one dares to step out of line. This kind of harmony is unsustainable. The children might eventually blow up or move far away, but the family unit will eventually break down. When examined below the surface, this pseudo-healthy family will function with strong roles and high fear in the children.

4

Were You A Family Hero
Or Family Scapegoat?
The Hand That Rocks The Boat

Your family role is behavior that is expected of you by others, principally your parents. It is the script written for you that enables you to fit comfortably into the family. You create a sense of who you are, your self-identity, based on these rules of engagement. If you follow the rules of your role, you feel psychologically safe and comfortable. You feel loved because you can expect acceptance and approval for doing what you are told. Your anxiety level is low. You have no fear of being shunned, isolated or unfairly blamed. Break the rules and you get shocked by guilt and shame. Even considering breaking the rules hits you with waves of anxiety and panic.

Families Do Not Operate On The Truth

Your parents' rules and expectations created an extremely powerful blueprint for your behavior. It was laid down when you were a small child, a time of extreme dependency and vulnerability. You are a blank slate at that time in your life, unable to survive without help so the rules of your role are your lifeline. They help ensure your attachment to the most important people in your life. They are carved into your psyche, and cemented into place by powerful emotions. Because these powerful emotions are are stored in memory and triggered by present events, these emotions can be activated at any time in your life.

It would be simple if you only had to follow the rules for your family role. However, other internal messages exist within your mind. You have natural reactions to what you observe and experience that may or may not mesh with the way you were raised. You may not be aware of these other reactions until a situation presents itself where your natural reaction and your family role clash.

All parents are imperfect. Just ask anybody's spouse. The problem is that people do not want to admit their weaknesses. In an equal relationship, partners challenge each other all the time about each other's flaws. But when a child sees a weakness and challenges a parent, it is like David going up against Goliath. The parent holds all the cards and has the authority and power to shape the child's behavior. This power differential forces the child to accept or reject the family rules. Having an ambivalent relationship with your family is unavoidable. Even when you disagree with them, you feel the pressure to align with them or else. Holding on to your authentic feelings can be especially difficult if it involves challenging your parents' weaknesses or exposing their insecurities.

Fault lines and unresolved issues are a universal fact of all marriages. The marriage is as imperfect as the people who are in it. It can only be some good and some bad. A couple has two choices: 1) Deny weaknesses exist and form agreements to not challenge each other, or 2) Challenge each other to resolve the problems. The latter path is difficult and often can bring the marriage to the brink of breaking up before relationships get much better.

As parents, your humanness means that you do some harm and some good to your children. There is no such thing as "I am the best mother (or father) in the world." Many people try so hard to be different from their own parents, but the sad truth is that they can't be too different than where they come from. Women often exclaim, "I'm sounding just like my mother!" The apple can't fall too far from the tree. Many of my patients find any similarity hard to gauge because they are the worst judges of how different they are from their family. They grew up in the system and are still blinded by it. Partners and children have the clearest perspective about how far from the tree a parent has been able to roll the apple.

Denial exists in some form even in the healthiest of families. Parents avoid doing any necessary marital work by silencing their children in one way or another. This occurs in all families, even those that are working hard to be as well informed, insightful and honest as they can be. This means all adults grow up with inner conflicts to sort out. Resolving emotional patterns that are ingrained from childhood takes a lifetime.

No matter how old you are, events in your life will always trigger memories from earliest childhood that cannot be erased. Emotions bring the past into the present. If the feelings that are provoked are large, or if you are reminded of multiple past experiences, you will have a strong reaction to the smallest of problems.

It is difficult to manage your own emotions as well as the voices of your parents in your head. Your authentic response is overwhelmed by the imprinted reaction of your parents. You can't tell healthy rules from unhealthy rules, or separate the emotions from past from the emotions of the present. All your emotions feel justified. Fortunately, over time, it becomes easier to identify your authentic feelings, and to experience less anxiety and confusion. The natural progression takes you from Family Role to Self For Others to Authentic Self.

Heroes And Scapegoats

When children see the truth and respond to it, but are met with emotional resistance from their parents, this puts them in a bind. For a moment, they feel angry that their reactions are not validated. But then anxiety kicks in. Will their observations simply be rejected? Will their parents get upset? Will they be severely punished? How badly will their reaction hurt their parents? Their natural anger gets overrun with the guilt and shame of potentially hurting their parents.

Children have only two ways to go: dig in their heels and suffer the consequences, or back down and swallow their anger. They either challenge their parents' denial or submit to it by staying silent or giving in. If they follow their natural anger, they may get rejected. If they ignore it, they lose their connection to their authentic feelings.

When kids play by the family rules, they maintain the connection to their parents. The problem is that the connection is dishonest. Submissive "good" children never can address their personal truth without splitting off their natural anger. They are taught to idealize their parents, so they don't have to address their genuine emotions. They are also taught to form dependent relationships based on blind obedience to the parents' rules.

Heroes

I will call the children who submit Heroes because they protect the parents from having to face the truth about themselves and about unresolved conflicts in the marriage. Heroes will even try to silence their siblings from speaking up to protect the parents. They are ruled by anxiety, guilt, and shame and deny their own anger. The benefit to living with this anxiety is they get to stay in Mom and Dad's good graces. They lose themselves, but maintain a family.

Generally speaking, Heroes avoid their anger to keep the peace, and have no empathy for those who do not. Heroes want to smooth things over out of fear that they will be labeled the angry one. But avoiding their anger just creates feelings of anxiety. Hero relationships tend to be rigid and full of obligations that are maintained by the threat of feeling guilt and shame.

Heroes avoid conflict in order to maintain their connection to the family and feel loved. This creates a blueprint that carries over into their other relationships, even after they are adults. When Heroes grow up, their relationships may be based on pleasing others to excess. disagreements make them feel afraid and ashamed. Heroes need others too much. To a Hero, being alone is a sign of failure and a reflection of their worthlessness. They aren't comfortable on their own because they only feel connected to others when they are keeping the peace. They are okay only of others are okay. Unless they learn a better way to handle their emotions, their adult Self for Others will be disconnected from their anger. They may be able to express anger in the service of others, but not in the service of themselves. An example is the mother who can fight for her children but be meek when it comes to standing up for herself. The blueprint set down in childhood will continue to affect their relationships outside the family as well, which usually is problematic and characterized by the avoidance of conflict and/or denial.

Scapegoats

I call the children who refuse to back down Scapegoats. Some children have such unhealthy parents that they can't gain acceptance no matter what they do. They have nothing to lose by being rebels. Others are born wearing their emotions on their sleeves. These children just cannot hold back the anger. A Scapegoat is usually referred to as the "problem child" or the "black sheep." Scapegoats take the blame for a problem that is not caused by them but is exposed by them. Unfortunately, the problem usually does not come up unless they are around to expose it, so they seem like troublemakers. Parents or even siblings might say, "Everything is fine until Cheryl comes around", or, "The family gets along fine as long as Matt is not there", or, "Lawrence starts all the trouble in the family", or, "There is always one bad egg in the bunch."

Scapegoats are no healthier than Heroes, even though they play a different role. Scapegoats know the truth, but there are no family rules for successfully representing it. When they have tried, they have been met with rejection and denial. The parents, rather than acknowledge the truth, blame Scapegoats for making up crazy ideas or being too sensitive. Scapegoats learn over time that nobody wants to hear what they have to say. They learn to hide their anger, but eventually, it bubbles over into rage, which supports the perception that they are the problem.

This unfortunate dynamic continues as Scapegoats grow up and it affects their adult relationships. Unless they find a better way to handle their rage, Scapegoats develop a Self for Others that is prickly. Trust is hard to develop. They feel alone and unsupported with their anger and tend to take matters into their own hands. This leads them to emotionally overload in a defensive or an even combative way that puts off other people, who then have an excuse to ignore the truth in what they say. They typically suffer more from depression than anxiety, easily fall prey to feeling hopeless or helpless. They have no reason to believe that they matter or will be heard. The cost to adult Scapegoats may be loneliness, self-blame, social isolation and suspiciousness. Instead of continuing to be the messenger of bad news and continuously the target of anger, they anticipate rejection and withdraw to protect themselves from harm.

The Story of the Jones Sisters: One Hero, One Scapegoat

Jim and Marie Jones have been married 24 years and have two daughters: Beth, age 20 and Pam, age 22. Jim and Marie's marriage has had its trouble. Jim has a history of alcohol abuse but has been clean for the past 10 years. He initially denied his problem and felt he was just a social drinker, but his supervisor felt differently. He told Jim he would be fired if he did not enter an alcohol rehab facility. Jim complied and has been sober ever since.

Jim and Marie came to see me because even though Jim was now sober, they were still not getting along. Jim would still pick fights about Marie's spending, and Marie would still buy whatever she wanted. Jim came to realize that he had been using alcohol to medicate his emotions that were still there. He also understood that in the absence of alcohol, he was at risk of trading addictions and becoming a workaholic. His job was high stress, and he could easily justify working around the clock if left to his own choices.

As for Marie, she came to realize that she was too passive about Jim's behavior. Marie avoided conflict at all cost and had been quickly overwhelmed by Jim's aggressiveness in the old days, especially after he'd had a few drinks too many. She coped with

Jim's anger by withdrawing and making snide, passive-aggressive remarks. Sometimes, she would turn her back and give him the Silent Treatment for days at a time.

The girls, Beth and Pam, reacted differently to the stress of the strained relationship between their parents. Jim had been drinking all their lives until he sobered up when they were aged 10 and 12; but even after that, they knew when their parents were disagreeing. Pam, the elder, had a personality like her mother's. She would console Marie when she was visibly upset by Jim's actions. She would avoid her father at all costs, and survived by being her Mom's best friend. Beth was completely different. She was more like her father and could not keep her mouth shut. When she was little, and Jim was drinking, she would call him out on it, and be sent to her room. She also tried to get her mother to deal with the problem, to no avail. Beth was the Scapegoat in the family and this label stuck with her. After Jim sobered up, any family problem still was blamed on Beth's defiant behavior. Beth was seen as the problem in the family, rather than Jim's frustrations and Marie's spending. Pam was the Hero who caused no problems. She was seen as the easy child who was sensitive and caring, a direct contrast to her younger sister, the troublemaker.

Both girls carry forward the scars of the family experience. Pam's Self for Others now experiences panic attacks in response to any conflict in her life. She is currently dating a boy, Joseph, who is aggressive like her sister and father. She admits that she is attracted to what she sees as his strength in dealing with the world, and hopes that she can learn to be more like him. Unfortunately, she defers excessively to him, and never challenges him when his behavior crosses the line from assertive to aggressive. This imbalance not only causes Pam to suffer but also has created a rift between Pam and her sister. Beth and Joseph do not get along. Pam does not know what to do and feels stuck in the middle between her sister and her boyfriend. She feels torn, wants to keep the peace, and is unable to take a stand with either one of them. On the inside, Pam feels angry with both Beth and Joseph, but this confuses her because she loves them both, and Heroes cannot be angry with people they love.

Beth's experiences as the Scapegoat in the family have not served her well either. She recognizes her anger but hesitates to express it in any of her relationships because she is so used to being punished for her opinions. Because of her personality, she can only hold it in for so long before it explodes at the other person in a rage. Beth has lost several boyfriends who felt she was too volatile, confusing and unstable. Beth is not actually insensitive or unkind, but her family role has scarred her. There is a reason she behaves this way, but her role as Scapegoat segued into a Self for Others that is difficult to get along with. She feels lonely, and would like a relationship, but hesitates to put herself in the dating world for fear that she will be unfairly treated. Like her father, she turns to work and has done well in her career. She is worried that she is destined to be a career woman without a partner or a family.

Pam and Beth illustrate how relationship patterns imprinted by your family role repeat in your life. These patterns are maintained by the blueprint that governs your responses. When you react to a situation, you are faced with a choice to behave one way or another, and you will default to your childhood role unless you learn to be more self-aware.

The Anger Dynamic

Siblings are forced to join one team or the other based on how they cope with their right to be angry at their parents. I call this process, the Anger Dynamic. It splits the family into two teams. The Heroes join with the parents to deny problems and avoid embracing the truth expressed in the anger of their siblings. Heroes who don't want to get involved or believe they can stay neutral still indirectly maintain the status quo. They simply have a quieter way of supporting the parents. The Scapegoats form a separate team. They challenge the status quo in order to survive. They hold onto their anger to prevent losing their authentic selves.

The Anger Dynamic is universal and how you align yourself defines the role that you play in the family. Everyone plays a Hero or Scapegoat to some degree. All kids need a way to cope with the suppressed problems that exist between their parents.

In-Laws And Out-Laws

The Anger Dynamic can erupt at any time over any issue, but it usually requires the presence of a Scapegoat to bring it out into the open. Scapegoats have a difficult position in the family. The family's response is to discredit the Scapegoat, so the truth they are calling out has no credibility.

The personal growth of other family members can increase the legitimacy of the Scapegoat's message and threaten to reactive the Anger Dynamic at any time. Scapegoats can be protected by the addition of new members to the family. What Scapegoats believe sometimes can be strengthened with the addition of new siblings, partners, or spouses through marriage. These new family members present a unique challenge. They have not been raised the same way and have a clearer vision about the truth in the family. These new family members may automatically be Scapegoats, and a Hero in the family may defect to their side. When children get married, they are under pressure from the family to conform, but often under pressure from the partner to rebel. As the spouses influence their partner to stand up for the truth, they may learn to embrace their anger and join in the Anger Dynamic with the Scapegoats. The family split widens even further as the two sides add members. In many circumstances, especially where the family denial is high, the new spouse gets blamed for influencing their new partner in the wrong direction. This is why new in-laws are often treated as outlaws and kept at a distance.

Healthy And Unhealthy Families

You learn to play a role in your family when you can't tell the truth about your feelings and observations. You act a part because you aren't allowed to be your Authentic Self. Roles exist when inner emotions are buried. When the parents and the rest of the family resist what you have to say, this naturally makes you angry. Do you hide your anger or persist?

In healthy families, children are encouraged to be honest, and they do not feel pressure to hide their natural reactions. Healthy rules allow children to develop strong Authentic Selves. They do not feel anxious about their right to discuss what they observe or feel. They are entitled to feel angry when their reactions are discounted. Children raised in these families know who they are, are open and honest about the strengths and weaknesses of their parents, and give their opinions equal weight to those of their parents. They are able to discuss, to compromise, and to blend the needs of others with their own needs. Because their opinions have not been stifled, they find it easy to problem-solve and to generate new ideas. Obviously, this is advantageous as they grow up and their Self for Others develops more and more relationships outside the family.

Whether a family rule is healthy or unhealthy depends on why it exists. Healthy rules are established to teach children the principles of relationships and morality. Even if children do not enjoy these rules, complain, or test limits, healthy rules feel right. Rules that make sense do not cause internal conflict in the long run. Ultimately, children accept healthy rules because they do not conflict with their Authentic Selves and they feel reasonable.

Unhealthy rules exist for the purpose of hiding faults and insecurities in the parents at the expense of the truth. They are rooted in denial. Examples of unhealthy rules are "you aren't allowed to be angry at your mother," or, "You may not fail and may never be lazy." These rules are unreasonable and make children angry. The kids have a choice; ignore the responses of the Authentic Selves and play the Hero, or hold onto their anger and risk being a Scapegoat.

If they choose to conform to family rules that forbid self-expression, Heroes grow up with an underdeveloped Authentic Self. They continue to play their family role and cannot recognize that there are alternative opinions and methods of solving problems than what they have been taught. These kids grow up doing as they are told without questioning, not only in the family but outside of it as well. Their Self for Others defers to authority figures that act as replacement parents, and they are unable to generate their own ideas.

In unhealthy families, denial is high and playing the Hero is heavily reinforced. Children are required to go along with what naturally feels wrong in order to stay connected. Over time, Heroes become literally who Mom and Dad want them to be. They no longer can even recognize their authentic responses. The truth is buried deep inside. Consistently playing a role for the benefit of others keeps the peace, but is very bad for self-awareness and self-expression.

John's Story: The Executor of the Estate

John, age 66, is the youngest of three siblings born into a moderately wealthy family. He has two sisters that are five and seven years older than he. Their father was an accountant with a large practice. They lived in an Upper-Class neighborhood in

Greenwich, Connecticut, owned another house at the Jersey shore, and had a large amount of money in investments.

From the outside, the parent's marriage seemed fine. John's father, Jeff, played golf every weekend, and Lillian, John's mother, went to the shore home whenever she could. His father would stay up in Greenwich most weekends while the family went to the shore. By all accounts, life seemed good.

Nobody seemed to notice that Jeff and Lillian spent as little time together as possible. Whenever John asked, "How come Dad isn't here? ", his mother would explain that his father had a lot of work to do. If they were at the shore, he needed to be at home. If they were home, he needed to be at the office. It wasn't until John was 11 that his oldest sister informed him that Jeff had been having an affair with his secretary for as long as she could remember. Both sisters had repeatedly objected privately to Jeff about his mistress without success. On numerous occasions when he had ducked out of family functions, they had gotten upset with him and let him know what they thought of him.

John was furious when he found out, told his mother what his sister had told him, and asked if it were true. John's mother replied, "I don't know," and walked away. It was clear she would not talk about it nor admit that it could be true. She wanted to act like nothing was going on. Her philosophy was "Don't ask, don't tell." Life worked for her that way, and she did not want to rock the boat. John, seeing there was nothing to gain by continuing to talk, suppressed his anger and never mentioned the affair again.

Several years later, John graduated from college, and his family threw a party for him. Jeff slipped out the door and was gone for several hours. John felt angry at his father's behavior and confronted him when he returned. To John's amazement, his father admitted that he had gone to see his mistress, who had a personal problem with one of her children and felt that she needed his help. John asked his father if his mother knew about the affair. Jeff replied, "I don't know. We don't talk about it." The message was clear to John. Nobody wants to talk about it. It's not a problem as long as nobody admits it is happening. Act like it doesn't exist, and it won't exist. Again, John swallowed his anger and went along with the charade.

Years later, Jeff died leaving John the Executor of his will. Before he died, Jeff told his son that he was selected was because Jeff knew he could count on John to do what he was told. With Lillian's approval, Jeff had created a trust leaving John in charge of the family's financial affairs. The stipulation was that John had to follow the advice of the family financial advisor regarding the family investments and shore home.

The appointment of John as the Executor did not sit well with John's two sisters. They felt that the only reason that Jeff chose John was because he always went along with everything and would do exactly as Jeff wanted. Plus, they felt they were being punished for standing up for their mother and challenging their father about his mistress. John's sisters also treated him badly. They would get together with their kids at the shore home and leave John out. They would even visit John's grown children, their niece, and nephew, and not inform John.

After Jeff died, the stock market crashed, and they lost 15% of their inheritance. The sisters blamed John for blindly following the financial advisor's advice, and they called the advisor several times to complain about John and the loss of money.

Occasionally, John would fight back. He wrote letters explaining the advice of the financial advisor and asked his sisters for some understanding about the time and energy it took to keep up with all of their mother's bills, taxes, and paperwork. But, in person, John would not bring up the subject, much to the dismay of his wife, Peg, who would get so upset that she would end up in a fight with John's sisters. John would try to calm things down, only to have Peg accuse John of failing to stand up for her. She felt that John's family was the cause of much aggravation in her marriage, and she could not understand why John was unwilling to protect her or him from the hostile sisters.

Peg was right in one way and wrong in another. John's family was the source of much distress in her marriage, but the real cause of the problem was John, not his sisters. John had always survived his family by being a Hero and going along with his father's affair. Even though he was now an adult, John kept recreating the pattern of conflict avoidance and blind obedience in all his relationships. The Anger Dynamic separated him from his sisters, and his family role now left him unable to be angry and defend himself from harm. John felt obligated to continue being the Executor because his father had wanted it. If he had turned down the task, he would have felt guilty about disappointing his father, even though he was dead. The mere thought of the guilt made him instantly surrender to the request. Likewise, he could not argue with the financial advisor because he was Jeff's agent and John had promised his father to follow his advice. An alliance with his sisters would be a violation of his commitment to his father.

John remains the obedient child, even though it costs him his relationship with his siblings and irritates his wife. He needs to remain the good boy at all cost. Instead of listening to his wife, he trivializes her advice by rationalizing that she loves drama and is looking to pick a fight. He thinks that her reactions reflect her aggressive personality and not his passive approach to life. He denies that he has a severe problem with conflict, and won't consider the need to change in any way. He tells Peg that she makes a big deal out of everything and needs to learn to get along better with his family.

John has never connected the dots. He does not see his pattern of conflict avoidance. He denies that he had a problem standing up to father, and feels his easy- going personality explains why he doesn't like to fight with people. To him, his sisters and wife are typical females who love to pick fights and create problems. John also learned from his father that a man can do whatever he wants, regardless of how it affects others. It was normal to be oblivious of family.

John's anger does surface from time to time, but in ways that he doesn't recognize. John is a passionate gardener and spends hours tending his vegetables. Regardless of what Peg or the children want to do, John disappears into his garden, leaving the family to fend for themselves. He has never noticed that the garden is his "mistress" and he says his time there benefits the whole family by providing food. He does not see the anger in his unwillingness to negotiate how he uses his time, and in the way, he disappears regardless of the impact on others.

Recently, a problem developed between John and a close friend, Eric. John had agreed to sell his car to Eric for a set price. Later the same day, a neighbor found out that John was selling his car and offered to pay several hundred dollars more. John agreed, but he did not tell Eric until he came over to pay for his car. When John informed him that he had already sold the car, Eric was understandably upset that John had broken their agreement and that he had not been given the chance to match the new price. John felt he had done nothing wrong and could not understand why Eric would react that way. He felt entitled to sell his car for whatever he could get, and he did not feel he had to get Eric's permission. To this day, Eric no longer spends time with John, who does not understand why his friend reacted the way he did.

John came to see me because his world had fallen apart. He was overwhelmed with anxiety. His sisters didn't speak to him, his wife was mad at him, and he had just gotten fired. It was all horribly unfair.

John had been a senior manager in a retail store, and there had been several episodes in which cash had gone missing from the cashier's drawer. The management team came in to review the situation and fired John for failing to address this ongoing problem. John could not believe that he was being held accountable for other people's mistakes. He felt he did not steal the cash, and he should not be punished for something he didn't do. He recommended that all the cashiers be fired and new ones hired – an idea that management considered ludicrous.

John could not see the connection between his own behavior and the reactions of others, so life seemed unfair and unpredictable to him. He only came to see me because he was running out of options. As we worked together, he began to see that his family role as a Hero had set him up to fail in his relationships in certain ways, but that he could change the outcome with greater self-awareness.

Gaining Self-Awareness

The more you know about yourself, the better you are prepared to make different choices and to change the repeating patterns that interfere with your life. Asking siblings, spouses, relatives, and family friends can give you some perspective on your family role. Another way to improve your knowledge of yourself is comparing yourself to others. It is often easier to see how other people's families influence their behavior that it is to see how your own family impacts you.

The strength of the emotions that bind you to your family role determines your Self for Others. Heroes are ruled by guilt and shame and lose their ability to stand up for themselves. They do as they are told and get rewarded for not being a problem. Scapegoats are able to hold onto their anger in the face of disapproval and stand up for the truth. Sometimes, they carry a chip on their shoulder from being ignored for years. This may make them trigger-happy when they feel belittled. With years of frustration behind them, they may appear too sensitive or volatile.

You project the rules of engagement from your family role onto every person you meet and reenact your family role in all your relationships. This tendency to play a role varies with the relationship. The more intimate the relationship, the stronger is the pull to follow the rules of love that you learned from your parents and family. You face stronger pressure to repeat the family role with your partner than you do with a friend. You emotionally respond like a Hero or Scapegoat more with your children than with business associates. You fall in line with your family role more in the face of your parents and siblings than you do with strangers. You live what you learn in the situations where it matters most.

Clarity regarding the requirements of your family role is essential to changing your identity for your Self for Others to your Authentic Self. Your fears are the chains that hold you tied to doing what others want for you, rather than being your natural self. Your anger outlines the path to your Authentic Self, although is often hidden or disguised. The better you can see all the emotions behind your thoughts and behavior, the easier it will be to tag their source and choose which to ignore and which to follow, and the more you can be your real self in all your relationships.

Knowing how your Self for Others works and the thoughts and feelings tied to it is critical to disengaging from it. Recognizing your family role that drives your Self for Others will enable you to know the enemy within and not be surprised by your own reactions. You can learn to ignore the voice of the Self for Others, no matter how strong, and listen to the voice of your Authentic Self, no matter how faint it has become. While you cannot change the messages of your parents in your head, you can learn to change which voice you choose to follow.

I wish I could tell you that you can drive your family role out of your mind completely, but that would be a lie. The blueprint is with you for life, permanently stored in your memory and activated at a moments notice. Fortunately, you can learn to manage it differently. You can learn to strengthen your Authentic Self and, over time, continuously improve your ability to be your real self.

Growing Up: The Continuum

By now you have probably noticed that there are different stages of self-awareness that we all go through on the way to becoming fully functional adults. Below is the process placed on a simple continuum. The goal is to reach the right end of this continuum, but in reality, most people do not get that far because they don't think that much about what it means to be an adult. They remain trapped in their Self for Others, run by their upbringing, all the while believing they are being true to themselves. By reading this book, and possibly getting some therapy if it would be helpful, you can learn to be emotionally honest and secure about who you are. You will learn to categorize all your emotions and express those feelings that reflect the real you as honesty as possible. Once you recognize your own authentic emotions, you will more easily see the emotions in others. You will become better at both representing yourself and emotionally listening to others. The independence and authenticity that you practice will enable you to create and maintain successful relationships both inside and outside of your family.

FROM CHILD TO ADULT: DEVELOPING SELF-AWARENESS

The natural progression as you mature looks like this:

Your **Family Role**	Your **Self for Others**	Your **Authentic** Self
The rules of your family determine whether you will be a Hero or Scapegoat.	Your family role affects how you behave when interacting with people outside the family.	Finally you learn to listen to your natural emotions and be your Authentic Self in the world.

ARE YOU A HERO OR A SCAPEGOAT?

PART I

Examine the five scenarios described below. Notice the different options that would characterize a Hero or a Scapegoat. Comparing your reactions to those mentioned will give you some clarity regarding your own family role and how attached to it you are.

1. The Family Wedding

You are the middle of three sisters. Your older sister has recently announced her engagement and already has made preliminary wedding plans. You are shocked to find out that your younger sister has been left off the list of bridesmaids to make room for the groom's sisters at the insistence of the groom and his family. While your two sisters have always fought, you feel that the bride-to-be is being unfair and insensitive to your younger sister. Your parents are equally outraged and feel their oldest daughter needs to learn how to stand up to her new husband and family. However, they have said nothing that might upset her.

Heroes want to keep the peace at all costs and don't want to cross anyone. As a Hero, you might:

1. Reassure your parents that you will not do the same at your wedding. Contact your elder sister directly and tell her the situation is hurting your Mom and Dad.

2. Tell the bride that you understand the position she is in.
3. Tell your parents how to manage your older sister.
4. Say nothing for fear of making things worse, or don't get involved at all since it is not your wedding.

Scapegoats are truth tellers, even if the truth is painful. As a Scapegoat you might:

1. Refuse to attend the wedding in protest.
2. Confront your older sister directly and tell her what you think about her plan.
3. Make a scene at the bridal shower.
4. Demand that your parents call the groom's parents.
5. Team up with your younger sister and refuse to cooperate with the wedding plans in any way unless a change is made.

Healthy Response

This situation requires knowledge of healthy boundaries to be respected by all. It is your sister's right to do what she wants on her special day, especially if she is funding any part of the wedding herself. However, as a sibling, you have an obligation to yourself to stand up against a decision that causes harm to another.

The boundary issue is, "Who should you talk to?" Your position as a sibling is to stand up for the truth, which is that the younger sister is being insulted and hurt. If either sibling asks you, you should give your opinion openly and honestly. You can suggest to each one that they should meet and talk about it, but it is not your job to structure the situation for them. Their bad relationship has taken years to make, is most likely a Hero-Scapegoat clash, and may not get resolved in time for the wedding. Also, these discussions should remain between the siblings and not the parents to avoid adding fuel to the clash of family roles.

---

2.   The New Baby

Your sister has just had a new baby and your mother, who lives out of state, is going to stay with her for several days to help out. Their relationship has been rocky at times, but you are glad to see everyone sharing this happy event. Unfortunately, the situation does not turn out as planned and your mother and sister end up in a fight. You are shocked when your mother decides to leave early. Your sister calls you on the phone to talk to you about what happened.

Heroes' side with authority figures and try to smooth things over. As a Hero you might:

1. Tell your sister that there are "two sides to every story" and you need to hear Mom's side before you can comment.
2. Tell your sister to leave you out of it and to go work it out with Mom.
3. Defend your mother and admonish your sister for not appreciating her help.
4. Call your Mom and sympathize with her.

Scapegoats are not afraid to speak up when they are angry. As a Scapegoat you might:

1. Call your sister to support her position because you have experienced similar difficulties with Mom.
2. Call your mother and tell her she was out of line.
3. Call your siblings to let them know that you support your sister's actions.
4. Warn your sister's partner about your mother's behavior.

The Healthy Response

Your job as a sibling is to understand your sister's position, not your mother's. If you feel your sister was wrong, separate the issues of what she said from how she said it. She may be right, but her delivery may have been hurtful. Maybe Mom pushed an old button that needs to go. If your sister was right, validate her right to be mad and have a discussion about how hard it is to not overreact to a parent's behavior. Do not call your mother and argue further. If she calls you, don't try to speak for your sister, but remind her that your sister's reactions can't be all wrong.

---

3.   Family Gathering

You, your two sisters, and brother have gotten together for a Fourth of July picnic in your back yard. Your parents live a distance away and have decided to stay home because it is too far to travel on a holiday. Your brother says he is angry that Mom and Dad don't make any effort to visit him. He has several small children and it is more difficult for him to come see them than for them to come see him. His complaint is that he often packs up the family to visit his parents, but they rarely reciprocate and are annoyed if he asks why.

Heroes do not want to rock the boat when there is a problem. As a Hero you might:

1. Ask your brother to stop badmouthing Mom and Dad.
2. Ignore him and talk to someone else.
3. Change the topic of conversation.
4. Defend your parents, arguing that they are old and have a right to make that choice.

Scapegoats call things as they see them to test the truth. As a Scapegoat, you might:

1. Support your brother by agreeing that Mom and Dad have always expected the kids to cater to their needs.
2. Call your Mom and Dad and ask them why they didn't attend the picnic.
3. Bring this up at the next family gathering with your parents and brother present, even if your brother has asked you to avoid the topic.
4. Make a list of how many times the parents have visited each of their children, and how often the children have visited them.

The Healthy Response

Your brother has a reason for the way he feels. Even if you were treated differently than he was, he isn't crazy and he isn't necessarily making things up. Listen and validate his reactions, encouraging him to address them with your Mom and Dad on his own.

---

4. Working Overtime

You are a conscientious worker who takes pride in your job. You have worked a lot of overtime lately and need a vacation badly. Your wife and kids are feeling neglected and you are fatigued. You finally plan a family outing and promise to join them Friday night out for dinner and a movie. At noon, you confirm the plans with your wife. At 3:30 PM, your boss rushes into the office and is frantic. He insists that the report you filed has errors and that he needs you to stay to correct them to make his deadline. Your boss has a history of claiming reports are inaccurate if they don't say what he wants them to say.

Heroes have trouble disagreeing with authority figures. As a Hero, you might:

1. Agree to stay to change the report, but don't call your wife to avoid a scene.
2. If your wife is disappointed, get angry with her for being a nag.
3. Ignore the coldness when you get home and go to bed.
4. Make excuses for not standing up to the boss and get mad at you.

Scapegoats are used to standing up for themselves and are able to use their anger. As a Scapegoat you might:

1. Confront your boss about being unreasonable and leave at 5PM.
2. Say yes, make a few minor changes, and leave at 5PM.
3. Tell your wife you have to miss dinner, but you'll still go to the movie.
4. Tell your boss that you already have plans.

The Healthy Response

This issue is about your work/life balance. The history of your boss's manipulation has not been addressed and it needs to be discussed at a future meeting. Because your boss has more power than you, you need to complete this particular report but request a meeting to discuss how to handle this issue differently in the future.

Regarding your wife, time is a resource that is shared by a couple. If an event changes the schedule, both parties have the responsibility to keep the other informed of a change. You have an obligation to your wife as a partner to keep her advised of a time change so she can reorganize her schedule as well. In the best of worlds, you would sympathize with her disappointment at not being able to go to the movies and accept as understandable and authentic the anger that she may direct at you.

---

5. Having to Visit a Family Friend on Your Vacation

You are going on a vacation with your wife and children, and really looking forward to some uninterrupted family time. When you tell your parents where you are going, they mention an old family friend who lives close to the resort, and, they ask you to visit him when you are there. They repeat the request several more times, saying that he is lonely and would appreciate your visit. Your wife is getting angry at the pressure and wants you to protect your time with your own family.

Heroes want to please their parents. As a Hero you might:

1. Make arrangements to visit over your wife's objections.
2. Not make any promises but feel so obligated that in the end you call and visit.
3. Ask your wife to challenge your parents because "they don't listen to me."
4. Avoid telling your parents about your vacation to avoid the conflict.

Scapegoats are aware of their own viewpoint and will defend it. As a Scapegoat you might:

1. Make no promises, then simply not visit.
2. If the subject comes up afterward, explain that one of their old friends is not a priority for you, and they should take care of this obligation themselves.
3. Confront your parents about ignoring your priority, which is relaxation with your family.
4. Ask why this person is so lonely and suggest some viable solutions other than ruining your vacation.

The Healthy Response

The issue is that your parents are not respecting your needs. They feel entitled to pressure you to put your needs aside and do what they expect of you. This is an example of where your needs as a couple supersede the needs of your parents. You would have a right to challenge the pressure they are putting on you and to support your wife's right to be angry.

ARE YOU A HERO OR SCAPEGOAT?

PART II

Rate how the questions below apply to you in a general way. Choose the number that most accurately describes your behavior most of the time.

1. I am dutiful and obedient to my parents' wishes.

5	4	3	2	1
Always		Sometimes		Never

2. I feel unfairly blamed for the problems in my family.

5	4	3	2	1
Always		Sometimes		Never

3. I am more comfortable leading than following.

5	4	3	2	1
Always		Sometimes		Never

4. I find it hard to trust others.

5	4	3	2	1
Always		Sometimes		Never

5. I fear failure.

5	4	3	2	1
Always		Sometimes		Never

6. I feel suspicious of others motives.

5	4	3	2	1
Always		Sometimes		Never

7. I like to direct conversations, spending more time talking than listening.

5	4	3	2	1
Always		Sometimes		Never

8. I am accused of fairly often jumping to conclusions or overreacting to problems.

5	4	3	2	1
Always		Sometimes		Never

9. I measure my worth by what I accomplish.

5	4	3	2	1
Always		Sometimes		Never

10. When I am involved, I take responsibility for the emotional reactions of others.

5	4	3	2	1
Always		Sometimes		Never

11. I am afraid that I will disappoint others.

5	4	3	2	1
Always		Sometimes		Never

12. I keep to myself when I am around my family, or find things to do in another room.

5	4	3	2	1
Always		Sometimes		Never

13. I have trouble relaxing if I am not doing something worthwhile.

5	4	3	2	1
Always		Sometimes		Never

14. I am always the person who points out the flaws in proposed solutions and people get mad.

5	4	3	2	1
Always		Sometimes		Never

15. My friends and/or partner accuse me of being too influenced by my parents.

5	4	3	2	1
Always		Sometimes		Never

16. I believe that people are only out for themselves.

5	4	3	2	1
Always		Sometimes		Never

17. I try to fix other people's problems for them.

5	4	3	2	1
Always		Sometimes		Never

18. I feel my family does not understand me.

5	4	3	2	1
Always		Sometimes		Never

19. I am quick to forgive and forget, and don't like revisiting old controversies.

5	4	3	2	1
Always		Sometimes		Never

20. I prefer to be alone.

5	4	3	2	1
Always		Sometimes		Never

Scoring:

1. Hero score, Odd Numbered Questions +_____

2. Scapegoat score, Even Numbered Questions -_____

3. Composite Score: Subtract #2 from #1 =_____

Plot all three scores on the continuum below to see where you stand. Each person has experienced family pressures to be the Hero and to avoid being the Scapegoat. A higher score indicates more pressure in one direction or another. The composite score shows you the level of identity with either role.

Hero						Scapegoat
Severe	Moderate	Mild	Neutral	Mild	Moderate	Severe
+15 to+11	+10 to +6	+5 to+1	0	-1 to -5	-6 to -10	-11 to -15

5

How Children Lose Their Spirit Of Independence And . . .

How To Overcome Learned Emotions

Your family role is one of the most important blueprints in your mind. As a young child, remembering what you need to do to please your parents is vital. It is your survival manual. Then, your family role gets extended to form your Self for Others, which dictates how you behave in any relationship. The role now serves as your emotional compass, your guide to all your relationships. However, it is a compass that doesn't read true north. It needs to be reset based on your own natural reactions rather than on the reactions of others. Ultimately, the goal is to go through life using the compass of your Authentic Self as much as possible.

Family roles are based on doing what you are told, even if you disagree, silencing your internal reactions of dissent, and promoting compliance to avoid fear. Roles prevent you from having a voice. They encourage dependency and make you submit to authority figures. Roles stop you from being an adult and blind you to your own authentic feelings. Roles require that you hide from yourself the very emotions that you need to form healthy relationships. They keep you behaving like a dependent child for life in your relationships with everyone. Roles promote dishonesty and destroy both families and marriages from the inside. They are destructive to marriages as they make the family a higher priority than the spouse. Roles are equally destructive to families. They separate siblings from each other. They create a civil war within a family, where the brother is pitted against brother or sister to maintain peace.

The task of being an adult is to grow into the capacity to form your own opinions and to defend them in the face of challenges from loved ones and strangers alike. This independence begins with overcoming the fear associated with not doing as you have been told. Being an adult means that you give yourself the right to honor your own authentic internal reactions. You do what you feel is right even if it is different from the way you were raised. If you break the ties that bind you to your family role, you become free to live your life representing who you are, fully and completely, in everything that you do.

The Story of George and Sheila: The Red-Hot Stove

Sheila and George had been married for five years. She married him against the advice of her parents who felt that George "wasn't like us." What that meant was that George did not have the same drive to succeed as Sheila's parents. Her parents were upper-middle class with high achievement aspirations. Her father had risen in the corporate world to be the Vice President of a Fortune 500 company. His considerable salary enabled them to live a life of luxury. When Sheila's parents insulted George, she would ignore their comments instead of creating a fight by coming to his defense.

George had no such background. He was an Activities Director at a local rehabilitation center. George loved his work and his people. Sheila fell in love with the care that he showed to his patients and to her. But Sheila's parents were right. George was not like them. His valued relationships, meaningful work, and had no interest in luxury. He was gentle, loving, kind, but not ambitious and driven like Sheila's parents. He would rather spend time with her at home than stay at work to earn overtime.

George's lack of interest in money created financial problems for the couple. As is often the case, the characteristic that first attracted Sheila to George became their biggest problem. Sheila also cared about people and was a social worker. Sheila still wanted the good life that she had known as a child and worked hard at her job so they could afford what she considered necessities. To George, time with Sheila meant more than nice car or new clothes.

The differences between them came to a head when their electric stove died. Sheila loved to cook and had always wanted a Viking stove with a ventilation hood. It's a very expensive stove, costing thousands of dollars and used by fine chefs in upscale restaurants. Sheila's sister had one, and Sheila felt entitled to one too, even though she could not afford it. George thought it was an unnecessary luxury item and wanted no part of financing any appliance other than the kind of normal stoves that everyone else used.

The stove became a sore point between the couple and the source of numerous arguments. Sheila knew it was expensive, but felt they could afford it by taking out a loan, just as they did when they bought their cars. George did not want the added financial pressure. He felt Sheila was being a spoiled brat who just wanted an unnecessary fancy stove just because her sister had one. Whenever Sheila mentioned the stove, George refused to talk about it. Instead, he would retreat to the study and watch TV for hours rather than argue with Sheila. Finally, Sheila got so mad about George's TV watching that she threatened to leave if he continued. During the last fight, they nearly came to blows, and she left to spend the night at her parents'. Once there, she cried about the problems with George, and her parents offered to buy the stove for her. Sheila was ecstatic. The next day, she went out with them, bought the stove, and had it delivered.

George, upset that Sheila had left, knew nothing about any of this. When the deliverymen showed up the next day with the stove, George flew into a rage, would not let the deliveryman into the house, and demanded that she return it immediately. Sheila got home just in time to allow the men to set up the stove in their kitchen.

This time, George left and went to his brother's house for the night. He refused to return home until Sheila returned the stove.

Sheila refused because she said it was a gift from her parents and George had no right to turn down a gift that was for her.

That started a cold war. Sheila came to see me over a month later because George had cut off all communication with her and was temporarily living at his brother's house. It was weeks since they had seen each other and Sheila was emotionally torn apart. She was mad at George for being so unreasonable about a present, but wanted him back and missed living with him.

SHEILA: "I am so confused at this point. I know that I still love George and want to be married to him. I just don't get why he is so upset with me. Don't my parents have the right to give me a present?"

ME: "I don't think the problem is about a present. I think it has to do with parents' interfering in a married couple's decision making."

SHEILA: "So you don't think my parents had a right to buy me the stove? They were just being nice. They know how much I wanted one."

ME: "Your parents offered because they didn't want you to be upset. That's what most parents do, try to make their children happy. But I am concerned about why you accepted the stove before you talked to George."

SHEILA: "Because! He would never have let me accept it. But I don't see how it is up to him!"

ME: "What do you mean by "let me accept it?"

SHEILA: "I mean that whenever we disagree, he goes off watches TV for hours until he gets his way. It drives me nuts. He doesn't work with me, so why should I work with him?"

ME: "Sounds like you are really mad at George."

SHEILA: "I'm not mad. I'm just upset with him."

ME: "What's the difference?"

SHEILA: "When you are upset, you still love the person. They hurt you, and you still care. When you are mad, you stop caring."

ME: "So if you were really mad at George, you would stop loving him?"

SHEILA: "I just don't care about him at the moment. I wanted to keep the stove, but instead of letting me enjoy it, he left home. He loses the right to have me care about him when he won't even participate in a conversation. Why should I care if he doesn't?

ME: "So you think the problem with the stove is a problem between you and George? I'm not sure George would agree."

SHEILA: "He wouldn't agree. He thinks the problem is about my relationship to my parents. He believes that they mean more to me than he does."

ME: "Do you think that is at all true?"

SHEILA: "No! Of course, I love my parents, but I don't depend on them. I have been out of my parent's house for five years. I work really hard. It's not like I call them and ask for help all the time."

ME: "You are talking about financial dependency. I think George is talking about a different kind of dependency. I think he is talking about your guilt if you disappoint them."

SHEILA: "What guilt? I don't feel guilty. My relationship to my parents is fine."

ME: "I think George would say that you don't feel guilty because you went along with your parent's offer. Do you ever disappoint them? Do you do what they want you to do? That is the right thing according to them. You and George are making decisions together based on what you both think is right. That's what a compromise is."

SHEILA: "George has always felt left out. I can't take responsibility for it any more. My parents have bent over backwards to make him feel included. He's the one who isolates himself."

ME: "I know that George retreats rather than fight back, and that is not a healthy or productive way to resolve a problem. Maybe he retreats because he feels it's hopeless to discuss decisions with you. He can't get you to admit that you are ruled by the opinion of your parents."

It turned out that Sheila lived with the pressure to embrace the "good life," as her parents call it, and was expected to work for the high achievements needed to create that kind of life. Her parents felt her grades were never been good enough. She was never pretty enough, thin enough, or athletic enough. Her parents thought that her choice of career as a social worker was a joke because it barely paid enough to even support her. It was important to Sheila to feel financially independent, but she would tacitly accept monetary gifts her parents sent her. When that happened, she would feel much shame and doubt. And would wonder if her parents were right about her shortcomings and her career. She lived in fear that she would be seen as a failure. She was in her thirties and had little to show for it. She was quietly angry but would never say anything to her parents.

While most parents don't have the resources to buy a Viking stove for their married daughter, this case is fairly typical of a marital problem that is being governed by family roles and obligations. George knows that he and Sheila share a set of values than are different from her parents' values. Sheila is conflicted about the differences she has with her parents and has never felt comfortable exposing how she feels about their values. She enjoys the luxuries they can afford, but she and George used to be happy without fancy material things. Sheila does not recognize that fear rules her.

George does not know how to cope with Sheila's denial. He retreats when he gets angry and gives up too easily. He acts out his anger by giving Sheila the silent treatment and a dose of her own medicine. If Sheila asks, "What's wrong?" his standard response is, "Nothing," and he walks away. He can deny problems, too. George and Sheila are more alike than they realize. George hides while Sheila avoids the elephant in the room.

By now you may be wondering about George's parents. He won't challenge his parents either, with good reason. George's father was a very opinionated man who married a very sweet but passive woman. George's mother never stood up to his father and lived in fear of him. George's role required that he follow suit. If George objected to anything, his father would verbally attack him, humiliate him by calling him names, and his mother would say nothing. George learned that silence was best when conflict was brewing. His retreat in his marriage was a repetition of what he had learned in his family.

Both George and Sheila are living their lives according to their family roles, but those roles are hurting their marriage. They can't solve problems because they can't be honest with themselves or each other. They have buried their authentic emotions. George is angry at his father's emotional bullying and his mother's failure to protect him but won't say a word to them. Instead, when conflicts arise in her marriage, he treats Sheila like plutonium. He feels safe enough to get angry at her, but he won't stay and talk through any differences. He prefers to wait it out until she relents, a method that leads to the build-up of much resentment in Sheila.

This case illustrates the emotional confusion created when partners are locked into their family roles and remain dependent on their parents to make decisions. The anger that is suppressed by both George and Sheila ends up showing up at the wrong time, the wrong place, and directed at the wrong person for the wrong reason. George was mad at both his Mom and Dad, but when provoked, he directed it at Sheila. His anger at Sheila's denial turned to rage so quickly that he would retreat to prevent himself from flying off the handle. Sheila was nothing like George's father. She would never humiliate him, but she was treated as if she were the same as his father. Unlike George's father, she was just frustrated that he didn't talk to her.

Sheila was equally guilty of the same dynamic. She was angry at the pressures to achieve in her family but had never said anything. She thought that would be ungrateful. Her anger at both her parents was like gasoline, lit by the match of George refusing to even talk about buying the stove she wanted. She felt justified in her being "upset" with George because his silent treatment made talking impossible. She did not ever see that she was angry at her parents, or that her rage was unhealthy. Her parents had done nothing wrong and were, in fact, being very generous, and George was the cause of the whole problem.

Neither George nor Sheila had truly separated from their families, and they had brought their roles right into their marriage. Both of them denied the destructive side of their families.

George agreed to come to therapy, although in the beginning, he wouldn't even look at Sheila. They learned to face both the good and bad in their families. As their awareness grew, they learned how to separate their anger at their family ties from their anger at each other. They became less afraid of speaking up to their families, and less defensive in their marriage as a result. Sheila began to challenge her parent's opinions more openly and to protect George from their insults. George learned to separate his anger at his father from his anger at Sheila. Once they learned to direct their anger where it belonged, George and Sheila learned how to accept and grow from each other.

Sheila ended up keeping the stove. She really did love it, and she used it to cook great meals that they both enjoyed. It actually became a positive symbol of working through the lowest point in their marriage, and a reminder to make mutual decisions without outside interference.

Nurturing Independent Thinkers

Family roles do not represent the classic American values of independence, equality, and freedom. These values can only exist when people have relationships that are not based on dependency or fear; when they are able to voice their authentic reactions and beliefs; and negotiate compromises with others when differences arise. When families are bound together by denial and unquestioned authority, the children cannot grow up self-sufficient and self-aware. If all the families in America were like this, there would be no independent thinkers qualified to run the country or even to vote. This would undermine the strength of our commitment to freedom, independence, and equality. A nation can only be as strong as the individuals and families that act as its foundation.

Each unit in that system- the individual, the marriage, and the family-must be built with the same organizing principles. A country is only as strong as the bond between its principles and its actions. If we believe in freedom and equality for all, but don't practice what we preach within our own families, children grow up scared and confused. They fail to cultivate the courage to protect our legacy of independence. When children are not encouraged to be independent, and to free themselves from the excessive need to please authority, they cannot become adults capable of fighting any enemy of freedom.

The People-Centered Family

Independent thinkers are not created in a vacuum. The tradition of independent thinkers must be nurtured from generation to generation because we are all born into dependency. Independence is our natural right, but it must be taught and encouraged by families and institutions. We need to put it into practice in our daily lives. Every day and in every way, the spirit of the American Revolution must be alive and well in every American family so children will learn to embrace their independence. Children live what they learn. If you teach them to think for themselves, they will live and love freedom and liberty. This upbringing requires a special type of family, a people-centered family dedicated to deliberately teaching this overarching concept and applying these ideals daily to every problem that arises.

A people-centered family does not create arbitrary rules to support the marriage and reinforce the authority of the parents. In a people-centered family, the husband and wife share power with each other and make decisions jointly in all things, operating with the organizing principle that two heads are better than one. They consciously create a marriage of equality, modeling for their children a relationship based on honesty and authenticity. As in all families, parents still make rules and children still test them. But in a democratic family, children are allowed to learn through trial and error and have the right to dissent respectfully. That right does not give them the power to decide. It gives them the right to question those in authority and requires the parents to work together to prevent an abuse of power. In a people-centered family, parents respect their children's right to dissent without taking it personally or as an affront to their authority. The children are learning to be emotionally honest. They are trying to figure out what makes sense and feels right to them.

Independent connections are the alternative to family roles. They can be encouraged in children by parents' who actively nurture independence. From the very beginning, the people-centered family builds relationships based on emotional honesty. The healthy parent recognizes that children may see the emotions of their parents more clearly than either parent sees themselves. They attempt to honor the truth expressed in children's reactions. Rather than automatically saying "No, that is not right," they honor what is true and correct about what a child says and explain what is incorrect. Parents do not purposely blind themselves to problems just to avoid unpleasantness. Both parents are committed to finding family-centered answers that support emotional honesty.

In the people-centered family, each stage of a child's growth into adulthood is treated as an opportunity to teach independence. The adolescent rebellion is regarded as a necessary stage of learning how to hold onto one's personal beliefs, yet still be respectful of differences. The adolescent typically makes mistakes of style, but their ideas have validity. For example, when teenagers believe their curfew is unreasonable, cursing out their mother is probably not the best way to get the point across. As children become young adults and learn to manage money, college, leaving home, starting a career, getting married and having children, the emotional reactions of every member of the family- parents, and children-are treated as valuable learning experiences and opportunities to form authentic, independent relationships.

Let me be clear about the kind of family that nurtures the spirit of independence. This is not a family without limits or boundaries. It is not a family that denies the roles and responsibilities of the parents and their need to use their authority for the health and welfare of the children. The family is a learning center for both parents and children. The marriage of the parents has checks and balances between the partners to ensure that decisions foster the spirit of independence rather than an abuse of parental power. Parents learn how to use their power respectfully, and to listen to the opinions of the children – no matter their age- before making decisions. This process acknowledges the truth in each child's opinions, with the understanding that children do not yet have all the knowledge or life experience they need to govern themselves.

One of the greatest aspects of our country is that it is a melting pot of people with ideas that have value regardless of the citizens age, sex, religion or nationality. A nation that trusts its citizenry must be made up of families that trust their children. The goal of the people-centered family is to find the truth by blending together the truths represented in each person's opinions. There are neither sides nor pre-conceived outcomes in the search for the truth. Everybody has a role, and each has some power. All are responsible to make things work and to cooperate with each other. Each child has personal freedoms that are earned through responsible behavior. Family rules are necessary to teach children the limits of personal freedom and the boundary where their right to act imposes an unfair burden on another family member.

The Independent Child

American children must be allowed to be free and independent in their thinking and actions. But becoming self-sufficient takes time. They first need to learn to trust their own judgment and to discern for themselves if there is truth in what they are being taught by their authority figures. They must learn to think on their own, critically evaluate opinions regardless of source, and not automatically believe what they are told by parents, teachers, ministers, or government leaders. In our current national climate, there is tremendous pressure to stay within the herd (e.g., peer pressure), to obey authority (e.g., the teacher, the policeman, the platoon sergeant), and to avoid individual thought (e.g., religion, business organizations).

To withstand this pressure to behave and think alike, the independent child must have an exceptionally strong sense of self. This strength is forged through the honesty of the family's discussions. Dishonest interactions are based on the denial of emotions. Honest exchanges promote discussion that includes all viewpoints and democratic resolution of conflicts. Honesty at home encourages the freedom of speech that Americans take for granted. Decisions that are based on the input of only the parents confuse and silence the children. Discussions that are not based on authentic reactions are the poison that weakens the children's sense of self and replaces courage with fear, doubt, guilt, and shame.

Consistent with the spirit of 1776, American children must be taught that it is acceptable to break the rules when they are abusive, outdated or based on inaccurate information. Starting at home, kids must learn to manage differences with others through respectful discussion and dissent. They must learn to honor their own thinking through without disrespecting others who think differently. If they break the rules, they must be prepared to accept the consequences of breaking the rules.

This does not mean that the American child gets to be spoiled or arrogant, be rude to authority figures, or not be held accountable to reasonable rules. It means that when they feel injustices exist, they must learn to speak for themselves and to articulately defend what they believe. They must use their own authentic reactions as a guide to find the truth in any situation. Children must learn the difference between reasonable and unreasonable ways to present their grievances to those in positions of power. They must learn to harness their quiet anger to overcome resistance and to use all their emotions to connect to others and to solve life's problems.

The Parent Centered Family

American families were not originally designed to teach independence. In fact, the structure of our family system has been a problem for centuries. A European parent-centered model of family life was stowed away in the minds and hearts of the first immigrants bound for America. This patriarchal family system was not based on independence and equality. Power was not shared between the couple. The father ruled the roost, and the mothers and children were expected to do as they were told. The early settlers had all been raised and indoctrinated into this type of parent-centered family.

This model worked well in a Europe ruled by the ultimate authority figures, monarchs and despots, and served the purpose of keeping children tied to the family to work the farm or apprentice in the father's profession. Parental power was not shared, mirroring the power structures of the authoritative and hierarchical political and religious systems of 18th century Europe. Members of the family who did as they were told were handsomely rewarded, especially if you were a first-born son, and any other children were also dependent on the system for their survival. The social fabric required dependency that was easy to transfer from a father to a teacher to a king. If you played by the rules and had the favor of the court, you could seek redress of grievances or request protection in times of war.

The parent-centered family is based on obedience. Authority is revered as the source of all truth. Personal freedom is sacrificed for security. Power rests in the father and secondarily in the mother. Parents do not disagree in front of the children. They maintain a united front, for fear that disagreement would weaken authority and invite disobedience, possibly even insurrection.

In this parent-centered model of a family, children are to be seen and not heard. The assumption is that children need discipline and must "toe the line" as they will do something terrible. "Spare the rod and spoil the child" excuses physical abuse. Children must be kept on the straight and narrow by any and all authority figures – for example, parents, teachers, priests and rabbis, and police. Children are required to listen to their elders and do as they are told. They are treated like wild animals who cannot be trusted to be reasonable or to have valid opinions. Encouraging children to be honest, or to voice dissent is seen as inviting defiance and acting out, behavior that threatens those in charge.

American families need to make the transition from top-down authority to a democratic approach that encourages everyone to speak. We value independence and equality, but we still use unbreakable chains of command in most of our families, schools, businesses, the military and so on. Where do children learn to exercise their judgment?

The way out of this quandary to listen to our authentic emotions to help us develop our individuality and independence. We need to honor our own reactions rather than blindly following the role that ties us to the way we were raised. We become free to follow our heart, stand alone if necessary for what we believe, and continue the fight until the mission is accomplished.

Emotions Are The Engine: Your Thoughts Drive The Car

Most people listen to what they say to themselves in their mind, their self-talk, all day long. When I ask them how they are feeling, they aren't sure. Some will say that they don't know how they feel. Still, others will say that they don't feel anything. But most of my patients are rarely aware of all their emotions. They don't see the emotional cause that gives rise to what they say to themselves.

This fact that your emotions are your most powerful and significant resource is a position that I will reiterate over and over in this book. In fact, the single biggest thing I have learned in my 65,000 hours of patient care is the power of human emotions. As I said previously, humans are emotional beings who happen to think, not thinking beings who happen to feel. You think and act to resolve the tensions created by your most powerful reactions, your emotions. You cannot understand yourself until you understand your emotions, and they may not be immediately obvious.

Your mind operates like a driver of a car. Emotions are the engine. All the power is in the engine. Your thinking is the steering wheel. Driving the car involves directing the power of the engine with the steering wheel. You can't negotiate curves at full throttle, so to solve life's problems, you drive at a speed that allows you to consider all your conflicting thoughts and feelings, and choose the direction that reflects your true self.

Why Your Parents Influence You Forever

Your personal history is uniquely yours. It is a product of your childhood experiences, and it never leaves you. It is your greatest blessing and your greatest curse at the same time. It is a blessing because it provides information that you can use to understand current events and to protect yourself from harm. You need it to survive and learn. However, your history makes you unable to experience life without bias or influence from the past. It becomes a curse because nothing is truly new to you. All events are seen through the lens of your past, which can distort what you perceive.

Your upbringing is always in your mind, embedded in your memory. Attempts to deny your past only blind you to its influence and increase the chance that history will repeat itself. The past is connected to every moment in the present through your emotional reactions. There is no experience in the present that does not have some connection to an event in the past. You can still have novel experiences, but they will always trigger some related memory.

Your parents continue to influence your reactions as an adult because your mind uses emotion to record your life experiences. Your emotions tag experiences as "important" and "unimportant" according to your parents' reactions. But your parents are imperfect people, so the rules you learn from them are some good and some bad. The bad rules are confusing and loaded with the fear of your parents.

Even when you are an adult, memory, boosted by emotion, gives your parents the God-like status they had when you were young and vulnerable, which makes it difficult, even impossible, to tell whether your reaction makes sense in the moment. It is hard to separate the emotions of the past from the emotions of the present. They all blend together, making it hard to tell if you are overreacting or reacting reasonably in the moment.

How Learned Emotions Are Created

Since your family role is your road map for survival, your mind must store a lot of vital information. It does this by laying down learned emotions in three ways:

1. Memories are tagged with emotion.

The more emotion you associate with any memory, the higher the likelihood that it will be remembered. Significant reactions from your parents are more emotional and therefore more important to remember, so you know how to please those who are important to you.

Emotions add that extra level of meaning so, you will remember what is critical for attachment and survival. Your actions and thoughts become tagged with emotion for the mind to remember what is critical for survival. Emotions keep the mind from becoming clogged with each and every occurrence. The amount of emotion you experienced as a child is directly proportional to the impact of any related situation in your life.

As an adult, emotions guide your actions to support the strongest attachment to significant others according to the way you were raised. When your thoughts or actions trigger a cautionary feeling, it is your mind's way of signaling what you need to do to connect and avoid rejection. What you do next is designed to relieve your fear, guilt, shame, anger or sadness. If you make the uncomfortable feeling go away, you feel like you are back in safe territory.

2. Competing emotions are suppressed.

For example, anger stands in direct contrast to guilt, shame, and fear. Anger is a strong emotion that creates pressure to push back and relieves the tension created by feeling afraid, guilty or ashamed. Joy and sadness can also weaken the effects of fear, guilt, and shame. If you are excited about something, you want to overcome your guilt or shame to embrace it and enjoy it. Guilt or shame would make you suppress that joy. Suppose your parents made a huge deal about eating cookies. Most likely you will feel somewhat guilty eating cookies, until the day you get mad and think, "I am now 27 years old. I think I know when it is OK to have a cookie!"

3. Your identity is based on actions that please your parents.

Initially, you see yourself through their eyes. As a small child, your goal is to stay connected to them, so your sense of who you love is based on your parents' reactions. If they are ok, you are ok. You need to remember what they want. Your sense of who you are fuses with what they want for you.. "I" is a confusing concept because your identity is based not only on what you believe about yourself but also on interactions with others. "I" often means "they," as in, "they told me." The sense of who you are is complicated and confusing, but it begins with the approval or disapproval of your parents.

An emotion is significant to you only if it originates inside you. For example, no one can make you feel guilty without your consent. If you say to yourself, "that person is just trying to make me feel guilty," you do not give any credibility to the guilt you may feel. It is put there by another, not internally generated by yourself. It is theirs, not yours. If you identify it as yours, then you will believe it and use it to guide your future choices and behavior. You must identify with your emotions to have them effect you

FEAR, GUILT, SHAME: The Big Three Learned Emotions

Strong emotions maintain and protect your family role and ensure your dependency on your family. I call fear, guilt, and shame the Big Three. Each independently creates great tension in the body. Ignoring your role will create anxiety while following your role will immediately reduce it. Doing the opposite of what you have been told, or even thinking about doing it, triggers all three of these emotions. The problem is that doing what you feel is right often conflicts with following the role you fulfilled as a child. These emotions are like warning sirens, letting you know that if you don't adhere to your role, you may experience disappointment, rejection or even abandonment. These emotions are intimidating because the child is that scared of separation from their parents, and encodes a large amount of emotion in the memories that are triggered. You re-experience that emotion whenever the same situation arises as an adult. You feel really scared, guilty or ashamed out of proportion to the true impact that any man, woman or child will have upon you as an adult.

The Big Three (fear, guilt, and shame) are the agents of your family role. They are important to understand if you want to break the ties that bind you to your childhood self and become independent. There will be many times as an adult when you will have to override these emotions to do what you feel deep inside is the right thing to do. The more you understand about these emotions, the easier it will be to stare them down and follow the path outlined by your authentic reactions.

FEAR

Fear is both learned and innate. The ability to feel the fear of a physical threat is innate and based on survival. If your life is in danger, you should feel fear. The inability to register it would expose you to possible death. The fight or flight response kicks into gear, and you react to save your life.

Unlike physical fear, the fear of separation is learned and based on experience. Events surrounding your relationships are imprinted in your mind by emotions. Collectively, your emotions tell the story of what it means to love someone, to care for someone, and to lose someone. Emotional hurt is based on a shift in the relationship, either due to conflict, or a complete loss of the connection due to death.

A special kind of fear, however, is the fear of separation. There is a strong irrational component to this fear. If a parent withdraws from a child without explanation, the child is not able to tell if or when the parent is coming back. The need for the parent is so great, and the child has little ability to understand time, that a temporary distance can be easily be misunderstood as a permanent loss. The simplest unexplained absences can terrify a child. This level of fear is stored in the child's memory to be re-experienced as an adult whenever the threat of distance appears in a relationship.

In most adult relationships, the size of the emotional reaction does not match the actual level of threat to the relationship. Many of my patients are confused and surprised by the level of fear that can arise in personal situations. There are some that panic for no apparent reason. Many freeze and become unable to "get the words out" when confronted with the need to tell people how they feel. Others will claim that they have no feelings or don't know how they feel. Many others will refer to feeling anxious without apparent cause, a condition known as "free floating anxiety.

Just for the record, I don't believe in the concept of "free floating anxiety." I believe that this experience is better understood as a fear whose root cause has not yet been determined. When I explore those kinds of experiences with my patients, I find that the root cause can be traced to a fear of separation. My patients may not readily identify the source of their fear as a specific threat to a relationship. To them, it feels more like a general threat. They tell me they are afraid that something bad will happen if they don't do what is expected of them. If I ask them to explain their fear further, they will say they are afraid their actions will cause some reaction from parents or others in the family that will change the relationship. They are afraid family members will be upset by their actions, and withdraw from them. Worse yet, they assume the separation will be permanent.

The magnitude of my patients' fears and the conviction that any damage will be permanent indicates how little this fear reflects adult experiences. Adults know that most mistakes in relationships can be fixed. Nearly all mistakes can be repaired with contrition and reparation. You say you're sorry and make it up to the person. Relationships change all the time. Trust levels ebb and flow. Distance grows and shrinks. Breathing space is necessary in good relationships. Friends come and go with change in circumstances. Nothing stays the same.

Many of my patients experience a great deal of unnecessary anxiety in response to any distance in a relationship, even the temporary distance necessary to resolve differences with each other. When you have a disagreement with someone, you need time to think about what the other person has said or done, especially if you disagree strongly. It takes time spent by yourself to reorganize your point of view and accommodate theirs.

When distance is necessary, many people can't handle it at all. They panic and irrationally believe the relationship has ended. This irrational fear exists in all of us because of our childhood dependency on our parents. To children, any distance is highly threatening because they need to be able to turn to their parents at any moment and know their parents are there to help. Eventually, the fear of separation lessens if the parents continue to go away but come back consistently, if the parent explains any absences to the child in a reassuring manner, and if the child has good care while the parents are absent. When parents are unreliable, fail to explain their absences to children, leave the child alone in a dangerous situation, withdraw without explanation, or are frequently out of control or unpredictable, children become more afraid of separation instead of less. This fear gets carried over into adult relationships.

Fear of abandonment or separation explains why so many of my patients are scared to death of conflict. This makes differences difficult to resolve and requires both many discussions and time spent apart to think about what is being said. Many of my patients panic whenever breathing room is required, and they surrender their needs before a true compromise is reached, so the problem continues to reappear. Alternatively, the person may continue to chase after the partner or friend relentlessly, and the relationship becomes so highly strained that the chance for a real resolution becomes lost.

Adam's Story: Fear and Divorce

Adam, age 28 is a sales rep for a pharmaceutical company. He makes over $75K per year and feels very good about his professional accomplishments over the previous six years. Two years after graduating, he met Monique, a technical writer, at a convention. They dated for a year and a half before getting married. The marriage lasted less than a year before Monique asked for a divorce. She claimed she couldn't live with Adam's temper any longer. Adam was devastated and could not understand why Monique wanted to leave after such a short time. He felt humiliated by the deterioration of his marriage and came to see me to cope with his distress. His job performance was suffering. He couldn't think straight, was having violent outbursts over small issues, and couldn't sleep.

According to Adam, one of the worst things was that he could not understand Monique's impression of him. Was he really such a bad guy that Monique would leave him after only one year? Whose fault was the breakup? Was he some kind of monster? Did Monique have a good reason to leave him? Adam was terribly shaken and confused by the whole fiasco. Adam could not tell if he was a good guy who was misunderstood or a bad guy who drove his wife away after only one year.

ME: "I know that Monique's request for a divorce was a big shock for you. When did you first notice that she was unhappy?"
ADAM: "That's just it! I didn't even notice anything was wrong. Everything seemed to be going just fine. We both worked a lot, but we had fun together on the weekends. Sex was great. We

fought a lot, but I thought that is what newlyweds did and just part of learning to live together. I just didn't see this coming…"

ME: "What did Monique say about the fighting?"

ADAM: "Monique said that I scared her. I do tend to blow up when I am mad. I take it and take it until I blow my top. I knew that wasn't good, but didn't think it was so bad that she would leave me."

ME: "I am not so sure that your temper was the reason that she left. There must have been issues that made you so angry. What else did she complain about?"

ADAM: "Monique was very rigid about lots of things. You had to do things her way, or she was not willing to play along. Like I had to go to all her family functions, but she refused to do the same with my family. She didn't like my family and wanted to spend as little time with them as possible. She also didn't think I made enough money. She thought I was lazy and could make more if I put out more effort."

ME: "Were things between you lopsided in her favor?"

ADAM: "I saw from the beginning that things were going to be her way or I could leave. I decided to try to please her, but whatever I did was never good enough."

ME: "No wonder you blew up after a while."

ADAM: "Yeah, I got to the point where I couldn't take it anymore. I felt guilty every time we fought, but that only made me try harder to please her. Never worked."

As it turns out, Adam's role in his family of origin was the "problem child." He was always unfairly blamed for problems between himself and his older sister. His sister was the "golden child" who could do no wrong. Adam was born with a hearing disability, and school was difficult for him. His father believed that Adam simply did not try hard enough and could be an academic success like his older sister if he wanted to. He never acknowledged Adam's disability and felt it was more of an excuse than a real difficulty.

Adam's problems in his marriage reveal the level of fear that ruled Adam's life when he was little. He lived in fear of failure and the shame that came with it. He tended to blame himself for anything that went wrong. His marriage became a repeat experience of his family. He was never good enough for Monique, but his tendency to blame himself prevented him from challenging her about the pressures she placed on him. Like his father, Monique saw Adam's character as the problem and wouldn't hesitate to blame him for anything and everything. Adam believed he was the problem, but his anger did not go away. Instead, it built up to the point of rage. This played right into Monique's hand. When Adam lost his cool, Monique was victorious because he was misbehaving, not her. His fear of his own anger was so deep that it ended up confirming his worst beliefs about himself.

Adam felt ashamed his whole life. This message was easy for him to believe. His parents always made him feel inadequate. He became afraid to listen to his anger because his parents would say he was "overreacting," even if all he did was complain about the way they were treating him. He learned very early that anger resulted in punishment, like his father screaming at him for "backtalk," taking away his car, or making him do extra chores. Now as an adult, Adam never acknowledged that he felt any anger. He barely knew when something bothered him. His anger would flash for a hot second, but immediately be buried by the fear of shame. This happened so rapidly he never even had time to register any anger at all.

Recognizing his anger was terrifying for Adam. In his psychological world, Monique was the reincarnation of his father. They used the same tactics, character attacks, shame, guilt, and bullying. Adam had even been programmed to see this as "love." He was used to this treatment from his father who told him he "loved" him. If he had been less afraid, he would have seen the problem with Monique from the beginning and avoided her.

Adam wanted Monique to come into treatment to work on their marriage. She came once but was unwilling to accept any responsibility for her role in the breakdown of their relationship. Why should she come to treatment when Adam was the problem?

Monique's refusal to participate began to wake up Adam's anger. Over time, he began to see that Monique's treatment of him was unreasonable. He also began to see how unfairly his parents had treated him and continue to treat him even to this day.

Adam divorced Monique and got better at challenging his family in a calmer, more self-respecting fashion. He learned how hard he was on himself. Happily, years later, Adam was able to take these lessons into a second marriage. He is healthier and happier than he could ever have been in a marriage to Monique.

GUILT

Unlike fear, guil*t* and shame are not natural emotions. They are learned reactions based on experiences with your parents. A polar bear will not eat you for feeling guilty. Strict upbringings breed guilt and shame. In fact, some parents embrace the use of guilt and shame to control their children and are proud of the fact that it works. They base this opinion on the compliant behavior of their child, not realizing that the true test of their parenting remains to be seen and is revealed by the child's capacity for work, love, and play as an adult.

Rational guilt exists when you break rules of reason. If you steal something from a friend, you should feel guilty. The guilt is reasonable because it is based on the Golden Rule: "Do unto others as you would have done unto you." If you don't like something done to you, you shouldn't do the same thing to somebody else. The guilt makes sense and is easy to comprehend. It tells you that you have made a mistake and need to make reparation to somebody for your actions.

Irrational guilt is a little different. Irrational guilt is based on breaking unreasonable rules. Unreasonable rules are made to protect the parents and not the children.

Cynthia's Story: Guilt and Control

Cynthia's mother was dead, and her father was an abusive alcoholic. Whenever he was drunk, and his kids displeased him, he did not physically harm them, but he would yell at them about how ungrateful they were. Usually, he threw in a lot of Scripture, so the children believed they were also failing God. By the time he finished his two-hour lectures about all he had sacrificed for his children, they would be exhausted and close to tears. They never knew what might set him off. It could be anything from the wrong facial expression to getting a phone call. They did not know what to do to avoid his wrath.

Cynthia's family role was based on irrational guilt. Her job was to keep Daddy happy. Anything that made Daddy unhappy when he was drunk would start the scolding about how hard he worked, how difficult it was to be a single parent, and how they should ask God for forgiveness. The kids never knew when daddy would get drunk, so they constantly felt a large amount of irrational guilt. Cynthia would feel extreme guilt whenever she spent his money, even on things like toothpaste or shampoo. She was afraid to spend time with her friends after school in case Daddy needed her, and bring her friends home was out of the question.

Irrational guilt highly influenced Cynthia's adult relationships. Her needs came last, behind those of her husband, children or even the needs of friends. She could not justify any time for herself and lived a life of great self-denial, which was not good for her or her family. Any time her husband encouraged her to do something nice for herself, she panicked. She would run into her irrational guilt and return to self-denial to relieve herself of that tension.

Cynthia finally became so exhausted being perfect for everyone else all the time, that she was hospitalized for exhaustion, and then referred to me. Treatment was based on using her authentic anger at the abuse she suffered from her father as the antidote for her guilt. The guilt was always going to be there. The difference was to use the anger to fight back, restore the right to have her needs matter, and create balance in all her relationships.

SHAME

Irrational guilt is closely related to shame but different. Guilt exists because you break rules, whether the rules are reasonable or unreasonable. On the other hand, shame has no basis in truth whatsoever. It is an emotion that reflects the worthlessness of the person, rather than a problem with something the individual supposedly did wrong. Shame is linked to feeling worthless as a human being, which is a lot harder to deal with than, say, breaking a window.

Many of my patients slide from experiencing irrational guilt into shame. My patients will often tell me: "I feel so bad that I did that." That is shame talking. Moreover, "feeling bad" is understandable if someone makes a mistake. I understand that they may feel bad when they make a mistake. Feeling "so bad" exposes a depth of feeling that is out of proportion to the mistake. Shame makes small things seem more significant than they really are. Shame also makes somebody feel worthless for merely making a mistake.

Shame distorts the human experience but is insidious because we believe it so readily. The only truth in shame is that it says more about your parents' imperfections that it does about your own. Shame is the imprint of their imperfections upon you. Children learn shame from parental overreactions to children's mistakes, not deliberate misdeeds, but errors in judgment from lack of experience. These are the UGLY responses that I discussed previously. The parents over-react based on their own issues, but children cannot be expected to understand that. First, they feel afraid, and with repeat events, shame becomes the lasting experience, with the children internalizing how they have been treated. They conclude that they must be truly terrible to have Mom or Dad react that much. It is their fault as it cannot be Mom or Dad's fault. After all, parents know best. After many shaming experiences like this, the children believe they should be ashamed of themselves just for existing.

It is worth repeating that shame says far more about the parents than the child. The parent should be ashamed, rather than the child. Let me make this point very clear. There is NEVER truth in shaming children, for example, ridiculing students for wetting their pants, or mocking a child's drawing, or criticizing children who try but cannot excel. Shame is a destructive emotion as a child and continues to be equally damaging to an adult. If children feel ashamed for what they have done, there is no room for learning by trial and error. We have to make mistakes to learn. When parents make children feel inherently worthless, each mistake opens the door for a rush of shame. How can a human being be worthless? Since when does a mistake define a person's entire value?

Since no parent is perfect, and all parents overreact sometimes to their children, the experience of shame is universal. We all feel shame from time to time. It drives much of human behavior and is often not recognized. Shame is hard to identify because it has many faces.

Nancy's Story: Feeling Unworthy

I once had a patient who filed for divorce from her husband of eight years, but couldn't pull the trigger to finalize the papers. Despite paying for her attorney and completing the documents, she could not bring herself to sign the divorce plea that would finish the process. In the meantime, she continued to see her husband who did not want the divorce. The truth was that he was very demanding and immature, and he always created drama as well as serious problems with money. But Nancy's reasoning was: "Who am I to judge? Maybe I am asking for too much, or expecting too much of him." "Maybe he can change if I just give him more time."

Nancy never recognized that her thinking was based on her own feelings of worthlessness. Her self-doubt went way beyond the guilt of hurting her husband's feelings. She felt ashamed that she was destroying her family because of her selfish needs. Whenever she considered signing the document, her shame and low self-esteem would surface. Who was she to ask for more out of her marriage? She would again see her husband to maintain some false hope of reconciliation that relieved her shame. Each time she spent any time with him, he would repeat the same behavior that made her want to leave him in the first place. She would initially get mad at him, but the shame would slowly creep in and destroy her ability to hold onto her anger.

Nancy's parents never wanted to have children, and her arrival was unplanned and unwarranted. Somehow Nancy was at fault for simply being born. Her parents were always irritated with her because she needed food, clothing, and attention. Nancy learned she deserved nothing in life. When she married at 16 to get out of her parent's house, she allowed her husband to call all the shots, even though he was usually wrong. It took her months to finalize her divorce and realize she was entitled to happiness.

Many things you say to yourself indicate the presence of shame. Self-doubt is often rooted in shame. People will say to themselves, "I'm not good enough" before they have even given themselves a chance to learn what they are trying to learn. They short-circuit themselves to relieve the shame. Others will blame themselves when there is no obvious explanation for a problem. They will say to themselves: "What's wrong with me?" to explain whatever is going on, rather than holding someone else responsible. Again, they do not see the shame in this question and listen to what they are saying to themselves without thinking about it. They are ruled by the invisible hand of shame and believe what they hear in their mind.

Shame can lead to low self-esteem. Self-esteem is high when the person knows who they are, can represent what they believe, and defend it against differing opinions. They get angry to fight back. Shame squashes anger in a sea of self-doubt robbing the person of their spirit and preventing the development of self-worth.

Overcoming Learned Emotions

The learned emotions of fear, guilt, and shame are extremely powerful. If you are like many of my patients, you are not used to sorting through your emotions. You tend to believe that whatever you felt in the moment is justified, and you blindly act to reduce tension created by your emotions. If you act to relieve the tensions of fear, guilt, and shame, you are being influenced by the past, by emotions that were ingrained in you years ago. This means you are being unduly influenced by the significant others in your life, especially your parents and family. Your behavior is actually being directed by your parents' beliefs and not your own. You choose to follow a path that you think reflects what you truly believe, but in truth, it reveals how you were raised. Without the awareness of where your emotions are coming from, you run the risk of imitating your parents, all the while thinking that they have little or no impact on you as an adult.

Overcoming learned emotions is vital to be your Authentic Self in all your relationships. It is also critical in creating independent connections, close relationships that are not based on dependency but on honest exchanges.

Your first experiences with independence are with your parents. You live in a state of physical dependence, which is linked to emotions like separation anxiety and fear or abandonment. For years your need for protection trump any feelings you have, and you internalize the beliefs and attitudes of your parents. As your need for protection decreases, you are better able to sort out your own beliefs and responses from theirs, and as an adult, you think you are free to believe what you want. But the blueprint of your family role never goes away by itself. You must make the effort to free yourself internally from the negative influence of your learned emotions. This can be a major struggle and confusion may reign amidst the voices in your head. You need to understand the enemy within to avoid any influences that pressure you into relationships based on dependency, dishonesty, and need.

Emotions Just Won't Leave

I'm sure you've noticed that an emotion does not disappear simply because you try to push it out of your mind. Some emotions can take over your brain almost completely – for example, falling in love. Others hover about like a mosquito you can't catch. Still others you may be able to stuff away fairly successfully, but they have not lost their power. Sometimes feelings surface that pose a threat to the family role. You know they are there. You can feel them, and admit them to yourself, but you are too afraid to act on them. You end up setting them aside to reduce your fear. You hide them to avoid them, like shutting the bogeyman in the closet. These emotions are hidden just below the surface of awareness and are terribly confusing.

The problem is that emotions you try to hide don't go away. They "leak". Emotions can present themselves indirectly using three pathways:

1. Acting out occurs when people's behavior exposes an emotion they refuse to acknowledge. An example is the people who hide their anger behind humor. They may joke a barbed remark, but when challenged, they will say, "That was no big deal. Can't you take a joke?" The jokester will not admit they harbor any anger or rage. Another example is people who are passive-aggressive. They refuse to say how they really feel but make veiled remarks, such as, "Oh, don't worry about helping me. You're much

too busy with your important work." They deny the obvious anger that fueled their remark. Yet another example is people who makes faces but when they are asked "What's wrong?" they will only say, "Nothing," or "I didn't make a face."

2. Dreaming is the second way of indirectly expressing hidden emotions. Dreams serve the purpose of processing emotion that can't be felt at the moment. You accumulate emotion during the day. The fuel for the dream is events that bother you more than you realize. At night, your dream machine takes over. The unprocessed emotion resurfaces and triggers memories that become loosely organized into a story you call a dream. Because you are asleep and not logically processing information, you are unable to organize the story to make sense. Your dreams take on a life of their own and may become weird and disorganized nightmares. Some dreams process emotions that you tried to shut into the closet years ago, but got reactivated by a present experience.

3. Sickness is the third way of dealing with hidden emotions. Any part of the body can be affected by the stress of emotions that have never been consciously addressed or processed. Chronic stress is linked to back pain, headaches, diabetes, heart disease, weight gain, gastrointestinal problems, depression, high blood pressure, insomnia, skin problems and autoimmune disorders such as fibromyalgia and more. Sometimes people self-medicate these problems using excessive sex, alcohol, or drugs which can lead to the even greater stress of abuse or addictions.

My wife's favorite phrase is, "Listen to your body because it is listening to you." Our emotions heavily influence our well-being, even if we aren't aware of them or try to ignore them.

Cathy's Story: Hidden Emotions Regain Their Strength

Cathy, age 48, came to see me shortly after her older sister, Francine, age 50, died very suddenly. Her death came as a shock to everyone as Francine had always been the picture of health.

Cathy and Francine had been close. At one point in their lives, they shared an apartment for five years as single women living in Chicago. They shared many experiences of city life, dating bad boyfriends, drinking too much, going to concerts, and so on. After they each got married, they went their separate ways. They saw each other at family functions, but distance had eroded their relationship over the previous ten years. Cathy now lived in Maine and Francine in Nevada with their husbands and children.

You would have expected Cathy to be distressed about Francine's death. Instead, she had no visible reaction. Cathy's husband, Bob, found this lack of response very worrisome. He knew the two sisters were close and couldn't understand why Cathy wasn't more upset. Bob encouraged Cathy to come see me.

CATHY: "I have trouble sleeping since Francine died and my irritable bowel has been giving me fits. I am in the bathroom every five minutes. I don't know what is wrong with me."

ME: "Bob seemed worried about you. Why is this?"

CATHY: "He thinks I should be sad and upset. Plus, I have no interest in sex. We fight every time he is interested. He takes it personally, but I just don't feel like it."

ME: "It sounds to me that your body is trying to tell you something."

CATHY: "I've never thought much about that mind/body stuff. What are you saying?"

ME: "I think it's possible that you are feeling more about the death of your sister than you are letting on."

CATHY: "Francine and I were close, but we haven't been a big part of each other's lives for years. I don't know why my body would react that strongly."

ME: "Do you miss your sister?"

CATHY: "Yes, I miss the good times that we had, but that was so long ago."

ME: "Sometimes when people experience strong emotion, they are afraid they might lose control if they give in to it. Could that be what's going on with you?"

CATHY: "Well, that could be true for me. I do know that I need to feel in control or I start to get anxious very fast. Bob and I fight about that all the time."

ME: "I think you become anxious when you are feeling deep emotion. It would be natural for you to feel deep sadness over the loss of your sister. Your body is letting you know how sad and frightened you really are."

CATHY: "Do you think that stress has anything to do with my lack of interest in sex?"

ME: "Yes. You shut down when you are overwhelmed by your emotions. It's your way of reducing the anxiety. The problem between you and Bob over sex is that you don't explain yourself and he takes it too personally."

By learning to pay more attention to her emotions, Cathy was able to begin the grieving process. She needed to face the range of emotions, from sadness to anger, that happen when you lose someone in your life. She confided more in Bob and learned to lean on him for support. Cathy also learned not be afraid to ask for help, something that had not come easily for her. Experiencing the sadness and vulnerability that went along with her sister's death, and realizing she could live through them, reduced her fears of losing control. When Bob and Cathy shared their emotions, those emotional experiences led them to feel closer physically, which in turn helped their sex life. They became a good example of what a very wise patient once said to me: "You need emotional intercourse before physical intercourse."

Cathy's denial of her emotions led to another problem. She was pseudo-independent. She thought that independence meant that you didn't rely on others and took care of things on your own. She was unable to open up to others because she could not protect herself from harm. If she were to get upset, she was afraid that she would be ridiculed for being weak. She had learned that lesson well in their family of origin. She remembered her parents telling her, "No tears. They don't help." So she would hold back her reactions, convinced that she was being strong. In truth, Cathy was run by her fear that stopped her from protecting her right to cry.

She had lost her true sense of independence and was run by her learned emotion.

6

There Are Really Two Sides Of You

Your Authentic Self And

Self For Others . . .

When patients come to see me, they are often confused by their own behavior. They cannot explain to themselves why they do what they do. For example, my patients may:

- Do something they know they should not be doing. They know better, so why are they doing it?
- Feel disconnected from their family, colleagues, or peers, even though they appear to be deeply involved with them. So are they or are they not part of the group?
- Act like different people in different situations. Why do they fold up like a lawn chair with some people, but boss others around?
- Be unable to make up their minds about certain choices. Why is it so hard?
- Feel closer to one child than another, even though they don't want to play favorites. Why can't they stop?

Your Self Talk

Many of my patients are unaware of the significance of their emotions. They know what they think, but not how they feel. Sometimes, they have been told that they are "difficult" or "stupid" and they take these two labels to heart even when they are not true. Or, they are self-aware enough to realize they are "stubborn" or "wussy", and realize this affects their experiences, but they still do not know what they are feeling.

To make things even more complicated, you'll recall that you have two sets of emotions: your authentic feelings, which are spontaneous, you're your learned emotions, which are set by your family role and operate your Self for Others. Situations trigger competing emotions, so your self-talk becomes an argument. If your family role wins the argument, you hide your authentic emotions to avoid the uncomfortable dilemma they cause. But hiding authentic emotions makes it so difficult to be human. When you are used to suppressing your immediate emotions, they are not available when you need them to function.

Ann's Story: The Good Girl

Ann is the eldest of three siblings. Unfortunately, her youngest sibling, William, is autistic. He was diagnosed at age 10 with Asperger's Syndrome, a mild form of autism. William was often distressed and behaved badly, but he was held to a different standard because of his diagnosis. Ann's parents did not know how to manage William very well and proceeded to spoil him at every turn. They gave him anything that he wanted and set few boundaries.

William now had not one but two problems. Not only was he autistic, he was immature and underdeveloped. He could not cope with frustration and became very demanding. Ann, 3 years older, was left to fend for herself. She saw that her parents were overwhelmed with William's care, and quietly learned that she would fit in by being the "good girl" who would not give her parents any problems. She became a dedicated people pleaser who would go way out of her way, no matter the circumstance, to help anyone whenever she could. There was a complete lack of balance between herself and others in all her relationships. She clung to pleasing others as if her life depended on it.

The simmering resentment Ann felt toward William exploded when Ann was working and on her own. Her parents had planned a vacation for their wedding anniversary and asked Ann if she would agree to take William for the week. During that week, William treated Ann miserably. He refused to listen to her, stole money from her, ate her special snacks and would stay up all night with the TV blaring. Ann worked long hours, and had to rise at 5 AM to drive an hour to work.

Ann couldn't take it anymore. She was tired of taking care of others and getting little back in return. When her parents returned from vacation, she told them everything William had done. Much to her surprise, her father backed William and blamed Ann for having little patience with a disabled person. Worse, her father called her selfish and told her she should be ashamed of herself. Her mother didn't even react. She just shrugged her shoulders and refused to disagree with the father.

Several days later, Ann woke up with severe chest pain and shortness of breath. She was positive she was having a heart attack and terrified of dying. She called out of work and drove herself to the Emergency Room of her local hospital. After a complete medical examination, the doctors ruled out a heart attack and diagnosed Ann with a panic attack. Ann was surprised that a panic attack could create such a powerful reaction in her body. It took the doctors a long time to reassure her that she was okay, and he was referred to me for follow-up care.

During our session we discussed her feelings about her home life, her brother, and the way her father had defended William at her expense. She admitted she had been angry, but then started making excuses for her father. She said, "He only wants the best for William and it has been hard on him too. I understand why he protects him so much." She expressed absolutely no anger toward her mother, and even protected her. When I stated that Mom and dad were a team, she denied it and said, "No way. My Mom has always taken care of me. You should try living with my father. It is his way or the highway. My mother has been my savior."

Ann was protecting her parents at her own expense completely, and denying her mother's role in the family problem. By not challenging them, she remained the 'good girl." Her panic attack occurred because the pressure of the truth about her life caused her anger to finally break through. But she didn't feel angry. She felt panic and terror.

After a lifetime of Ann being patient, her brother's increased aggressiveness toward her became the catalyst for her reaction. This scared Ann at a deeper level that even she understood. She cannot acknowledge her anger that has built up over living the family dysfunction her whole life. I spoke with Ann over several visits, reassuring her that her hidden anger was reasonable, but it threatened her family role. Good girls were not supposed to get mad or put pressure on parents. If Ann admitted that she was mad, she would have had to acknowledge the truth about the favoritism in the family as well as the inequality between Mom and Dad.

Ann's treatment is ongoing. We are still discussing Ann's position as collateral damage in a family already overwhelmed with a difficult problem, and her right to feel and use her own authentic reactions.

Your Authentic Self

Your Authentic Self is based on your natural reactions which are immediate and unfiltered. They spring from a subconscious source that makes you react both intellectually and emotionally in a way that makes sense to you. For both the heart and the mind, in a very simplistic way, things either feel good or feel bad. If something feels bad, then there is something definitely wrong somewhere. You may not know exactly where the problem is, but you know when something doesn't feel right. You naturally get angry in those situations. Anger is the natural reaction to this confusing and uncomfortable situation. It is your authentic warning signal that there is a problem to be solved.

It sounds surprising, but sadness and anger form the emotional core of the Authentic Self. Whenever a problem arises in a relationship, there are actually two problems. The initial problem is somebody's behavior toward you. A person may have done something to mistreat you, ignore you, take something that is yours, etc. Anger is the natural reaction to this problem. A secondary problem also exists. The relationship has now changed because of the problem. You may trust the person less because they treated you badly. Sadness is the natural reaction to the loss of trust and threat to the relationship. Sadness exists because of the desire to maintain the bond.

Mad and sad dance together in a way that keeps both emotions under control. Their purpose, somewhat counter-intuitively, is to promote joy. These two emotions operate most effectively when they are linked together because they enable you to both solve a problem and maintain the relationship at the same time, a process that brings joy.

Think of a time when someone hurt your feelings badly. If the situation is significant enough, you feel so sad that you are at risk for slipping into depression. Then your anger comes alive because you get mad about the way you were treated. You may become energized by being mad as well as sad.

Similarly, think of a situation that made you hopping mad. Underneath the anger, you probably feel sorrow and a sense of loss because the relationship has been damaged. Feeling your sadness can prevent the anger from turning into rage by choosing to address the problem more carefully.

Both sadness and anger indicate there is a problem, and they help you enjoy life and solve problems. Collectively, they are your real gut instincts. You can trust them. They are linked to your sense of truth. They are the real you, part of your Authentic Self.

Your first reaction to being put in a situation that feels bad to you is anger. You were taught in childhood that your anger is unacceptable, so you quickly suppress it. However, your anxiety kicks in immediately and continues to warn you that there is a conflict between what you believe (your authentic emotions) and what you have been taught (your learned emotions). The stage is set for a battle between your Authentic Self and your family role, or your Self for Others.

Anxiety is like the warning siren of a fire truck. Immediately fear, guilt, and shame punish you for even thinking that you might consider making a choice that would violate your role. If you capitulate to the rules of your family role, you'll feel better, a sense of relief in the short term. But your Authentic Self will have lost the battle. That is never a good thing because you will have to suppress your authentic reactions to reduce your anxiety. You gain relief at the expense of your real self.

Lisa's Story: The Fearful Lesbian

Lisa, a nurse, managed the staff of an entire hospital department. She described her problem in the following way: "I have over 40 people who report to me. I have written up and even fired several nurses without blinking an eye. People respect me and do what I want them to do. Yet, every time I meet with my boss, I turn to jelly inside. All I can say is "Yes, ma'am," and do whatever she wants. I know that her suggestions won't work, because she does not know what is going on, but I give in to her all the time. I feel like a wimp when I am around her. What is wrong with me? Am I really that weak? Which one is the real me; the one who manages her staff or the one who can't stand up to her boss?"

As it turns out, Lisa had been greatly affected by her mother's illness when she was a small child. Her mother was diagnosed with multiple sclerosis (MS), a neurological disease that left her mother disabled and exhausted. In addition to handling her schoolwork, Lisa cared for her mother as much as she could. Her father would encourage her and praise her for being so caring and loving toward her mother. Lisa's father did not realize that he was promoting a role-reversal where the child becomes the parent to the parent, (what is called the *"parentified child"* in psychological terms). He thought it was good for Lisa to take care of her mother, and thought she enjoyed doing so. He did not realize how damaging it was to her psychological health.

Lisa's family role required that she take care of her mother and deny her own wishes and needs. She lost her childhood to her mother's illness and became an adult prematurely. She became over-responsible for the care of others, and irresponsible in the care of herself. Lisa was able to see why she could not challenge her boss but could challenge her subordinates. She had been raised to obey authority figures, always. But when it came to taking care of her own needs, that was not allowed. Her family role only enabled her to be in the service of others. She did not have permission internally to be in the service of herself. That was against the rules.

There was another element to Lisa's story. Lisa realized at an early age that she was a lesbian. She was attracted to girls even in elementary school, not just as friends but also romantically. Memories of her sexual fantasies at an early age involved physical exchanges with women. She once mentioned this fact to her mother who was horrified. She threatened to disown Lisa and throw her out of the house if she ever dated a woman. Then she told

Lisa's father who told her that homosexuality is a sin and against God's commandments.

Lisa buried all of her authentic feelings. She could not risk upsetting her sick mother and being the black sheep in the family. She dated many boys to cover her real interests and be acceptable to the family. She even went as far as having sex with a boy. The experience was not satisfying to her at all, and only confirmed her suspicions about her real orientation.

After we had already spoken several times, Lisa came to see me with an announcement. She had fallen in love with a woman at work who loved her in return. Lisa was thrilled but was also having nightmares and headaches. She was too afraid to tell her parents that she had a girlfriend. Lisa had invited her new female partner, Tammy, to move into her apartment with her, and was both very happy and scared to death that her parents were going to find out.

LISA: "I know I have to tell my parents about Tammy, but am worried about upsetting my mother and having my father yell at me again about the Bible. I'm also afraid I will just lose it with them and feel terrible about it afterward. I know that I didn't choose to be gay. I was born that way. But they don't see it that way. They think I am going through some phase of hating men. It's infuriating."

ME: "Tell me what angers you the most about your parents' reactions."

LISA: "I resent that my needs don't matter to them. I have always had to adjust for my mother's MS, and my father expected me to do that. It made his life more comfortable."

ME: "That doesn't seem fair. He was the adult and had the responsibility for your mom, not you. How did you react to that pressure?"

LISA: "It didn't seem like pressure at the time. It was just me being me. I enjoy taking care of others. I became a nurse for a reason, and I am good at what I do."

ME: "You strike me as sensitive and caring. I bet you are a really good nurse. It's just that you were a child and it's not good for a child emotionally to have to care for a parent."

LISA: "I didn't even think about it. My Dad had to go to work, and it just seemed the reasonable thing to do."

ME: "It was convenient. It just wasn't healthy."

LISA: "So what was my Dad supposed to do? We didn't have enough money to bring in help."

ME: "You were just a kid. How did you know there wasn't enough money for that?"

LISA: "My Dad told me."

ME: "That is exactly my point. A parent shouldn't be talking to their kids about their finances. It scares children and makes them worry."

LISA: "You're right. I used to worry about money all the time, and I still do. It makes Tammy crazy."

ME: "It sounds to me like your father had other options."

LISA: "I never thought about it before. It just seemed like it was something I had to accept. I had no other option."

ME: "You didn't then, but you do now. You're a grown woman, but you are still making excuses for your father. There's no reason why he can't support your relationship with Tammy, yet you aren't angry enough to push back at him."

LISA: "Nobody is allowed to push back at my father. That just doesn't happen in my family."

ME: "Maybe that's why you have the headaches. Your body is telling you that it's time to stand up to your parents and ask them to support you. The health of your body and your relationship with Tammy both depend on it."

After many sessions during which Lisa learned to face her fears, she was finally able to come out of the closet and tell her parents about Tammy. At first, it did not go well. Lisa's parents were horrified and didn't talk to her for several months. Lisa described that time as one of the most difficult in her whole life. Her guilt and shame for being gay and being the family problem seemed to rise with each passing day. She leaned on Tammy during this period. Tammy was incredibly supportive and helped her to keep pushing the guilt away by reminding her of her right to be what she was born to be.

After several months, Mom and Dad relented. They realized when Lisa didn't call or come to visit that they were about to lose their daughter. They talked to several of their friends who supported Lisa and chastised her parents for being so judgmental.

Lisa's mother finally called her. Lisa was glad that her parents finally accepted her choice, but she remained upset by what she'd had to endure. Lisa had been forced by her parents to live with an enormous amount of guilt and shame. After coming to see me, she had an internal battle to find her anger to beat back the shame. She had to hunt for all her anger to overcome her excessive feelings of responsibility for her mother's health, as well as the shame imposed on her about her sexual orientation. Lisa and I will continue to discuss the effects of being a parentified child and getting in touch with her authentic feelings to manage these reactions in future situations and relationships.

Finding The Truth Within

A positive aspect of anxiety is that it is activated in response to something. Behind your anxiety, there is an authentic response, even if it was only for a nanosecond. This response is the real you speaking to you. When your natural reactions are not aligned with how you were taught to behave, you must do something to reduce your inner turmoil. The good news is that the turmoil only exists because there is an authentic emotion that gets stirred within you. Even if you are not sure of what you are feeling in a given moment, you are feeling something. Anxiety is a sign that you internally know something doesn't feel quite right.

The innate reaction within you is your truth. It defines your uniqueness. Some have even referred to this reaction as your "Light within," and assigned it religious significance. Quakers believe that it is the presence of God within you. It is not necessary to be religious to appreciate that an emotion that wells up from deep inside you is highly significant. It is the real you trying to come out. To deny it would be to deny yourself.

Your authentic response to a situation may be strong enough to override your fear, guilt or shame, but usually this requires life experience and awareness. Sometimes your authentic responses are so threatening to your family role that you immediately hide them from yourself. The problem is that you can't really fool yourself. You know they are still there. You can feel them, even admit them to yourself, but you are too afraid to act on them. Despite recognizing that they are there, you end up setting them aside to reduce your fear, guilt, and shame. You cut the connection to your real reactions, or water them down to the level required to make them acceptable to others. The emotions of the Authentic Self always exist, but are often pushed to the back of your mind, not only when you are little, and the situation is life or death, but also when you are older, and the emotions should no longer be stuffed away.

For the Self for Others to form, the Authentic Self gets nearly buried at an early age. Your mind hides your authentic feelings. Anxiety is the signal that your family role is going to bombard you with fear, guilt, and shame. These emotions are the friends of the family role because they keep your behavior on the straight and narrow path outlined by your parents. Your Self for Others is an artificial identity that kicks in when your unscripted, natural response conflicts with how you have been taught to respond. If your authentic response is considered out of line, you feel anger. This is a threatening emotion that morphs quickly into anxiety. You must make a decision. Do what you want to do, or do what you "should" do? Is this "should" what you believe is correct, or what you have been told is correct? You may hear the voice of your parents inside your head saying, "Don't do that!" Then your Self for Others takes up the judgment, and your self-talk says, "I could never do that. That's just not me!" The statement is confusing because it is not really about you, but about the person your parents expect you to be. The phrase, "That's just not me," does not come from a natural reaction of anger, and does not reflect the real you at all.

When you play the family role to reduce your fear, guilt, and shame, there is a cost to yourself: the loss of your authentic reactions that keep your relationships in emotional balance. Unfortunately, the lost emotions that are stuffed deep down into your mind are the very emotions that you need to be authentic as a person. They are not actually bad or harmful. They are only scary because they got labeled that way whenever your parents react strongly to your childhood responses of yours. Authentic responses reveal the real you. It is critical for you to recognize them when you are making decisions that reflect the real you, and not decisions based on childhood fears about parental approval.

Rachael's Story: Never Look Back

Rachael, age 27, came to me as part of a court-ordered treatment plan for driving while drunk. However, what she really wanted to talk about was her relationships with men, so that's where we started. Rachael asked me, "Why do I always seem attracted to bad guys who end up hurting me? Am I self-destructive?" Rachael had recently had a series of relationships that all ended the same way. In each case, she would take great care of her boyfriends no matter how they treated her. She would excuse their behavior by telling them, "I understand," and not make demands for equal consideration in return. In every case, the man left and blamed her for the breakup. After the fact, she realized that she stayed too long in each relationship. Rachael couldn't understand why she didn't learn her lesson and why she kept repeating the same scenario over and over.

When we talked about this problem, I asked Rachael if she ever felt angry at the imbalance in each relationship. She acknowledged that she would get mad, but whenever she stood up for herself, the boyfriend would get angry back, and she would go silent. She would give in whenever she felt that she was hurting her boyfriend's feelings or she became scared of losing him.

Rachael felt torn in two. One part of her would be mad and want the current boyfriend to understand how she felt. Another part of her would feel bad for him, and would not want to lose the relationship. Usually, she did whatever she had to do to hold onto the relationship, rather than be alone.

Rachael was confused by the weakness of her anger and the strength of her shame and guilt. Her rightful anger would surface but quickly fade to feeling sorry for the boyfriend. She did not recognize that she had been raised to be ashamed of her anger. She would say that she "felt bad" if she continued to argue. Staying felt right and leaving felt wrong, even though the problems in each relationship never got solved and kept reappearing. She was unable to end them and continued to the bitter end until the boyfriend finally had enough and dumped her.

127

Rachael felt she was a wimp. She used a personality trait to explain her behavior, instead of blaming the way she was raised. She had an excessive attachment to her family role and always heeded the shame that maintained it. Her Self For Others was overdeveloped while her Authentic Self was very weak. She was too afraid of her authentic anger to use it effectively to help herself.

I was not surprised to find out that Rachael learned this fear in her home with her family. If she disagreed with either her mother or father, they would withdraw from her, leaving her confused and full of guilt. Withdrawing love from a child is even scarier than lecturing or yelling. Unable to understand the problem, Rachael told herself she was expecting too much from her parents, who were trying to do their best and had her best interests at heart. She remembers thinking that she was an ungrateful kid who did not appreciate all that her family did for her.

Rachael's guilt and shame were very effective in burying her anger. She hid her mad behind sad. She would never admit that she was angry. If you asked her, she would say, "I'm not angry. I am hurt." Without her anger to help her turn the situation around, her sadness would turn into depression. She would numb her overwhelming sadness through substance abuse. She was prone to bouts of binge drinking and smoked marijuana on a daily basis. While she could not admit that she was angry, it was easy for her to admit that she was depressed. To her, depression was acceptable. Everybody was depressed about something. The last thing she wanted was to be known as an angry person.

With each failed relationship, Rachael was heading closer to a confrontation with her authentic emotions. It came one night after doing too many shots out late at night with her friends. She made a bad decision to drive while drunk and got into an accident. Fortunately, no one was hurt, but she did receive a summons for Driving Under the Influence (DUI). Her alcohol blood level was 0.12, well above the 0.8 maximum.

After her journey through the court system and rehab, Rachael ended up in my office. After months of our working together, she was able to embrace her anger and began to use it to restructure her relationships. The task was not easy. Many of the people in her life pushed back at the "new" Rachael. She was no longer a dependable doormat. Her friends claimed she was not herself any more, and she lost some of them. Her family didn't like her *"mouthiness"* and wondered if her treatment was making her worse instead of better.

Rachael held onto her newly recognized anger and it paid off. She made new friends and eventually met and married a healthier man. They built a relationship based on authentic feelings, and remain married to this day. Rachael's parents still want the "old Rachael" back and never understood the pain and suffering hiding her emotions had caused. Rachael now knows better and is willing to accept the consequences that maintaining her right to have a voice and be authentic may bring. The benefits far outweigh the misery of her old lifestyle.

Growing up is the process of pushing back against your fears to unearth your authentic reactions and learning to heed them in all situations. Your goal is to use your authentic emotions as the guide to create relationships that validate the person you really are, not the child your parents were able to manipulate.

As an adult, you no longer need to follow the rules of your family role. You are free to make your own rules once you can understand which emotions to follow and which to ignore. The people in your life do not require the same behaviors as your parents. Your actions do not mean the same thing to them as they meant to Mom and Dad. Yet, even as an adult, you can't help but have those feelings as they are imbedded in your memories. As an adult, you will always have to manage the competing reactions inside you, and make a choice between which set to follow.

Your Self For Others

The universal experience is that we all have two selves. There are not three, or four, or ten. There are two. As a small child, we create an identity through our relationships with significant people in our life, especially our mother and father. We create an identity that wants to please, wants to stay connected to the family, and is willing to override any opposing emotions to remain in the good graces of our parents and other authority figures who become parent substitutes. We develop a family role, which evolves into our Self for Others.

Your parents were able to control your behavior using the learned emotions of fear, guilt, and shame. You were not born with these responses already programmed and part of your repertoire. Your parents introduced you to them through your family role that became internalized to form your Self for Others.

Your Self for Others stores all the information that you need to know to hold onto the relationship to your parents. When you behave the correct way, there is harmony in the family and you feel secure. When you behave the wrong way, your parents are angry and you feel afraid, guilty, and ashamed. These are very strong emotions, and are the basis for the Self for Others. They are activated to keep you from breaking free of your expected behavior, not just within the family, but also within all your relationships. Years of living with your family train you how to maintain the peace in your parents' marriage, not how to express your own emotions.

Which Emotion Is The Right One

Once you become an adult, you can anticipate many situations about which you will feel conflicted. A visit to see your mother-in-law, moving far away, or even just buying a birthday present may become fraught with decisions. On the other hand, internal conflicts may happen without any apparent cause, seemingly "out of the blue." You can be cruising along in life and trusting what you see and do. The next minute, something changes, and you can't make sense of what is going on inside of you.

Your Self for Others is accustomed to getting its way. You grew up needing your family role to survive, so giving in to fear, guilt, and shame is a well-worn path. At the same time, your authentic emotions reflect the real you. Sometimes, you know that your natural reaction makes sense, but you are intimidated by the strength of the guilt and shame it provokes. All of your emotions feel genuine, so how can you tell which ones to follow? As my patients will often say, "How can something be right when it feels so wrong?"

When my patients experience a conflict between their Authentic Self and their Self for Others, they often ask me if they have multiple personalities. The answer is no. What they do have is two competing relationships. The first is your relationship to yourself. The other is your relationship with your parents, family and significant others. Each of these relationships is associated with different emotions. In the best of times, these two emotional fields overlap. What you feel is right and authentic is consistent with the way you were raised. When these two emotional fields are incompatible, they pull apart. This causes anxiety, which leads to fear, guilt, and shame. Splitting into the two selves is a natural reaction to fear, as the Self for Others attempts to silence the Authentic Self. The stakes are high. You may have to risk disappointing your family and endure the potential separation from them that might occur to honor your Authentic Self. Without having a model of the mind to explain this phenomenon, it can be a very disturbing experience. It can feel like the mind operates on its own without your control.

A century ago, scientists had a name for this experience. They believed that there was a little creature inside of you, a "homunculus", that told you what to do. People believed this explanation because that was exactly the way they felt. Fortunately, modern psychology offers a little better explanation. You are programmed by your family experiences. An imprint is created in your memory that acts as an autopilot setting. Fear signals a warning whenever your natural reaction clashes with the way you were raised. Your autopilot selects the appropriate memories to pour on the emotions of guilt and shame that have been learned and rehearsed through years of experience, following the rules laid down by your parents. It is not a "homunculus" inside of you. It is the memory of your parents' rules represented by your voice inside of you reminding you of what your parents would have wanted you to do in this situation. It happens automatically so it feels like you have no control over your mind. And it happens so fast that you feel you are running to catch up to reactions that are occurring at the speed of light.

Anger can often create this sensation, and some of my patients explain this experience using religious terms. Some people believe that anger is the work of the devil, while the family is the source of all good, and therefore is allied with an angel. This is the undeveloped perspective of children who idealize their parents for survival and assume that what their parents have told them is all good and always in their best interests.

As uncomfortable as it may seem, this is not true. The devil inside you is actually the fear, guilt, and shame, emotions imprinted on your vulnerable mind that reflect the imperfections in the way you were raised. Invariably the lessons you learned from your mother and father contained some flaws. They taught you some good rules and some bad rules. The bad rules protected the parents from their own anxieties and were not designed in a healthy way for your well-being. The bad stems from the insecurities of your parents, the humanity in every parent passed on from their parents. Making this even more devilish, the bad rules are not acknowledged by the parents and are actually denied, which results in lying, labeling, over-reacting and explanations that don't make sense.

These bad rules are embedded in your family role and make connections full of anxiety and tension. When you do what pleases your parents, you feel good, not because it is the right thing to do, but because it calms your fears of displeasing others. The learned program is the unhealthy part of your upbringing, the true devil inside you.

Your relationship to your parents sets the stage for the inevitable split between your Self for Others and your Authentic Self. The same ties that bind you to your family also keep you in bondage to guilt and shame. Families' nurture and hold us back at the same time. Breaking free of the ties that bind, honoring your right of independence, is necessary to form healthy relationships based on emotional honesty and authentic reactions.

If I refer back to the angel/devil dichotomy, independence is served by the angel, not the devil as some may incorrectly think. The angel assists your authentic reactions, simple honest emotions like joy, sadness, or anger. When you are angry in a healthy way, you are trying to solve a problem. You are not trying to hurt anyone. You can trust your natural anger. When fear causes it to be held back, it finally comes out in a storm. The work of the devil is reserved not for authentic anger, but for its progeny, rage.

Mike's Story: Life / Work Imbalance

Mike, age 42, was a stockbroker who specialized in high-risk investments. He loved the competitive nature of his business despite the difficulties created by the swings in the market and the many governmental regulations. He was aggressive and focused at work, feeling that he had to take advantage of the upswings before the next down cycle occurred.

The way Mike conducted his business was the way he conducted his life. He was driven to win in everything, from work to golf to a simple table game with the family. This negatively affected all his relationships. People in the office were afraid of him. His wife and children were constantly upset that he didn't listen to them and made no time for them. Even when he was at home, his brain was thinking about work.

Mike's wife, Louisa, insisted that he come to see me. Mike felt that he did not deserve to be treated "like some nut." He felt angry for being misunderstood and being used. He expected people to understand the toll that his work took on him. He was totally confused by the failure of people to make adjustments for him.

After Mike and I got talking, he admitted he was aware that something wasn't working in his relationships. He had no close friends and was unable to enjoy family time. He recognized that everybody around him was saying the same thing, so there had to be some truth in what they saw.

Mike was confused. He knew that he didn't listen well to others and that his work made him insensitive to their needs. But he felt too emotionally exhausted by the demands of his job to behave any other way. Mike loved his wife and children and knew they counted on his income. This was the only way he knew how to provide for them. While one part of him was ashamed for destroying himself and failure to emotionally care for his family, the other part felt driven to compete and loved the money and recognition that being a top producer gave him. Mike was unable to compromise his style of working, so there seemed to be no resolution to his problem.

I can summarize Mike's history in one phrase: high achievement family. Success was measured in money and/or fame by virtually everyone in Mike's family of origin. Mike's wife did not come from money nor did she put a high value on material things. She wanted connection and companionship. Mike fell in love with Louisa because she was different. She provided the missing piece in Mike's life. He could cry with her, feel vulnerable with her, and did not need to prove himself to her. He felt safe with her.

Mike put a high value on Louisa's ability to nurture him. He knew that he had to nurture her in return or their marriage wouldn't work. If he could not take care of her as she did with him, she would get emotionally exhausted, or have an affair, or fall in love and leave him. The problem was the damn pressure he felt to perform and show his family and the world that he was successful. Not only was his work highly competitive, but he was paid solely on commissions and didn't make any money if he didn't make the trade. His fear of failure consumed him. He would lie awake at night planning his strategies and worrying about the future. He understood what Louisa meant when she said that his head was always in the game, but he didn't seem to be able to stop it.

Mike was not sure if he actually wanted to stop it. He couldn't tell if he liked the money and the lifestyle he created or whether he had just grown up expecting to live that way. He loved the closeness that he felt with Louisa, but wasn't sure he could give up his job and income for her.

Mike did not realize that his real motivation was relief from the fear of failure. His Self For Others works to avoid shame, especially public humiliation. He feels a cold sweat whenever his boss posts the sales figures for the week. When Mike and Louisa take a (rare) vacation, it takes Mike several days to get off his cell phone and wind down. His authentic feelings emerge whenever he is alone with Louisa and has his mind clear of work. He feels real joy, not the joy that comes from making a trade or posting the top income figures. He does feel sadness whenever he thinks of losing Louisa to the pursuit of money. The problem is that the draw to his Self for Others is incredibly strong, and at home the rewards of a comfortable lifestyle have taken the place of his presence. The path of least resistance is to continue to feed the work dragon, give Louisa what is leftover emotionally, and hope that the advantages of the lifestyle and early retirement outweigh the disadvantage of a possible divorce.

I can imagine several outcomes for Mike. At the rate he is going, a heart attack would not be a surprise. Changes in the market could affect his income dramatically. Louisa is getting closer and closer to giving up on him. Mike is unlikely to change unless circumstances change around him, and he is betting everything on things staying the same – which they never do.

A trial separation might allow Mike's Authentic Self to come up for air so he can rearrange his priorities before he dies or gets divorced. He may decide a new Lexus is worth the risk. Or he may realize that once lost, family time can never be replaced.

7

The First War Of Independence

Winning The Battle

Between The Selves . . .

Being a healthy adult is a little like playing the childhood game of hide and seek. You hide your natural emotions as a child to fulfill your family role. As an adult, you pay a price for not having those emotions around. You lose the connection to yourself and survive by giving others what they want. To be true to yourself, you need to go on the internal journey to reclaim those emotions.

The journey through your mind is difficult, confusing and scary. It is easy to feel that you are fighting against yourself and not knowing what to do next. To prepare you for this fight, let's take a step back at this point and see what you now understand about yourself. From the discussions so far, you now know that all normal people have two selves. They are called the Authentic Self and the Self For Others. Each of these identities is organized around two competing sets of emotions. and reactions.

The Authentic Self is based on your natural reactions. I will refer to these emotions as the primary emotions because they are innate. These include simple emotions like joy, surprise, sadness, and anger. Not everyone gets the same joy out of the same things. Not everyone feels the same level of sadness from loss or change. The strength reflects your individuality, the qualities that make you who you are and what people remember about you. Your emotional responses are as unique as your fingerprint.

Sadness and anger are the core emotions of the Authentic Self because they protect joy. When mad and sad operate together, the person is

35

maximally organized to give voice to their beliefs, defend those beliefs, and still respect the other's opinion. Relationships based on these exchanges are authentic, validate each person involved and endure overtime. These are the independent connections that you need to make marriages last, raise healthy children and create a family that celebrates equality and freedom for all its members. They are the source of true joy in your life.

The dependency and fears of childhood cause you to suppress your natural emotions and lose the connection to your Authentic Self. Without a strong internal presence to your authentic reactions, your identity is usurped by an alternative identity, the Self For Others. This self is rooted in the family role given to you by your parents. You look to them to tell you what the truth is. Your job is to go along with what they say. When you do as you are told, you avoid encountering the fear, guilt, and shame that is activated when you don't do what you are told. You remember these episodes and encode the rules required to keep your parents happy.

The emotional base of the Self for Others is the fears of the scared child coupled with the guilt and shame born of parental disapproval. These emotions are learned. When you operate in this mode, your sense of self is organized around them and not yourself. You play a role that they designate, and this role forms the blueprint for the rules of engagement with significant people in your life. It is not the real you, but an automatic response designed to relieve felt or anticipated fear, guilt, and shame. These emotions are strong and confusing. If you feel strongly about something, doesn't it mean that it is your true thoughts and feelings? Not necessarily. The strength may not reveal how you truly feel, but how strongly your parents felt about a given subject. The strength of the emotion makes you confused about who you are and what you are supposed to do.

The issue is further complicated by your parents' insecurities. What they taught you was a combination of reasonable and unreasonable. Some of what you learned is based on truth and rules of reason. As a result, the fears that arise in any given situation as an adult are rational. The guilt that you feel as an adult for breaking rules of reason is also rational guilt. The guilt is rational guilt because you may have broken a reasonable rule.

While this consistency may be true for natural emotions, this is not the case with learned emotions. Learned emotions are riddled with the fears of your parents. These unreasonable rules are built into your family role and incorporated into the Self for Others. That role is not designed to be reasonable. It is designed to maintain the denial of your parents' insecurities and to protect the marriage from conflict. The unreasonable demands are based on your parents' own fears, some of what may have been passed down to them by their own parents. They pass those fears onto you through the strength of their irrational reactions. These reactions impact you because of the power of the need to please. You learn to believe that there is truth in staying true to your role because your behavior may greatly upset your parents and you feel strong doses of guilt and shame. Despite some niggling knowledge that what you are doing is not the right thing to do, the reaction is too hard to overcome at the moment, and you do as you are told.

Confusing the Selves

The concept of self can be confusing. Consider the following commonly used phrases about the self: "I don't know who I am; I want to be myself; I need to find myself; I want to be true to myself; I am mad at myself; I need to prove myself." Each of these phrases implies that there is something invisible about the sense of self. What is this elusive concept called "the self"? Is it defined by what you do, what you say or what you feel? Do you define it by your talents, values, and skills? Does it change when you are around other people? If you want to be yourself, who are you when you are not yourself? If you need to find yourself, where is it hidden and how do you find it? Who are you when you are searching for your real self? What is your true self and equally important, what is the fake self? If you are mad at yourself, what self is mad located in to direct it at yourself? How can you have no self? Who are you when you are acting without a sense of self?

You must first learn to recognize the differences between your two selves to decide which self to be. The need to stay in your role blinds you from realizing that there may be other reactions going on inside of you. You may not even realize that you are not being your real self. These questions need to be answered to better understand who you are and the decisions you make in any given situation.

The Case of Barbara: The Elusive Self

Barbara was a 43-year-old woman referred to me by her friend. Barbara confided in this friend about an affair she was having with a co-worker and the confusion that she felt. To give you some history, Barbara has been married to Craig for 18 years. She has two children with him, Allison, age 16, and Gregory, age 13. Until last summer, Barbara's life seemed very ordinary and traditional. She had attended Catholic schools and earned her BA in English from a Catholic college. She got a job in an ad agency writing copy.

It was there that she met Craig who was an executive in the agency. They fell in love, got married, moved to the suburbs and had the two children shortly after that. They were raising their children in their Catholic faith and were involved in all the children's activities from soccer to PTO. They had money in the bank, savings accounts for the children's college tuitions, and were building a pension fund. By all counts, they were living the American dream.

Barbara went to work part-time when Gregory was 10 and Allison was 13. She felt stifled at home but felt comfortable that she had provided a stable foundation for them during the 10 years as a stay-at-home Mom. She enjoyed returning to work and loved her new job. Her work was stimulating and provided much needed time to converse with adults. Her job required her to interact regularly with her team that included a co-worker named Allan. Barbara spent many long hours with Allan and all the team servicing the needs of the clients. Advertising was a demanding business, and she loved rising to the challenges that came at her.

Over time, Barbara's need to interact with Allan began to bother her husband, Craig. Barbara was continually texting Allan and the entire team, even on the weekends. Barbara would apologize for the interruptions but justified it as a necessary evil if she was going to stay in this line of work. Craig began to suspect that Barbara was developing romantic feelings for Allan. Whenever he would raise any issue, Barbara would accuse him of making things up, being insecure and possessive. She discounted his reactions and thought he was making a big deal out of nothing.

Craig felt differently. He thought Barbara was over-invested in her work and were neglecting he and the children. After a particularly annoying series of texts, phone calls, and meetings, Craig told her: "If you spent half the time talking about us as you do about Allan, our marriage would be great."

Barbara should have heeded Craig's warnings. At the most recent Christmas party at a local restaurant, Barbara had several glasses of wine and was feeling no pain. Allan asked her to out for a nightcap after the dinner to a bar to listen to some jazz. While at the bar, Allan leaned over and kissed her. Barbara, much to her surprise, didn't pull away. In fact, she returned the kiss even more passionately. The two of them left the bar, went to Allan's apartment and had a wild night of passionate sex.

Barbara didn't realize how late it had gotten. She returned home at 4:30 AM. When she checked her cell phone on her way home, she noticed that Craig had called her several times looking for her. When she got home, she carefully slipped into bed. Craig got up the next morning and was furious. He didn't bother to wake her and headed to work. When Barbara finally awoke later in the morning, she awoke to an empty bed. Surprisingly, Barbara was not scared or filled with guilt. She felt nothing. She had coffee with her confidant later in the day and told her what had happened last night. Her friend found it unusual that she wasn't scared or guilt-ridden, and suggested she come see me.

The following exchange occurred between Barbara and I on the first visit:

ME: "What do you make of the fact that there was no reaction on your part after spending the night with Allan?"

BARBARA: "I'm not sure. I am so confused about what happened. If you had asked me even that night at dinner if I wanted to have sex with Allan, I would have said, "No way!" I would have completely denied even the idea. I was totally shocked by my own actions. I just don't know what got into me that night. I was not myself."

ME: "Tell me more what you mean by the phrase, "I don't know what got into me that night."

BARBARA: "I felt possessed like I was out of control. I know. I made choices that night, but I didn't feel like there was a choice. I felt driven to him and just went with it. I am scared that I might do it again if I am around Allan."

ME: "Craig was obviously upset with you. How do you feel about that?"

BARBARA: "I know that what I did was wrong. I would not like it if Craig cheated on me. I know he has a right to be angry with me, but I just don't care. That also is not like me. I normally care too much what others think about me, especially Craig. That's why I am so confused about my reactions or non-reactions if you like."

ME: "When people cheat on a spouse, they are not protecting the relationship from harm. It is typically a hostile statement about the state of the relationship. Are you angry at Craig over something?"

BARBARA: "We have been married for 18 years. There is a lot about Craig that makes me mad, but there is also a lot of good. He is a good father and provider. He can be insensitive and cares more about his job cares more about the kids than about me. I have come to accept that I can't change him and need to get over it."

ME: "Maybe your affair is telling you that you are having trouble getting over it."

BARBARA: "Are you telling me that I am angrier than I realize?"

ME: "Your actions may be telling you that."

BARBARA: "How come I don't feel angry at him? Life day today is pretty much the same. I don't go around being mad all day long. Why can't it be as simple as I wanted to have a good time and needed some release?"

ME: "Your affair is significant for several reasons. One, you acted out of character. You have no history of being promiscuous as a teenager or adult. You believe in being married and having a healthy family. You don't believe in having affairs or lying to people. Second, you don't have any of the typical reactions that I'd expect. You aren't feeling bad, ashamed or guilty. You describe it as feeling nothing. Third, what you did was an impulsive act. There was no forethought. Acting impulsively, unlike yourself, and not feeling any remorse all concern me."

BARBARA: "What exactly are you concerned about?"

ME: "When people act in that way, they are typically acting out hidden emotion. I am concerned that you store your anger and it forces its way out through your action. The typical path to experiencing your emotions is blocked by anxiety... We need to find out where the anxiety comes from that makes you split off from how you feel. I am concerned that you don't understand what your behavior means."

Organizing The Selves

Barbara's case is not unique. If you remember the example from my own life in a previous chapter, I experienced the very same thing. The origin of my panic attacks was the anger from the pressures that I lived with and didn't know I had. The fears of letting people down made me suppress that anger. The fears were exacerbated by the trauma of that golf accident with my brother where I was now more afraid than ever of doing harm to someone. I was now scared to death of my anger and couldn't acknowledge it to myself. I had to suppress it to do what I was supposed to do, what others expected me to do.

My sense of self was welded to my family role, and I didn't even know it. In that sense, Barbara and I were very much alike. We both had a warped sense of self, attaching strongly to our Self For Others and burying together our authentic emotions and our identity with our Authentic Self. We both had literally thrown away who we really were and replaced it with what others expected us to be.

In Barbara's case, she was not aware of the struggle for her identity. She had spent a lifetime following the rules, and that was who she thought she was. Her family and her religious training taught her what to do, and she never questioned authority. Doing what others told her to do made her feel calm inside. As a result, she identified with her family role. That was her job and her lot in life. She accepted it willingly because Mom and Dad would praise her for being the child that they didn't have to worry about, the one who always did the right thing. The mere thought of rebelling and acting up brought fear and terror. The subsequent guilt and shame would shut her down completely and remind her to stay in line. Her authentic reactions were nowhere to be found unless you were looking for them. They did surface in the occasional stray thought about wanting to do what others got to do or a flash of anger if she was taken for granted. It never lasted long and doing what she was told brought great relief and an identity that made both she and her parents proud.

Her Authentic Self finally emerged that night with Allan, but it was too threatening to initially admit to herself. She could not explain what had happened and remained temporarily shut down when she first saw me. She could not explain to herself why she had cheated on her husband. Her affair showed her that she was angrier and more unhappy in her marriage than she had wanted to admit to herself. She was asking herself to live a life at home that was unfulfilling and required excessive self-denial.

Conversely, she loved the validation that work gave her and wanted more because it was so lacking at home. Craig was more invested in his sports teams and his work than his wife. While he was an excellent functional partner on the surface, he neglected his wife' emotional needs for validation. A storm was brewing in their marriage. The affair brought the cat out of the bag. She could no longer deny that she was more emotionally upset than she realized.

Barbara is an example of a person in extreme denial and an accident waiting to happen. Eventually, the emotion breaks through. After her first visit, Barbara went through a prolonged period alternating between being really mad and really sad. Craig distanced himself from her even more. She asked him to come to participate in her treatment, and he refused. Her parents did not react well. They did not know what had gotten into her and thought she was having a nervous breakdown. Her world felt like it was falling apart. The only place she felt herself was at work and with her kids.

Craig's resistance to come to treatment eventually doomed the marriage. As her authentic emotions emerged, Barbara no longer accepted the time that Craig devoted to his work and his sports. She started doing more things with friends and family, and her children. Her interest in staying in the marriage got less and less as her husband offered no option to resolve the imbalances that existed. Barbara wanted desperately to preserve the marriage for the sake of her children. As she wrestled with her authentic emotions, she came to realize that her children were being harmed by the hostility in the home and that neither she nor her children were living a healthy life. I am happy to say that Barbara is now divorced, living the life of a single mom with her children, and is far healthier and happier than she ever was while married. She is now free to form new independent connections to her family and any potential partner, and better understands how to raise her children to hold onto their Authentic Self.

Stages Of Finding Your Authentic Self

Most people are more aware than Barbara of their competing emotions. Barbara was stuck in denial, the first stage of finding yourself. Barbara's path to finding her Authentic Self had to wind its way through her denial and suppression of her natural reactions. Most people would have registered the fear of the attraction to another man and the threat it might pose to a marriage. There might have been more recognition of the chemistry between them at work and any sexual fantasies about Allan. She would not admit her attraction to Allan, let alone engage in any thoughts about having sex with him. The mere thought would bring such terror and internal panic that her mind would use the autopilot setting to dismiss them instantly.

The second stage to finding your Authentic Self involves fear. The path to finding your true reactions may run you into fears that you may have to face. As a child, you typically respond to this fear by surrendering your reaction and doing what you are told. As you get older, there is an increasing pressure to "be yourself." This phrase means that you do what you feel is right rather than follow what you have been told by authority figures in your life, from parents to teachers to religious leaders. You come to this realization gradually after many challenges that you bring to your parents. This testing phase heats up during adolescence as children branch out and experience life in other families through interactions with friends and activities.

This stage is commonly called the adolescent rebellion. You learn through trial and error how to stand up for what you believe and represent yourself to your family. This process gradually shifts your identity from your Self For Others to your Authentic Self. You grow yourself up into an adult by taking the risk to honor yourself, to be yourself in all that you do. You learn to fight your fears and not surrender to avoid disappointing your parents or extended family.

Learning to recognize your anger when it first occurs is the last step to complete the shift of your identity to your Authentic Self. This is a process of learning how to use your anger effectively. This is where the mad/sad connection comes into play. Each buffers the other and organizes the healthiest response. This is difficult to do and requires much practice. Your relationship to your parents becomes the safest place to try your anger on for size. You learn through trial and error how to solve a problem without hurting other people's feelings. This is the outcome achieved when you can hold mad and sad together.

In a healthy family, a parent doesn't take the anger personally, facilitates the independence, and teaches the child how to keep the sad tied to the mad. In the unhealthy family, the parent sees the child as disobedient and defiant and stunts the psychological growth toward independence. If the parent succeeds at squashing the rebellion, the child's identity fuses with the Self For Others. These teens become adults who survive by giving others what they want and are unable to be authentic. Their relationships remain dependent and unfulfilling. They become people like Barbara who live lives that are based on pleasing others to excess and denying the right to any of their most basic needs.

The Battle Between The Selves

The demand for growth toward independence creates an internal war to capture your identity. The war is waged between your emotions. In a nutshell, the mad/sad of the Authentic Self is pitted against the guilt/shame of the Self For Others. You hear this battle in the self-talk of the internal war within. To get a clearer picture of how this operates, let me describe what goes on in the average mind of my patients. You can hopefully use this model to help you in your own search for your Authentic Self.

The battle begins when fear is triggered by an authentic reaction that challenges the role that you are required to play. Fear starts a cascade of emotional events. Fear attacks the bond between mad and sad. Instead of feeling both emotions at the same time, you begin to hide one emotion behind the other. If you hide your sadness behind your anger, you are prone to rages. Rage causes damage to the relationship, a loss of self-respect and ultimately gets buried under a pile of guilt and shame. The same weakening occurs if you do the opposite. If you hide your anger behind your sadness, you retreat rather than react. You deny that you are angry, describing it as "hurt" rather than anger. You are more comfortable expressing the sadness, but the anger remains denied.

This gap between mad and sad opens the door for the rush of guilt and shame from the Self For Others. The Authentic Self is defenseless. Your anger is hidden, unable to be used to protect yourself and you succumb to the guilt and shame. In either case, the problem that caused the initial reaction doesn't get solved. You are left to accept what is unreasonable and lose your ability to represent yourself. You resolve the tension of this conflict by conforming to the rules that you were taught and making choices that keep you in your family's good graces.

Not everyone wins this battle all of the time. Some never get started and pay the price. Others begin the battle as an adolescent and run into so much trouble that they give it up. They regress to being the obedient son or daughter and depend on others to tell them what to do. The fall into their role and stay stuck repeating their role in every relationship in their lives, for the rest of their lives. Even if they stay the course as an adult and continue to fight the good fight to preserve their Authentic Self, a person can regress at any stage in their life and return to the comfort of the family role. If enough stress is applied, the family role remains a permanent source of temporary comfort.

The Never-Ending Battle

Keeping your Authentic Self present is a struggle for your entire life. It's one battle after another, winning some and losing some. Each time you win, your Authentic Self gets stronger. Each time you give in to your family role, your Self For Others gets stronger.

Facing that fear is so much harder than people realize. It is difficult to stand up for yourself and be different than where you come from. Freedom requires risk. There is always a cost. On a relationship level, the cost is often being alone. Challenging those you love often results in some temporary distance while the relationship changes and adapts. Standing up for yourself makes you face the fear of that separation. You cannot appreciate the cost of freedom until you have personally experienced it.

This struggle to honor yourself is a universal experience. It begins with the dependency into which you were born and hopefully ends with an independent adult capable of being honest with themselves and representing how they feel in all relationships and situations. There is a myriad of problems for human beings that evoke this struggle. Some people have to honor their birthright sexual orientation, regardless of how their family feels about homosexuality. Some people are born with handicaps and must learn to not blame themselves for the limitations imposed by their disease. Some are born with learning disabilities that may go undiagnosed. The child may get unfairly blamed for not trying hard enough or blamed for lacking the motivation to study and work hard. Some may end up in a rehab center before they are willing to examine the impact of her family system on their emotional well-being.

All people have to battle the history with their families to be who they want to be. This is their first taste of freedom and independence, hard won by waging a war within themselves to fight the family influence and be themselves. This is their personal war of independence, an experience needed to embrace independence, freedom, and equality in their relationships and in their lives. Some learn from their life experiences. They are able to get beyond their limited knowledge of their own feelings and get to the emotional root cause of their actions. They are able to stare down their fears, ignore their guilt and shame and go down the path that feels right to them. They change. They come out of the closet about more than their sexuality. They live a life of balance and develop healthier relationships.

Others lose the fight and pay the price. They continue to feed themselves a diet of shame. They continue to be confused about who they are and deny the impact on relationships and emotional connections. It is only those who do the work that get the reward.

My Personal Struggle For Independence

I personally know how hard it is to grow an Authentic Self and create honest relationships. You know from a prior chapter about my history of growing up in a high achievement family and the demands made on me to be the family Hero. My Self For Others was well developed in response to that pressure. I had to learn to grow my Authentic Self. I believe I have strengthened my Authentic Self each time I have taken the risk to challenge others and stand up for my beliefs. One of the most difficult situations that I have faced had to do with my family of origin and the management of my elderly parents. I was in my late 50's at the time. These situations are never easy and, like marriages, reveal all the stains on the family carpet. You may recall from the discussion in a prior chapter that I suggested that a family must all join together in the Anger Dynamic in order for siblings to develop closeness as adults. By coming together, the collective truth about the family is exposed, and each of their respective Authentic Selves become reinforced. Like a healthy marriage that supports each partner's independence, the sibling relationship can be a source of truth about the nature of the family and the common experience of the parent's good and bad sides. It can be a source of comfort and support to be authentic and independent as an adult.

The aging of my parents provided the challenge to my family to unite around the Anger Dynamic. To provide some background, I am the third of four children. I have two older sisters, who are only 16 months apart, the eldest being 7 years older than me. I have a younger brother 3 years younger than I. We were two different families separated by both sex and age. It didn't help that my father was heavily biased toward males. He didn't know what to do with girls and couldn't wait for the day that he had a son. My sisters were treated as if they had less value and took their anger out on each other. They were like oil and water. It didn't help that my eldest sister was given the job of surrogate baby sitter. Since both my parents worked together, my oldest sister was expected to care for her younger sister despite being only 16 months older. She would tell me that my mother used to say to her over and over: "You are the oldest. You have to take care of your little sister."

My eldest sister resented being treated that way. She let my parents know this by acting up wherever she went. She had a fabulous sense of humor and was prone to do practical jokes that would get her into a lot of trouble. This infuriated my father and gave him more cause to pick on her. Whenever she would get mad and say that she was being treated unfairly, my parents would dismiss her and tell her that she was the problem in the family. When she wanted to go to law school after college, my father told her that law is for men and not women and refused to help her finance her education.

My eldest sister experienced the classic Scapegoat role. Whatever she did was never good enough. My second sister took an opposite tack to fit into the family. She became Daddy's little girl, even with a nickname. My oldest sister didn't have a nickname. If she did, it usually began with a curse word. My second sister did whatever she needed to do to be the perfect daughter. She was bright, studied hard, and made no waves. She was a classic Hero child who, unlike her older sister, made her parents proud.

When I came along, I fit the Hero mold better than she did for one simple reason: I was a male. She couldn't compete with my athletic achievements, and we were both equally smart, so I won on both counts. I don't remember having any animosity toward her. In fact, I felt sympathy that her achievements weren't given the same weight as mine. She never felt like a threat to my primary position as the Hero.

My younger brother was born with dyslexia, and his feet turned in. Both issues limited his ability to perform athletically and academically as a child. As a result, he too never posed a threat to my status as the primary Hero. He got to be the baby in the family who was able to do what he wanted and fly under the radar. He had a great sense of humor, was easily liked, loved music, and was fun to be around. He looked up to me, and I watched out for him as my younger brother. I thought we were a normal family.

There were many issues throughout our lives together that exposed the roles that we played and the unhealthiness in the family system. The allegiances and loyalties formed along the Hero/Scapegoat lines. My eldest sister was the one who created all the problems. My parents would come to the other three of us to ask us what to do with her, only serving to cement the fact that there were two camps in the family. There was the good ones and the bad one, the one that my parents couldn't understand and would complain about.

To avoid the pressure, my eldest sister ran away to California. She fell into a bad relationship with a man who stole thousands from her and left her with a huge debt. My parents gave her the money to get back on her feet but silently resented her. They would openly discuss that with we Heroes, but never to my sister. They would deny that they treated their children differently and claimed to have no favorites. It was not a healthy situation and was ripe to explode over time.

That time came with the aging of my parents. They did not age gracefully. They refused to acknowledge any of the cognitive changes that began to affect them in their early 80's. Eventually, both my parents were diagnosed with dementia. My mother developed classic Alzheimer's disease, while my father's cognitive decline was more typical of a vascular dementia. They both died at age 90, having spent the last 5 years of each of their lives requiring full time custodial care in the home.

Along the way, my mother and father stubbornly held on to their independence. My second sister supported their right to do as they wanted. She felt they had earned that right, regardless of how unhealthy or risky they acted. I pushed for a neuropsychological evaluation to assess their level of risk, but that went undone. My parents and sister wanted nothing to do with that as it might prove that they needed more help than they were willing to admit. My father continued to drive well into his late 80's despite having numerous accidents. We were waiting for him to kill somebody or himself with his car. He nearly lost his realtor's license for failing to comply with state regulations regarding the return of initial deposits. He needed somebody to gently step in, but he refused to give anybody an opening.

This whole situation blew up one Christmas when my eldest sister came home from California for the holidays. The day she was leaving, my father gave her a letter documenting all the loans that he had given her, including the cost of Christmas presents from past holidays. In my father's typical indirect style, he handed her the letter and asked her to open it on the plane. When she asked him what was in the letter and he didn't respond, she opened it directly in front of him and read it. She couldn't believe what he was doing and got very angry. She acknowledged that she did owe him the loan that he had given her, but not all the monies that he had listed in the letter. When she asked my other sister, she agreed with my father. She told her that she had been helping my father do an accounting of outstanding money owed by his children, and that is what they had come up with together. My eldest sister was livid, left for California and wanted nothing to do with either my father or her sister.

When my oldest sister called me to tell me what they had done, I now had to take a stand. I knew that remaining neutral was not an option. I believe that you are either part of the solution or part of the problem in a family. There is no option for "I don't want to get involved." It was clear that I needed to take a stand. It was also equally clear that my father was demented and not acting like himself. He was typically very generous to his children. He had helped us all like he had helped my sister when she got into trouble. He had loaned me some money for the expenses of my first book. He had transferred the equity in an investment property to my second sister. He never did help my brother an inequality that I felt needed to be rectified to be fair. He refused when I brought it up to him. This was not the father that I had known my whole life.

The next time I visited, I challenged my parents directly over what had occurred. My mother burst into tears, as this was the first time she had heard what my father had done. My mother knew that he had hurt my sister very badly and was angry for not being informed. My father became angry at me and was appalled that I would support my eldest sister. My younger sister continued to defend what they had done and saw nothing wrong with it. Despite knowing that my father was a terrible bookkeeper, she trusted his numbers and felt he had a right to rectify the loans that he had made. Her perspective was so skewed by her attachment to them that she could not even consider challenging my father's position or seeing the truth in her sibling's reactions. She was blinded by the strength of her overdeveloped Self For Others.

Part of what made it all even more confusing was that my father never made it clear that the loans needed to be repaid. With me, he said, "Pay me back when the book sells." The book sold well but did not cover the advance, so there were no profits with which to repay him. He had never brought it up to me, and I thought there was no problem. Plus, my second sister accused me of failing to repay a construction loan from 25 years ago that I know I had repaid to him with interest one year later. If his numbers were wrong with me, I knew that the numbers were most likely wrong with my other sister as well.

My stand changed my relationship to my family forever. My eldest sister and I were now more bonded than ever in the Anger Dynamic. My relationship with my second sister grew very distant and continues to be superficial to this day. I went through a period of distance from my brother who supported my second sister for a period of time. After a while, he made some steps to support my position that enabled us to repair the relationship over time and enjoy each other's company once more. Sadly, my two sisters never were able to come together. They did visit together once before my sister died recently after a yearlong bout with lung cancer, but their relationship remained strained to the end.

My position with my father and sister helped me believe in myself, but the journey was not easy. I initially felt very depressed about the distance but felt that my anger was righteous. It cost me dearly as I was now treated by my father like one of the Scapegoats. I was a Hero fallen from grace and he no longer trusted me. Despite my medical knowledge, I was not given any role as medical proxy and was not given any further information about their finances. It was like I was cut off and thrown away. I had to decide whether I would surrender to get back in their good graces or stay the course. My Self For Others was pulling me in the direction of dropping my objections, but I couldn't do it. My Authentic Self wouldn't allow it. I felt that I had to stand up for what was right, and this situation was clearly wrong. I continued to visit my parents as they became more disoriented, but it was never the same. It was clear my father had emotionally disowned me. To him, I was a traitor who turned on him.

I learned in that difficult period how to be more comfortable in my own skin. Said differently, my Authentic Self grew stronger through that sad ordeal. I never doubted the truth about what had happened, but the sadness was sometimes overwhelming. I did learn to hold my mad and sad together and grew a stronger belief in my emotional reactions. I also think my strength helped my older sister hold onto her anger better than she had before. Even through the course of her yearlong bout with cancer, she didn't waiver in her position and shared it often with me. It made us closer despite being further emotionally from the rest of the family. In the end, I believe we both won our respective battle for independence.

Wiffle Ball In The Backyard

In contrast to the sad and difficult story about my eldest sister, I have another lighter experience to share that illustrates how the battle between the selves can emerge in the smallest of life events. Sometimes, the right thing to do is not so clear. During a visit to my daughter and her family in Apex, North Carolina, my 6-year-old granddaughter asked my wife and I to play wiffle ball in the backyard of their home.

To understand the background to this story, I must first digress to discuss my competitive nature. I have always liked to compete. I like to compete more than I like to win. I will try to do the best that I can in all situations. If my opponent is better than me, good for them. If I win, good for me! I am not a sore loser. It's a game to me, and that's all it is.

I have wondered if my competitiveness is part of my temperament or is part of my need to prove myself to others. Beginning with my parents, being competitive brought me accomplishments and admiration from them. However, I do know that I would be competitive no matter how I was raised. It seems part of my innate personality to engage with others and situations to the fullest. So is my competitiveness connected to my Self For Others or my Authentic Self? If overdone, and I am insensitive to others at that time, I could see that my natural propensity could become fueled by the extra meaning assigned by my parents. If that were the case, then I would be running on anxiety and make decisions to compete at all cost to reduce my fears. If I were truly just competing for the fun of it and being authentic, I would be comfortable and enjoying myself.

There is one other issue that will come to play in the incident I will describe below. I am old school when it comes to competition. I do not believe in giving trophies for participation unless the children involved are disabled. I believe that learning to be a good loser and the sadness that it brings is as important for a child as being a winner and experiencing that joy. Protecting the child from competition robs the child of experiences to grow and learn about themselves. The challenges of competition teach you how to face your fears and overcome your doubts. It's an educational experience if done correctly. If it is an opportunity to inflict shame by coaches or peers, it is not a beneficial experience, and nothing good comes of it.

So back to my wiffle ball game in my daughter's back yard. Each of us took turns being up at bat while the rest of us played the infield or outfield. When I come up to bat, I hit the ball as far and high as I could. I hit several over the trees in the backyard and had to go into the neighbor's yard to retrieve the ball. I was enjoying myself. Bria was having fun too. I would chase her half-heartedly down to first base and celebrate her getting on base, stealing a base, or scoring a run. It was just plain simple fun in the afternoon sun.

At one point, I was standing in the outfield when Bria hit a long pop fly, an amazing hit for a little girl. True to my competitive nature, I ran it down, caught it, and threw it back to the pitcher. My daughter and my wife looked at me with horror. My son-in-law started to laugh. My daughter scolded me for catching the ball. She wanted me to fake it, drop it and let her round the bases to score a run. I had robbed her of an opportunity to have some fun.

Let's examine my decision to catch the ball more closely. As I started to run to catch it, the thought did go through my mind to let the ball drop. I remember a series of thoughts, including my belief that children shouldn't be coddled and weighed that thought against the idea of letting her run the bases. I decided to catch the ball. My daughter thought it was a bad decision and showed my ultra-competitiveness. She felt that I let my own need to perform and prove myself to others win out over the needs of a little girl to feel good about what she had accomplished. She felt my fear cost her child a good time.

I still have mixed feelings about that event. Was I being true to my Authentic Self to catch the ball or was I being driven to succeed by my Self For Others? I certainly could have let the ball drop. It just didn't seem like the right thing to do. If I judge whether I reacted in a healthy way by my daughter's reaction, then I was certainly wrong. But if I judge my actions by my daughter's reaction, aren't I being excessively influenced by another in that case and isn't that giving in to my Self For Others? How do you tell where the truth is?

I do know that my granddaughter and I have fun together and she loves to spend time with her "crazy grandpa." Like her mother, she was mad at me for catching the ball. I explained myself to her, and she seemed to understand my choice. Not so with the rest of my family. They tease me about it to this day, and part of me wonders if they are right. Another part of me doesn't agree with them. Which part holds the truth and which part is my real self?

This event happened 8 years ago, and I am still grappling to face the truth. It's why my family continues to tease me. They are trying to remind me to avoid my Self For Others and to honor my real self. If I look inside for the truth, I have to admit that I am trying to justify something that, down deep, I know was unhealthy. If I am honest with myself, I gave in to my family role and let my Self For Others take over. It has a strong influence over me. It is a trap I can fall into at any time in my life. The reason I know that is true is because I find myself trying too hard to convince myself. The truth keeps trying to rise to the surface, and I have to work too hard to push it back down. I know that I have some beliefs about the value of competition, but those beliefs need to be introduced in a planned fashion, not created by a spontaneous and impulsive decision that is justified after the fact. I also have to face the fact that everyone else had the same opinion, including my 6-year-old granddaughter. While you have to be careful not to surrender to the crowd, you must also give significance to what they say, especially if it resonates with the niggling truth inside of you. This is why vigilance is so important. The Self For Others fits too nicely, and the Authentic Self can be hard to find.

Key to Winning the Battle

There are five keys to winning your personal battle to be your Authentic Self. The first is the knowledge of emotional dynamics, the interplay among your competing emotions. The second is an awareness of your personal defenses, hiding your emotions from yourself and learning to play detective to rediscover them. The third is the belief in your natural reason, the truth that you feel after discerning the difference between your natural and learned emotions. The fourth is the courage required to face your fears and take the risks to honor yourself. Fifth and last, you need to stay vigilant lifelong to avoid being taken by surprise by your automatic responses. Let's examine each of these five keys more closely.

Emotional Dynamics

You now know that people act to relieve emotional tension. To understand yourself and others more completely, you need to see the emotions behind the actions. You need to be able to see fear rather than assign character traits to yourself and others as explanations for behavior. You must look behind the fear to see the competing emotions and self-statements from the two selves. The loudest voice in your mind may not be the voice of your real self, and the truth may lie in the softer voice. Understanding how emotions work gives you the ability to stand up for yourself despite doubt and fear.

Defenses

Each of you is born with psychological defenses that you use to hide your natural emotions. These defenses work well initially, but the emotion leaks out over time and affects what you say or do. While you may not be able to instantly access your natural reactions, you can learn to recognize their presence indirectly. How they leak out from under the defenses is an important piece of information for you to recognize the disguised form of your natural emotions.

You may recall from a previous discussion how mad and sad interact. I have many patients who do not feel angry when the situation calls for it. They will hide it behind sad and call it hurt. Some may just feel anxiety when they are actually angry. In each of these instances, the person must say to himself or herself: "I know that I hide my anger, so when I am really afraid, I know that I need to treat it as a signal. It is telling me that I am angrier than I realize and need to figure out what could be making me so mad." Since the awareness of how your defenses operate is so critical to becoming independent, I will devote the whole next chapter to discussing how psychological defenses work.

Natural Reason

Your ability to believe in natural reason is probably the most significant key to winning your independence. You need to trust that your reactions make sense, even when they conflict with the opinions of learned scholars and powerful authority figures. The truth stands alone and is more significant than any person's role or education.

You will often hear people say that you should "trust your gut." The problem is that your gut is poisoned by the imperfections in the way you were raised. Just because a given act may bring disapproval and disappointment from your parents does not necessarily mean that it is the right thing to do for you. It certainly is the right thing to do according to your parent's way of doing things, but may not apply to you in this situation. Your gut can only be trusted if you can tell the difference between your learned emotions of fear, guilt and shame and the natural emotions of joy, sadness, anger, etc. You can trust your instincts provided you can tell the difference between your instincts and the instincts of your parents. I will talk more in a subsequent chapter about the significance of natural reason, and its importance throughout the history of mankind to help you become even more convinced that your natural reason is the path to the truth.

Courage

Listening to your natural reason, especially if it is the quieter voice in your mind, takes courage. It is always easier to follow the path of least resistance and do what others want you to do. Especially when others have more power than you do, it is always easier to give in and go along. Rocking the boat is more difficult. You don't know what to expect or how you may be hurt from choosing the option that feels right to you. It takes courage to take the risk to push back or take the leap of faith required by a given choice.

Courage comes from the strength of your emotion and your personal values. The angrier you become, the easier it is to act. If you combine the level of emotion with a moral imperative, you can't help but react. It propels you to take the risk because not doing something feels worse than the fear of doing something. It gets to the point where you feel you have no choice but to do the right thing, what feels right in your heart and mind even if others object.

Vigilance

I talked before about the need to remain vigilant throughout your life to the power of your family role. Your family role reduces anxiety and makes you fit into what others want. There is great comfort in that role. It will always tug at you when you try to make a decision, especially if you have to "go against the grain." Vigilance helps you to prepare to face down your Self For Others. Surprise gives an advantage to the Self For Others. If you become confused, it is easy to retreat to the default setting of the family role. With vigilance about your ever-present role, you can strategize better how to internally push back against your fears to maintain the independence that you have gained.

8

The Grown-Up Game Of

Hide And Seek . . .

How Your Psychological Defenses Work

The journey to live an emotionally authentic life on your terms requires you to know how the mind copes with your emotions. From previous discussions, you know that your natural emotions pose a threat to the childhood attempt to organize a self through pleasing others. I called this identity your Self For Others. To forge this self, the mind is required to hide your natural emotions. These natural emotions are the enemy of the Self For Others, a force that breeds independence rather than doing what you are told.

In order to compete for attention within your mind, your natural emotions must be either muted or hidden from awareness. This is the job of your psychological defenses. You develop them at a very early age to cope with the fears of separation from your parents. Your mind constructs a system in response to a fear that suppresses or completely hides your authentic reactions. The type of defenses that are used is based on a combination of genetic and environmental factors. You are born with a unique response to fear. Some people flee while others stand and fight. Your choice is most likely tied to the strength of your temperament and modified in response to the severity of your parental reactions to your natural emotions.

When you need your natural reactions as an adult, then you will need to know how to find the natural emotions that are hidden by your defenses. This is the adult game of hide and seek. You seek to find the natural reactions that were buried as a child. Your defenses are built to serve your parent's needs and maintain your family role. As a result, they are the continued impact of your parents on you in the present moment. They are a permanent part of your personality. Even as an adult, these defenses remain in operation and are often triggered in response to fear without conscious thought. They are childhood scars that impact you throughout your life. They determine the rules of your own hide and seek game.

There are two features to psychological defenses that work to your advantage and give you access to your hidden emotions. The first is that no defense works absolutely. Emotion, especially natural emotion, is so powerful that it breaks through the stoutest of defenses. As I mentioned in a previous discussion, some emotion begins to leak out over time and affects your behavior. Learning to recognize these indirect expressions enables you to read your behavior to infer the presence of your emotion. This skill can be learned and improved with practice.

The second feature that helps you find your authentic reactions is that your defenses can be modified with experience. When you expect a catastrophe to occur and nothing happens, the defenses get weakened. Over time, the defenses are no longer needed. You begin to react differently to the fear that signals the fight between the natural and learned emotions. Change occurs because you learn how to doubt the doubt. Said differently, you learn to take the risk to honor yourself despite the fear. You get better and better over time learning to override the fear and do what you feel is the right thing to do.

Alcohol and drugs can artificially reduce your defenses. The emotion that gets exposed when you are intoxicated or high is real and not created by the alcohol. If a person is an angry drunk, they were angry long before they started to drink. The anger is not in the bottle. It is in the person's mind waiting to get exposed. Especially when drunk, the person is not prepared to manage it nor even accept it. People will often blame the alcohol for embarrassing statements or crazy behavior. They might say, "That was the alcohol talking. I didn't mean it." Like the sign in the bar says, "In vino veritas," translated from the Latin as "There is truth in wine."

In a normal state of mind, your defenses blunt your emotional awareness. You can learn to recognize the operation of your defenses and dismantle them. In the remainder of this chapter, I will discuss the different types of defenses and how they work. I hope that this knowledge will enable you to surface how you truly feel and use these emotions to operate as an independent person in all your relationships.

Case of Bruce

Some people have very little access to their emotions. Their defenses are so tight that the person doesn't know how they feel in any given moment. This lack of emotional awareness is a very common human experience. Consider the case of Bruce, a 35-year-old patient of mine. Bruce has been seeing therapists for years to help reduce the overwhelming insecurity that surfaces in many social situations. His insides jump whenever he feels left out of social events. As an example, he may see his neighbor talk to another neighbor, but make no overture to talk to him. In that moment, he feels anxious and worried that he is not liked in his neighborhood.

That same reaction often occurs in other social settings. He internally panics at a party when his wife seems to be joking around and having a good time with another male friend. He gets anxious at a business meeting when another colleague gets compliments from his boss, and he gets none. Bruce manages his anxiety in those situations poorly. He makes sure that he gets noticed by inappropriate behavior that he thinks is funny, behavior that has gotten him into trouble in many situations.

Bruce knows that these reactions are not normal, but has little idea how to fix them. He asked one of his former therapists, "How do I fix my self-esteem?" The therapist replied: "I know this may sound hokey, but if you look in the mirror each day and say good things to yourself, eventually you will come to believe them." Bruce never returned to that therapist. Bruce asked me the same question. My response is buried in the ensuing dialogue between Bruce and I during one of his sessions:

BRUCE: "I get that I have this problem, and I get that it makes me do and say stuff that gets me into trouble. I just don't know what to do about it."

ME: "What exactly do you see as the problem?"

BRUCE: "I feel anxious and insecure all the time, especially when I compare myself to other people. I need an answer that is better than say positive things to yourself. I don't need magic. I need a real answer."

ME: "My answer is that I don't think you know yourself emotionally. Your fear silences your anger when you know something is wrong and makes you define what you do by the reaction of another. You need your own emotional compass. When you do that, you will feel good about your decisions or actions and stand up to other's criticisms. You will feel stronger inside."

BRUCE: "What anger are you talking about? I only feel fear."

ME: "Your fear is based on pleasing others because that is how you survived as a child. The world you came from was not emotionally safe and fell apart. That fear is hardwired. It makes you hide other reactions, like your anger when you are treated differently than others. The anger registers but it gets lost in the fear."

BRUCE: "I don't feel angry when my boss compliments somebody else. I only feel afraid."

ME: "I understand that you don't feel the anger I am talking about, but I guarantee that is there, even if for only a split second. It as natural as the pain you would feel if I dropped a rock on your foot. You may say, "That's okay," but you would not be able to deny the pain. Same thing here."

BRUCE: "OK, so if I buy that the anger may exist, how do I use it when I can barely feel it?"

ME: "You look for it and try to hold onto it. It takes work, and you get better and better at it the more you try. It's the work of therapy. Getting better means you grow the percentage of time that you can catch the anger. There will be plenty of times that you miss it and you need to be patient. The fear is hardwired, and it will always be there to trap you. With practice, you can learn to doubt the doubt and feel more secure."

Bruce's case illustrates how confusing emotions can be to people. Bruce sought professional help to fix his low self-esteem. He saw self-esteem as a "thing" like a medical condition that is cured by treatment. Bruce isn't prepared to do this work. He wants somebody to prescribe a solution. He wants it fixed.

Bruce's answer lies in an area that he doesn't expect. His low self-esteem comes from his lack of knowledge about how his mind processes emotion. He has a fragile sense of his Authentic Self, as his Self For Others was overdeveloped to cope with the emotional chaos that existed in his family. His guilt and shame act like an electric current that shocks him if he does not do as he has been told. He is further confused because he blames himself for the way he was raised. He does not see that these emotional reactions have been trained into him. Because he feels them, he believes they originate within himself and represent what he believes. He is unaware of himself or how his feelings control his behavior.

Bruce needs to learn a whole lot more about himself, his emotions, and the way that the mind works. Knowledge of his family dynamics, the family role that he was required to play will help Bruce to define who he is from who he was told he was supposed to be. He needs to be taught about the quality of life experiences and the two sources of human emotion, his natural reactions and his learned responses. He needs to learn to dismantle his defenses that hide his emotions. He needs to understand what happens when fear arrives and how to look beyond his defenses to find his authentic emotions.

The Unconscious Mind

Bruce is an excellent example of the need to understand how your mind works with both hidden and experienced emotions to achieve the goal of being authentic and creating independent connections. Emotional life is confusing. Mother Nature played a cruel trick on you. She gave you emotions to let you know what is important but forgot to give you the training manual to figure out how to use them. This book is that training manual.

For your defenses to work, you need a place in the mind to store emotions outside of your awareness. Some refer to this area of the mind as "the back of your mind." It has also been called your "unconscious mind," the portion of your consciousness that stores emotions that cause anxiety. This structure of the mind is very controversial. Sigmund Freud, M.D., a European physician who practiced in the early 1900's, made his place in history from his elaborate descriptions of the operations of the unconscious on human behavior.

Freud believed that the emotions stored in this area were so powerful that they would shut the mind down if they were to be experienced. Freud's beliefs about the nature of the unconscious were based on his theory that unconscious emotions were associated with the powerful instincts of sex and aggression. These instincts were assumed to be destructive to mankind, leading Freud to posit that all human beings had a death wish, an instinct he called "Thanatos." In Freud's view, the unconscious was this place where dark emotions lurked that threatened to destroy the individual. His teachings formed the basis for modern psychiatry and influence the prevailing view of medical professionals to this day.

Other psychological theorists that followed Freud did not agree. These neo-Freudians as they were called, did not assign the same negativity to the unconscious mind. My experiences as a psychologist for the past 33 years have led me to agree with this latter group. The spokesman for this philosophy was Harry Stack Sullivan, M.D, an American psychiatrist who practiced twenty-five years later than Freud. Sullivan believed that the emotions stored in the unconscious were derived from the child's fears of separation from the parent. They were a constructive response to a threat of abandonment by one's caretakers, a high anxiety situation for a child who is dependent on a parent for survival.

This theory assumes that humans are biological creatures whose instincts for survival are strong and adaptive. They are not destructive. In fact, the more you understand and use these powerful emotions, the better you can survive as an adult. The stability of your relationships, the key to human survival, can be improved by using your emotions to be honest, and authentic.

Sullivan believed that these emotions were closer to the surface, stored in the pre-conscious and accessible with increased awareness of your emotional life. He did not believe that people would decompensate from recognizing these stored emotions. In fact, he thought just the opposite. Sullivan believed that experiencing these emotions was critical to learning how to change your behavior as an adult. Accessing these emotions would enable the adult to learn that people do not have the same expectations for your behavior as your parents. He felt that you could learn to separate what happened to you as a child from what happens to you as an adult. Sullivan coined a term, "corrective emotional experiences" to describe this process of learning how to separate your emotions based on childhood experiences from those generated by present-day situations.

Working With Your Emotions

Psychologist's ideas about the unconscious mind are essential for two reasons. One, you need to understand your unconscious and not be afraid of it. You have a place in the mind that gets automatically loaded when fear strikes. It's like the operating system in your computer. You aren't aware of the operations, but you know that a program exists that acts on your information. You program your mind to react to what scares you as a child, and that program kicks on whenever fear is detected. You store the emotions in the unconscious or better labeled, the pre-conscious child.

As an adult, they no longer have to scare you. It is like a haunted house at Halloween. You experience fear if you visit one as an adult, but you know somewhere inside you that there is no real danger. The fears of a child were real. Those authentic emotions could cause a separation between you and your parents, a scary thought for a child. As an adult, you no longer have to get your parent's approval. They are just like you. They do some things right and some things wrong. The fear as an adult is a memory of bygone times, rational as a child but irrational as an adult.

The second important point about the unconscious is that you can access emotions hidden there in two ways. First, the authentic emotion has to register in the mind to trigger the autopilot program that activates the defenses and hides the emotions. As you will see in the subsequent discussion, defenses differ in the level of access that you have to that initial flash of emotion. Defenses are built to handle different levels of fear. Some defenses are so strong that the flash of authentic emotion is gone in a nanosecond. Others hold onto the reaction for a while before it is shoved to the back of the mind. This is important to understand because it can be the first point of change for you. If you can catch the emotion before it is hidden, you can use it in your relationships. I will talk more about this in a subsequent chapter on relationships.

The other access point to your authentic reactions opens up after they have been stored. Defenses are not airtight. They leak. You can learn to recognize the leaks and indirectly access those emotions. For example, you may start procrastinating on some task. This is often a sign of fear that you will disappoint someone with your work. Once you know that your fear signals the threat of shame, you can mobilize your anger to defend what you are going to do. You can learn to read the procrastination as a signal to teach yourself how to access your hidden emotions. You can win the hide and seek game.

There are a few common elements to understand about the nature of your emotions and the operation of your defenses. Four general reasons make human emotion so complex and difficult to understand. For one, you learn to hide in your pre-conscious mind some of your emotions as a child and must learn to find them again to function well as an adult. This is what I have called the adult game of hide and seek. Second, you often experience your emotions on delay. They are not often available when you need them. You have to wait some of the time to know how you honestly feel in a given situation. Third, your emotions are rarely experienced alone. You feel multiple emotions at the same time. Sorting through them takes time. Fourth, you can experience a rush of emotions all at once. You store emotion in your memory to use your past experiences as a guide to understand the present. When you experience emotion, you can experience a cascade of emotions from the past and the present at the same time. This experience is called "flooding." You flood with the emotion from the past whenever the present triggers an emotionally loaded memory of what has gone before. Flooding is an overwhelming experience that shuts down the mind, prevents any rational thought and sends you into overload, making understanding even more difficult.

Types Of Defenses

Now that you understand the nature of the unconscious and how your mind handles your emotions, I want to expand your understanding of the nature of your psychological defenses and how they work. Your defenses are your way to suspend your primary reactions. Suppression of emotion is the outcome of all defensive processes.

Each person is born with a unique set of defenses to hide emotional reactions. You are pre-programmed to use one of two sets of defenses based on the fight or flight response. This response is the biological survival mechanism innate to humans. There is a psychological equivalent. Your mind responds to the presence of threatening emotions with either fight or flight. In both cases, there is a range of defenses to handle different threat levels. High fear requires a strong defense and the emotion is locked away. Low threat activates a lower level of defense. The emotion is present for a period of time before it is suppressed.

The Flight Defenses

The Flight defenses are organized to enable the mind to run away from emotion, to avoid experiencing any of it. Denial is the core of all flight defenses. Denial operates to shield the person from awareness of a particular emotion. Denial comes in mild, moderate and severe forms depending on the level of threat. Mild anxiety causes emotion to be suppressed. The emotion is experienced for a short period of time while you find a way to understand what is going on. You can use intellectualization or rationalization to convince yourself that whatever happened is not that bad and/or not your fault. Another defense that results in suppression is projection. Projection occurs when the person attributes to another what is actually occurring within them. For example, a person who is angry will accuse another of being angry and avoid examining their own reactions.

Higher levels of fear require stronger levels of denial. Avoidance is one such defense against moderate levels of fear. If you stay away from people, places, or things that upset you, you don't have to be upset. You don't have to feel anything and can even deny that you are afraid of whatever you are avoiding. Grandiosity is another defense to handle moderate levels of fear. It is considered a stronger level of defense because of its negative impact on relationships. Grandiose people will often say that nothing bothers them and will tell others to "get over it." They fail to admit weakness or failure that will bring an experience of sadness. Typically, grandiosity is a mask for intense feelings of inadequacy that can be denied. The individual doesn't feel the shame of being inadequate because they are so busy convincing others that they have it all together that they don't even notice.

Another type of avoidance reaction involves the misuse of religion. Rather than advance the concept of spirituality, religiosity, as it is called, is used as a defense against the truth. The individual hides behind religious beliefs to deny reality that is occurring and avoid the need to acknowledge any emotional reaction.

These types of defensive reactions can negatively affect the quality of the emotional exchanges in relationships. Stored emotion leaks out in a variety of forms. Facial expressions, voice tone, loudness, and body language are just some of the many ways that hidden emotion becomes visible to the observer. These indirect expressions short-circuit communication and cause glitches in human information processing. Communication primarily occurs at two levels. There is an exchange of facts and exchange of feelings. The feeling base is contagious, but can only occur when there is an understanding of the emotion that is being communicated. When feelings are denied, you don't know what to do with the information that you are receiving. The sender is denying that it is being sent, but the emotion needs to be understood to know the meaning of the facts. Communication becomes distorted, disrupted and breaks down.

People use terms in ordinary conversation to describe this confusion. They will say that another person "doesn't get it" or refer to them as "clueless." When you use these terms, you are describing people who keep their emotions hidden from themselves. Their emotional exchanges become superficial. Denied emotion limits the ability to nurture and validate the emotions in an exchange. You can't connect to that person, can't "get on the same page." The superficiality protects the relationship from engaging in exchanges that may lead to conflict and disconnection. These individuals resort to "parallel play" experiences, engaging in activities together that pass the time but do not result in greater understanding of each other. They cannot engage in "heavy" conversations that require emotional listening and emotional self-exploration. They live life avoiding the emotions of others to hide their own emotions from themselves.

The highest level of fear is managed by defenses that involve what is called "splitting." The denial is so strong that the emotion is split off from the person's awareness and the damage to relationships is severe. This is a different process than what goes on when you feel split in two, like the angel-devil on my shoulder experience. This is a normal and universal experience. In that case, you are aware of both sides of yourself. You hear self-statements that reflect the multiple emotions that are challenging each other. Splitting is not the normal experience. In the case of splitting, there is very little or almost zero awareness of the presence of emotion. This type of defense is called dissociation because the emotion is separated from normal consciousness. It is sealed behind a wall created by the mind to protect the individual from an overwhelming level of emotion.

Dissociation can cause experiences to occur that are scary to the person. In states of extreme anxiety, the person can experience depersonalization where they feel they are having an "out-of-body " experience. Some of my patients have described it to me as looking down at themselves or seeing themselves from across the room. They feel like they are losing their mind. When it occurs without obvious explanation, it can be very scary to people. Extreme forms of dissociation include fugues, multiple personalities, and Post-Traumatic Stress Disorder. In these cases, there is an extreme level of denial to the point where the person is unaware of their emotional states. A person in a fugue will disappear for a period of time and have no awareness of what occurred during that interval. I had one such patient leave his home and go to a hotel where he slept for four days. His family found him and woke him up. He had no explanation for how he got there or how long he had been away.

Multiple personalities are formed to store different levels of an emotion. For example, there are levels to anger, ranging from frustration to annoyance to rage. There is a personality to handle frustration, another to handle annoyance, and yet another to handle rage. Each of these personalities do not recognize the presence of the others, nor do they share any of their emotion. The person constructs a wall around each one to protect the exposure of their level of emotion. The individual affected by this condition operates in all the different personalities and has no memory for any of the events experienced in the altered states. They live life like a strobe light experience, with gaps between experiences that can't be explained.

In Post-Traumatic Stress Disorder (PTSD), traumatic events are dissociated and hidden from normal awareness. Wartime experiences, severe sexual or physical abuse create emotions that need to be packaged to protect the mind from overload. Current events trigger the emotions, and they dump into the person's awareness at unexpected times. These are called flashbacks and cause the person to decompensate temporarily when the emotions flood into them. The pressure on the defenses creates a condition called hyper-vigilance. Hyper-vigilance is a heightened state of sensory awareness where all the senses are on high alert to protect the person from threat. In these cases, people are startled by shadows, sounds, and smells. They feel like their skin is crawling. Many experience sensory overload and are often misdiagnosed as being psychotic.

Fortunately, these conditions do respond to psychotherapy over a long period of time. Each therapy session becomes an opportunity to experience some emotion that is threatening. Over time, the person learns that their worst fears do not occur and the fear is reduced by corrective emotional experiences. Treatment takes years to reduce the fear. The memories and the emotions remain, but the person's response to their own emotions becomes more manageable.

Case of Beth

I once treated a woman named Beth early on in my career as a psychologist who showed me that the relationship between your mind and body is complex. I think Beth taught me more about psychology than I taught her. Beth, a 42-year-old woman, first came to see me with a weight problem. As we worked together on her weight, it became apparent that she had many other life experiences that were difficult to explain. Her husband would claim that she is gone for hours at a time without explanation, often leaving the 10 and 12-year-old girls alone in the house. In response, Beth would claim that her husband is lying and she would never do that to her children.

As I got to know her better and better, other more bizarre incidents began to happen. One day, a neighbor told Beth's husband that he had seen her recently in the local bar, hanging out and being seductive with several strangers. When her husband confronted her the next morning, Beth was confused and upset. She could not understand why he was angry with her. She denied she had been in the bar, had no memory of any such event, and was outraged that he was implying that she was out cheating on him.

As the story turns out, Beth had a history of severe childhood abuse and had developed a dissociative disorder to cope with her emotional reactions to her abusive past. She had created multiple personalities, each one formed to manage a different level of emotion. There were some who were very sarcastic, others who were physically combative, and one who would protect her at all cost. Marriage had created the need to manage these emotions more directly. It caused Beth to split apart even further to cope with her emotions and hide them from her husband. Because of the overwhelming emotional load from the abuse, the only way Beth could function would be to split the emotions into little pieces and create a personality to cope with each level of reaction.

Not only can hidden emotion force the mind to create distinct boxes for every scary emotion, it can dramatically alter the physical body. One day, I get a call from Beth's physician for a consultation. In the past, he had noticed that Beth would be allergic to a medication one day and be able to tolerate it a week later. On this particular occasion, he had discovered an abnormality in her EKG, a test of electrical activity in the heart. When he called her back in for a retest, the abnormality had disappeared. A month later, he retested her again, only to have the abnormality reappear.

He called me to discuss whether her dissociative condition might explain what he had found. As we reviewed the timetable of these events, we were able to piece together that Beth's body was altered by her emotional states. She would be allergic to medication in one state, and not be allergic in another state. Not only did her emotional states dictate her response to medication, they also apparently affected the electrical activity of her heart. She actually had a cardiac condition in one emotional state that would disappear in another.

Beth is facing a long uphill fight to be healthy and integrate all the emotional pieces in her mind. Each therapy session is an attempt to take the emotion of the moment and process it as much as possible before the dissociation is triggered. I could actually see the transformation occur in Beth, as she would move from the sadness of a child to being an aggressive bully who would physically threaten me. By experiencing the emotions that were locked up in each personality, Beth could integrate slowly the emotional pieces into her Authentic Self. I could tell when that happened as she could recall the prior experience and retained the memory of the event. Years of sessions like these resulted in Beth being able to handle the emotion of everyday life and the flooding of emotion from her abuse. She learned to process this emotion and use it to solve problems. She became less afraid of herself and more comfortable in her own skin.

The Fight Defenses

There is a second class of defenses that I will call the fight defenses. The distinction between fight and flight defenses is somewhat arbitrary as all defenses shield the person's awareness of their emotion. Flight defenses are designed to avoid. Fight defenses are designed to divert the emotion, an attempt to wrestle with it. The purpose is to engage the emotion in some indirect form to redirect it to an activity that occupies the mind. Unlike the flight defenses, there is recognition that something is wrong with their body or themselves, but the underlying emotion is hidden from view.

Like the flight defenses, there are mild, moderate and severe levels of fight reactions. "Bad habits" are an example of a mild fight defense. The person may bite their nails, rub their fingers or feet together, pull on their face or hair, blink excessively, bounce their legs up and down, tap or drum on a surface or engage in other forms of nervous expression. Each of these behaviors serves the purpose of reducing or managing anxiety. Repetitive motions reduce tension and distract you from what is really bothering you.

Obsessive or compulsive rituals serve the same purpose. Making sure that shoes are aligned in the closet, checking and double checking if lights or appliances are shut off before you leave the house, your showering and grooming routine, are all examples of rituals. Doodling, getting on the scale repeatedly to weigh yourself, and hoarding are more obsessive rituals that serve as fight defenses. They reduce tension through repetition of a set of behaviors. The ritual comforts the person, and they feel anxious if the ritual is interrupted. Obsessional thinking can serve the same purpose. The person ruminates over a topic endlessly, repeats non-stop the same phrases, or has a song play continuously in their mind.

As you may recall from my personal life story, my mind used fight defenses to keep my emotions bottled up. As a young adult, I was battling with the possible shame that I would experience from failing to live up to my hero role that I was expected to play in my family. I was supposed to be the doctor in the family that would validate my parent's claim to the upper class. I was well on my way until my authentic anger finally surfaced. I didn't feel the anger or the shame. I only felt the anxiety that would drive me to study obsessively and be overly conscientious. People admired me for those traits and ignored the signs of emotional distress and anxiety. As the battle between my anger and shame built, my obsessional thinking distracted me from those emotions. I would repeat a name over and over or replay the same song in my head until I felt like I was going crazy. It was not until the anxiety crippled me during college that I began to have an awareness of the true emotions that were driving me.

In addition to obsessive-compulsive rituals, there are other low-level fight defenses that numb emotional distress. Substance or lifestyle abuses signal the presence of significant anxiety. People can eat, sleep or drink too much when their anxiety levels rise. Sex, porn, alcohol, drugs, video gaming, smoking cigarettes, shopping and gambling are just a few of the lifestyle behaviors that can serve as a defense to hide underlying emotions. The activity has to have sufficient stimulation to maintain the person's attention for extended periods of time and prevent the individual from recognizing the emotion that drives the behavior. They are easy to justify because there is a normal level of activity or substance use and a fine line when you cross into unhealthy use.

A moderate level of fear can trigger somatization, the storage of emotion in the body. In somatization, the body's normal functions are interrupted by fear. In a previous section, I discussed that there are three levels of bodily function that can be affected by the storage of emotion: the voluntary muscles, the involuntary muscles, and the immune system. Suppressed emotion causes malfunctions of involuntary muscles like migraine headaches, muscular twitches, and tics. An example of an involuntary muscular problem is Irritable Bowel Syndrome, where the colon spasms in response to anxiety. Female sexual dysfunction can result from rigid muscles in the vagina and failure to lubricate. Male sexual dysfunction can similarly result from diminished blood flow into the penis restricted by the impact of muscular tension on the vascular system.

Autoimmune diseases can develop from prolonged muscular tension. These can range from the inability to fight infection, to rate of healing, to diseases like fibromyalgia and diverticulitis.

Self-blame is another moderate level fight defense. It is often employed to fend off significant levels of anger or shame. With this defense, you are aware that you are upset but unsure with whom you are upset. If asked, you might admit that you are upset but describe it, as "I am angry at myself." You can acknowledge the anger but only if is directed at yourself. This prevents the admission of anger at another that might result in conflict and a possible change in your relationship. It's far easier to blame yourself than risk being alone.

Severe fight defenses can be frightening. Rage reactions can cover sadness or deep feelings of inadequacy. If you feel pushed to expose some hidden emotion, you can fly into a rage to silence or discount the other person. The cost to the relationships is high as the individual focuses only on the rage to the exclusion of experiencing sadness. Severe levels of obsessive-compulsive behavior can hide deep emotion. Severe skin picking can result in doing damage to the face and other body parts, a condition called Body Dysmorphic Disorder. Cutting using razors or other instruments is yet another fight defense. The person who cuts has exhausted all avenues to resolve their feelings and need a high level of distraction to quiet their mind.

Both the fight and flight defenses are triggered by fear of the exposure of deeper emotion. They are defenses to reduce anxiety. They are dramatically different than psychotic or bi-polar behavior. These conditions are biologically based and can be made worse with the normal anxieties created by human relationships. The psychotic and bi-polar behaviors are not defenses. They are medical conditions that require medication for treatment of the biological factor and psychotherapy to treat the emotional/relational issues.

Case of Ben

I recall the case of Ben, a sophomore in college whose experience was eerily similar to my own story. I remember thinking that my personal experience gave me insight to identify what was happening to him very quickly and get this boy back on track. Ben's physician referred him to me after seeing Ben at the request of his parents. Ben's roommate at school had contacted Ben's parent as he had not seen Ben for several days and was worried for his safety.

He told them that Ben had not been himself lately, so the parents went to school to find out what was going on. Ben had returned to his dorm room by the time his parents got there but was evasive about where he had been or what he had been doing. The family decided together to bring Ben home and have a consult with the family doctor. After meeting with Ben, his doctor became worried. Ben seemed disconnected and unable to coherently answer any questions put to him. The doctor was worried that he was having a psychotic break and sent him to me to evaluate.

After my initial interview with Ben, I understood why his doctor felt that way. In the first appointment, Ben clutched onto his parents and refused to talk. He wanted his parents to remain in the office during my interview. He could barely talk, had a wild look in his eyes, and was incapable of explaining what was going on inside of him. He would mumble words that made no sense and blankly stare at me. He looked like a deer caught in the headlights.

Ben's parents and physician were terrified because Ben had always been a compliant child who never got into any trouble. In high school, he hadn't been the best of students, but seem well adjusted and got by in school like his two brothers. There had never been any reason to suspect that Ben had a mental health problem. There was a reason for that. Ben was smart enough to know that the less he told people, the better life was. Back in high school, Ben kept any problems he had to himself. He did not feel his parents would understand and wondered if they would be disappointed in him. If asked how things were going, Ben had the same one-word answer: "Great."

Now things were not so great, and Ben couldn't hide it any longer. Ben's capacity for critical thinking had gone out the window, and he had no idea what was happening to him. The more we talked, the clearer the problem became to me. Ben was having a severe panic attack to the point where his internal thoughts were like a runaway train. He could not stop them and was scared by his inability to control his mind. He felt that he was going insane and was not going to let anybody know.

I discovered Ben was overwhelmed at the college but wanted to return and complete his studies. If he quit, he felt that he would be a failure and let his family down. Both his brothers had finished college and it was reasonable to expect that Ben would follow suit. However, Ben's courses were much more difficult than he expected, and he was in over his head. He had isolated himself from his friends this past semester because he spent all this time studying and had not taken time off to have fun. Ben knew he was failing at least two courses and had just completed taking midterms, two of which he failed. He did not know what to do and spent days walking the campus trying to figure it out. He did not know whether to admit defeat and withdraw or stick out the semester and run the risk of getting F's in two courses. Suicide came to mind from time to time and scared Ben even more. He was grateful to his parents for coming to rescue him and was looking forward to finding out what was going on inside of his head.

Ben was experiencing significant failure for the first time in his life. His fear of letting down his parents, and the potential embarrassment with his friends, created more anxiety than Ben could handle. His thinking capacity had been overwhelmed by his emotional state, temporarily shutting down his ability to function in the world. He was the human version of a deer in the headlights. It was an incredibly scary occurrence for Ben. He could not deny his emotion and was overwhelmed by it.

Ben had never struggled with his emotions before college. High school was simple and easy for him. He had good friends, two older brothers who loved him, and parents who cared. He had no reason to think anything other than life was fine and he would go down the same path as his brothers. He had never had problems before, had always felt protected by his family, and did not suspect that he needed to be anything different than what he was. He never understood those kids who complained about their parents. His parents were "great," and life was "great."

The struggle with grades in college came as a shock to Ben, and he was totally unprepared to cope with it. Life to him was a party, and he expected the same in college. He was active in his fraternity and felt a close bond with his Greek brothers. His father owned a family business, and all the brothers were expected to join right out of college. His life seemed set until he hit the wall.

Ben's panic attack was a result of his shame at falling off the track that had been laid for him by his family. He was underdeveloped emotionally as he had grown up in a protective bubble. Denial and avoidance had been his coping strategies, and they were no longer working. He had a long road ahead of him to understand the source of his emotions, the depth of his shame, and the need to reorganize himself. He had no ideas about the naturalness of the adolescent rebellion and had never understood how his friends in high school could get so angry at their parents. Ben's journey required him to more closely examine why he went to college, his future plans and entertain whether he wanted to go in a different direction than had been laid out for him. Did he really want to join the family business or was this an easy way to avoid taking any risks? In sum, Ben needed to grow himself up and be who he wanted to be, even if it cost him a cushy job with his family.

Conclusion

Ben's story is a story of how denial could not keep back the emotional wave that hit him in college. Your defenses will be different than Ben's, but it is important to know what they are to retrieve the emotions that they hide. You don't want to be surprised like Ben and collapse under the weight of accountability. You will not use all the fight or flight defenses that I have just discussed. I presented a smorgasbord of defenses so that you see and understand the particular ones that you use. The intent is to have you examine your own behavior and recognize the type of defense that your mind employs when your anxiety level rises.

Understanding how to read these defensive reactions is critical to discovering your authentic emotions that are hidden from your awareness. Once you have freed the authentic emotions from the defenses, you can now form independent connections that are based on honest emotional exchanges. Using these hidden emotions will be critical to managing your emotions in the future and restore the set of reactions necessary to fight the influences of your family role.

9

Birth Of A New American Psychology
How The Founding Fathers, Not Freud,
Got It Right . . .

Independence is not an easy idea to embrace. On a personal level, it has a bad reputation. People mistake it for being selfish, distant, and caring only about oneself to the exclusion of others. This is a false impression. Independence in personal relationships is based on authenticity. You are authentic when you are emotionally honest with yourself and with others. True intimacy requires the presence of an Authentic Self to offer to the other person.

The basic dilemma with independence is that people want to be free, but also connected to a group. You need others to survive but don't want them to tell you what to do. However, human beings fade in isolation. You need yourself, and you need others, and the two needs are sometimes opposing. You survive because you trust what you see and defend your rights. You want others for support and validation. You suffer because balancing those needs requires loss in one direction or another. If you surrender, you lose yourself. When you stand up for yourself and act independently, you risk alienating a significant other. Somebody important to you, like a parent, sibling, friend or boss may disapprove of your beliefs. If you defend those positions and do not surrender, you risk being alone. You take the chance to be targeted, discredited, and worst of all, ignored.

The ability to be independent requires you to embrace your Authentic Self and the natural reason that it requires. It is an acquired taste. When you are young, you are insecure and believe that older, wiser people know more than you do. As you collect life experiences, you learn to trust yourself more and more. You begin to challenge authority and reserve the right to believe differently than what you have been told. While there is some truth in the adage that age brings wisdom, there is equal truth in the concept that natural reason is vital to survival.

This struggle between your own ideas and what your elders taught you is challenging on both a personal and social level. Ideas backed by emotion can change the world. They can cause individuals to speak out against injustice, inhumanity, and inequality. Ideas like independence, liberty, freedom, and equality destabilize the status quo. You are asking people to break bonds and form new ones. To do that, you must risk losing something, like money power, status and face the new unknown.

That is why a simple idea like natural reason can evoke such strong reactions in some people. Rebellions throughout history often occur because of an idea or philosophy from an individual who represents the common cause challenges the prevailing political and religious ideologies of the time. The idea takes root because others emotionally connect to it. The emotion becomes contagious, and a rebellion ensues.

The simple idea that the common man has innate knowledge for self-survival is a powerful idea and a source of conflict and revolution throughout history. What makes the concept so controversial is the idea that the truth lies within the individual and not in some higher power or authority. The individual decides the answers to many of life's problems for themselves. That idea seems pretty benign until you realize that it flies in the face of many of the recognized authority figures in the world, from parents, teachers, and doctors to presidents, kings and religious leaders. That simple premise takes power away from those in charge, empowers the voice of each person, and puts power back into the hands of the people.

Giving power back has never been an easy task, especially for those in charge. In fact, as history has shown, it has typically required a revolution. Wherever there is social unrest, the voices of natural selves are trying to be heard. Anger is the natural reaction to man's inhumanity to man. The same anger that is the root of your Authentic Self surfaces collectively wherever human injustice is present. Where there is a violation of human rights, you will find anger. Anger is the natural response to inequality, neglect, dishonesty, greed and many other problems that result from an abuse of power. Anger is the voice of independence and a threat to authority.

Your connection to anger should be as normal as breathing and as natural as joy or sadness. Anger tells you that a problem exists. Solve the problem, and the anger goes away. Unlike these other natural emotions, the problem is that the presence of anger activates fear. When the child's natural reactions are met with disapproval from the parent, the child becomes afraid that the parent will pull away. If the parent doesn't reassure the child or reinforces the fear by showing severe emotional distress, the anger becomes loaded with anxiety. Your mind as a child creates a program to warn you of impending danger. Whenever your anger flashes, a rush of anxiety is not far behind.

The ancient Greeks were aware of this problem with anger. Aristotle, the famous Greek philosopher, once made a statement referred to as "Aristotle's Challenge." He said: "Anyone can become angry – that is easy. But to be angry with the right person, to the right degree, at the right time, for the right purpose and in the right way – this is not easy". (Nicomachean Ethics). Aristotle's quote implies that he knew that anger gets suppressed and experienced in delay. When a person continuously stores their anger, it erupts in rage. Rage scares everyone, including the person who is raging. It reinforces the idea that anger is scary and that bad things happen when you are angry. This fear of anger is universal.

Throughout the course of human history, politically astute people willing to assert their needs have gained power by using people's basic fear of their own anger against them. If you can keep people afraid, you can control them. It becomes the source of exploitation of the masses. This control is only temporary. Once people begin to believe in themselves, revolution is not far behind. The power of human emotion eventually rises to the surface and fuels a rebellion against injustice.

Anger is often confused with rage. Anger is different than rage that may fuel a mob mentality. It is a civilized response to being mistreated. It is righteous anger to heed the voice of the people protecting their natural rights and liberties.

The Spirit of 1776

This very process happened in early America and eventually led to the American Revolution. By the middle of the 18th century, the American culture of independence was firmly entrenched and creating civil unrest. The issues of taxation by the English crown became both an issue of self-determination and economics. Some historians have argued that the English law that denied the colonists the right to use their own currency, called "script" was the primary fuel for the American Revolution. Colonial trading companies had to buy English money and pay interest to conduct their business. The injustice of this law and its damage to American interests created deep resentments that would foster the need for rebellion to protect the natural rights of the American people.

The spirit of rebellion in the colonies reached a fever pitch by the 1770's. The anger at the mistreatment of colonial needs by the English crown had to break through the fear of challenging authority and the power that it represented. For many, it was more than the fear of challenging the power of the British Empire. There were emotional ties to the Crown.

These were loyal British subjects who were raised to believe in Mother England. Separation was equivalent to rejecting your parents and running away from home. After much debate and anguish among the delegates from each of the colonies, the Declaration of Independence was authored in 1776. America was born in righteous anger. The collective desire for independence overrode the fears of reprisal.

There was one Founding Father who became the philosophical voice of the American Revolution. Thomas Jefferson, the author of the Declaration of Independence, was a noted author and legal scholar of his time. He had written many treatises and laws for the State of Virginia, including the Bill of Rights for the state. Jefferson's writings contained more than political ideas about government and the right to self-determination. They revealed a deeper philosophy about the nature of man and a commitment to the concepts of natural rights and natural reason.

Jefferson took issue with the idea that natural rights were given by the King to the people. The words he chose to use for the Declaration of Independence show the growth in the belief in natural rights and natural reason that first began with the Magna Carta and extended to the English Bill of Rights. The document begins with words that establish the natural rights of all people that come from God and not bestowed by a king:

"When in the course of human events, it becomes necessary for one people to dissolve the political bonds which have connected them to another and *to assume among the powers of the earth the separate and equal station to which the Laws of Nature and of Nature's God entitle them*, a decent respect to the opinions of mankind requires that they should declare the causes which impel them to the separation.

We hold these truths to be self-evident that all men are endowed by their Creator with certain inalienable Rights that among these are life, liberty and the pursuit of happiness..."

According to Jefferson, the truth was now self-evident. For a concept to be self-evident, you must use natural reason to understand it. Knowledge of the truth is innate. You are born with it. It doesn't need to be taught or given to you.

Jefferson must have known of the significance of the phrase, "self-evident" because they were not the words that he had originally chosen. He had originally written, "we hold these truths to be sacred and undeniable." Most likely with an assist from Benjamin Franklin, the term, "self-evident" was introduced. This idea reflected the Quaker tradition of the reason being self-evident in all men, a prevailing thought in the Pennsylvania region at the time. (David Fischer, "Liberty and Reason," New York, Oxford Press, 2005).

This idea was not only radical for its time; it remains radical to this day. The Founding Fathers had a completely different way of looking at people and human nature. They believed that the common man was a wise soul that had innate knowledge. Wisdom was based on common sense. People didn't need an almighty sovereign telling them what to do. They knew what was good for them and could govern themselves. They could follow their hearts and trust their judgments. They instinctively knew what was right and as a people, could make decisions in their own best interest.

This was the view of man that the Founding Fathers embraced. This made the American Revolution so much more than a political rebellion. It was a philosophical and psychological revolution, introducing a belief system to the world that had not previously been considered. It gave birth to the importance of independence and assigned new significance to natural reason within each individual. It became the core of the American mind, defining what Americans believed that was different from everybody else. Equality to Americans meant that every individual was important and contributed to the melting pot that made America unique. The vote of the toothless, uneducated frontiersman had the same value as the vote of the landed gentry. Every man had value, and every man contained some measure of the truth.

Restoring Trust In The American Way

Americans belief in this core principle became eroded over time. Too many Americans have lost the capacity to trust the legacy of the Founding Fathers, the gift of natural reason. I believe that this issue lies at the heart of many the problems Americans are facing today. Americans need to decide which path takes them back to be able to trust themselves again. The time has come to make a choice between the path of fear or the path of anger.

I believe that America needs to return to the path of anger to rebuild the spirit of independence. Embracing your emotions is the key to restoring that trust in yourself and resetting the compass to point toward independence. Anger is the antidote to fear and shame. When you embrace your anger, your fighting spirit is rekindled. You push back because you trust your reactions, trust that something is wrong simply because it feels wrong.

The Old Psychology

In order to change course, Americans and any freedom loving people must change themselves. They need to stare down their fears to embrace their core emotions. They need to learn to trust themselves again. They need to move from a world based on roles to a world based on the exchange of emotion. They need a new psychology that embraces human emotion and how to use these basic reactions to forge lasting bonds with the significant people in their lives.

Americans need a New American Psychology that teaches them what independence and freedom mean within all their relationships. They need a psychology of self and family to rebuild the nation on American principles of freedom and equality. They need to have American marriages where power is shared. They need to raise American children within a family that teaches them to be independent and to respectfully challenge any emotional abuse of power. They need an American psychology that teaches them to trust themselves, share themselves, and build relationships based on the common values of equality and freedom for all.

To be consistent with the Founding Father's beliefs, the core of an American psychology has to rely on natural reason. Traditionally, this has not been the basis for most personality theories. Traditional psychoanalytic psychology created by Sigmund Freud, M.D. stands in direct contrast to the concept of natural reason. Freud's theory was a distinctly Old World model evolving out of the culture of Austria post World War I in the 1920's. It was a theory that addressed how a man related to himself, his fears and his impulses.

In stark contrast to the beliefs of the Founding Fathers, Freud believed that man's basic nature was based on a death instinct, thanatos that rendered man unable to be trusted with his own well -being. According to Freudian thought, mankind was viewed as self-destructive. Absent was the idea of natural reason. Man's behavior was to be understood as intra-psychic conflicts between pleasure needs fed by sexual and aggressive urges clashing with social norms. Freud's ideas became widely accepted by the medical establishment, and his influence continues to be significant to this day. One only has to look at the common expression, "Freudian slip" to understand how much it permeates modern thinking about human nature.

Freud's ideas were easy to accept because they provided scientific support to the nature of man espoused by the Judeo-Christian traditions. This philosophy has been used for thousands of years as the basis for understanding the nature of man. Freud provided a psychological framework to continue the long-standing religious tradition of distrusting man's basic nature. According to traditional Christian theology, mankind was tarnished with original sin and required God's mercy and grace to be saved. Essentially man was bad until proven good. Consistent with a Freudian perspective on instincts and emotions, anger, sexuality and other basic human needs formed the basis for the Seven Deadly Sins. These are lust, wrath, gluttony, greed, sloth, envy and pride.

With eternal damnation as the consequence, no wonder people were afraid of their impulses, desires, and themselves. Thanks to Dr. Freud, they now had a more modern and pseudo-scientific explanation that fueled the very same fears. Human problems now had nothing to do with emotional dynamics especially fear, situations, or lack of knowledge. People created their own problems for unconscious reasons and therefore could not be trusted.

A New American Psychology

In the new millennium, the idea of natural reason is being threatened with extinction. Fear is at a high level and driving people to believe what they are told by authority figures. They are losing the belief in themselves and their natural reason. This process must be reversed for Americans to embrace their core principles and live life the American way.

To return to your American roots, you must first start with yourself. You need to understand yourself in a new way. The Old World psychology eroded your belief in yourself and natural reason. It trapped you in your fears, leaving you to numb away the fear with an obsessive preoccupation with work, money, alcohol, drugs, gambling, sex, cell phones, social media, and the Internet. The loss of real connections and honest emotional exchanges created a void that people filled with fear, greed and the pursuit of material goods. They surrendered the basic values of truth and honesty in both personal and business relationships. They have become morally bankrupted because they are running so hard from themselves.

In addition to distracting yourself from your own natural reactions, the Old World psychology has taught you to blame yourself to explain your shortcomings. You became overdosed with guilt and shame. Without knowing how to manage your own fears, you understood them incorrectly as character or motivational issues. A child who doesn't study is automatically seen as lazy. The worker who doesn't try very hard is lacking motivation. The mother who drinks too much wine night after night is weak willed and doesn't care about her children. The fat person is lazy and has no self-control.

Character traits are an easy way to understand yourself and others but are based on a psychology and philosophy of man that is decidedly un-American. You misunderstand yourself and why you do what you do. You become prone to blame yourself for events or choices that are better understood within the framework of natural reason. You misunderstand the actions of others because you misunderstand yourself. Trait theories explain differences in human temperament but do not go far enough to provide an explanation for the role human emotion plays in human behavior. Trait theories lead to a superficial understanding of yourself and others. You understand these problems superficially because you have not been trained to understand emotional dynamics. To understand the person, you must understand the emotional root cause of their behavior. People act to release emotional tensions. If you are too busy ignoring your emotions, you won't be able to recognize those emotions in others until you can recognize them in yourself.

Natural reason provides an alternative construct to understand yourself and others. If people act to protect themselves and survive, they you must understand fear as a root cause and other emotions in order to understand yourself and others. So what is the root cause of fear? If you look beneath the surface of your fears, you will often find that your own anger is the source of your fear. You have been taught to look at it backward, that there is fear behind anger. I think it works the other way around. You get angry first, and then become afraid of how the anger may change your relationship to others if you act on it.

When you get challenged with a problem, you naturally want to fight back. Anger is that low level reaction that tells you that there is something wrong, that a problem exists that needs to be solved. Somebody is treating you badly, asking for too much, wanting to take something from you that is yours, making demands on you without giving back in return, taking you for granted, and a host of other interpersonal problems. When you suppress your anger to cope with these problems, the anger does not disappear. It is stored for later use. When the next event occurs that makes you angry, you open the flood gates that lets loose the stored emotion from your memory. When you flood with emotion, your anger turns into rage. What begins as a natural response to a problem comes out like a shaken can of soda. You want to yell, scream, and hurt people. You fly into a rage, and your anger becomes unproductive. Nothing gets solved, and people get hurt.

Rage reactions scare everyone. When you over-react, you lose respect for others and yourself. You can't defend your rage because natural reason tells you that you would not want to be treated that way. Rage generates fear, guilt, and shame, and makes you lose faith in your anger. There is a wicked cycle being repeated. Natural anger that is suppressed turns into rage followed by guilt and shame that only confirms the very fear that got the cycle started.

Nowhere is this more universally true than in your relationship to your parents and family. As a small child, you simply react. You yell when you don't like something and get mad when you felt mistreated. In response, your parents discipline you for getting angry. They teach you to be afraid of your anger, to surrender to their way of doing things, and punish you if you refuse to cooperate. You learn that anger creates disapproval and distance from those you love and need. You are taught to fear your anger. Guilt and shame rush in to make you doubt your right to be angry. You lose the connection to the emotion that is your protector. You surrender so you are not alone.

The loss of the belief in your anger has many consequences. You become disconnected from yourself and your emotions. Without understanding how to find the truth within yourself, you tend to look to others for answers. You succumb to the demands of authorities who pretend to have simple solutions to complex problems. You subject yourself to the abuses of power without complaint and believe what you are told. Without being able to look within, you are led like sheep to solutions that serve the needs of others. You lose control of yourself and your ability to make others accountable to you.

The American Way

The theoretical base for a truly American psychology resting on natural rights and natural reason has existed for as long as America has existed. Back in the colonial era, psychology was slow to develop as a science, and its truths buried in philosophy and religion. The roots of this American psychology go back long before Jefferson penned the Declaration of Independence. It started in the colonial universities that played a large role in disseminating knowledge of philosophy and psychology during that period.

At Princeton University in New Jersey, the philosophy department developed a school of thought called "Scottish Pragmatism." John Witherspoon, President of Princeton, and a Scotsman himself, and signer of the Declaration of Independence was the leading proponent of that philosophy. Scotch realism advocated the application of common sense in philosophy. These philosophers maintained that certain intuitions were self-evident and discernable by introspection of one's consciousness. The human senses were the guide and provided much information about the world that could be understood using natural reason. Witherspoon authored a series of sixteen lectures on the Common-Sense School that were widely read in that period.

After over fifty years of being overshadowed by Freudian psychology, a truly American psychology based on natural rights and natural reason reared its modern head in the post-Freudian period of psychology in the 1950's. At that time, an American psychiatrist, Harry Stack Sullivan, M.D. developed the interpersonal school of psychology. Interpersonal theory blended concepts of psychoanalytic thought with natural reason and applied them to human relationships.

Like Witherspoon and Jefferson who predated him, Sullivan's psychology was distinctly American and consistent with the philosophy of man adopted by the Founding Fathers. He believed that man's behavior was purposeful and not self-destructive. Fear of separation was the core of human fear and man's behavior could be understood as an attempt to reduce this anxiety. To Sullivan, human emotion resulted from the imprint of significant relationships. The universal source of conflict was the battle between the individual's reactions and the reactions that were trained into them by their parents, a natural split between natural reactions and learned reactions. Anxiety was the signal that those two elements were in conflict and a choice needed to be made to either face the fear or act to reduce it.

If you compare Freud to Sullivan, it is easy to see why Sullivan's ideas took years to gain popularity. There were reasons Freud was so widely accepted. He was saying in scientific terms what every minister and priest had been saying for years. Religious leaders talked about original sin, and Freud talked about the "id." Both referred to the side of man that could not be trusted. Freud was also a medical doctor, a member of the medical elite, and his arguments were well written and very persuasive.

The same was not true for Sullivan. Like Freud in his day, Sullivan was a product of his time and life experience that undermined his credibility. Dr. Sullivan suffered from schizophrenia and was often hospitalized in the very same hospital in which he practiced, St. Elizabeth's Hospital in Washington, D.C. He was a doctor one day and a patient the next day. He was also a gay peace activist in the 1950's, both issues offending the establishment views of his time. His writings were difficult to read and remained hidden until rewritten by an editor, Helen Swick Perry. Between his mental illness and his political views, it is surprising that Dr. Harry Stack Sullivan's interpersonal theory gained any acceptance at all.

Thanks largely to the work of Dr. Sullivan, the foundation for a New American Psychology has existed for some time. Passed along and extended from Witherspoon to Jefferson to Sullivan to me and now to you, it is time to unearth it and use it now to understand yourself and others in a new way. This is the psychology that embraces American values and is based on an American view of life. It will define a new path that not only helps you reorganize yourself based on your natural reason but also defines the way to build independent connections to others.

Basic Tenants of the New American Psychology

Independence resulting from using natural reason is the cornerstone of the New American Psychology. Separation and individuation are encouraged to forge relationships of emotional honesty rather than dependent relationships based on obligations held in place by guilt and shame. Attachment occurs based on healthy emotional principles rather than the relief of fear of parental rejection. All relationships are based on the same principles of freedom and equality for all. These principles guide marriages and families to adapt to the growth of the family members and the addition of new members like in-laws and grandchildren. They form a psychological base that is uniquely American to understand yourself and others and build lasting relationships that form the backbone of a free society.

An American Psychology must rest on the Jeffersonian building blocks of natural reason and natural rights. Natural reason is used to understand Emotional Dynamics. It helps to navigate the defenses and separate natural from learned emotions. Natural emotions are based on natural reason and create independent people who build independent relationships. Independent relationships are formed by honest exchanges between authentic people.

Authentic people value each other's reactions as each reaction is assumed to be purposeful and needs to be understood. There is an honest attempt to combine the truths in both positions. All parties look to find the gray rather than choose the black or white position. Thoughts and feelings are mutually given credibility. Natural rights are honored as all parties practice the right to be heard, to value the truth in both positions, and to resolve differences through negotiation and compromise. Equality means that both parties have equal status, and conflicts are resolved until both parties agree to the outcome.

In order to fully understand the application of this new American psychology to your life, I summarize below a list of the seven tenets of this approach to human behavior:

SEVEN CORE PRINCIPLES OF AMERICAN PSYCHOLOGY

1. Mankind Uses Natural Reason To Solve Life's Problems.

Natural reason is based on the idea that each individual contains the truth within to make decisions that are purposeful and not self-destructive.

2. Healthy Human Behavior Is Based On Natural Rights.

Natural rights include the freedom to express your thoughts and feelings and expect them to be assigned value. Natural rights imply that human beings have the right to share their reactions with others.

3. Applying Natural Rights and Natural Reason Promotes Independence.

Human beings are born into dependency as the default state. They must separate and individuate to ascend to their natural state of independence.

4. Emotional Dynamics Drive Human Relationships.

Human beings are feeling beings who happen to think, not thinking beings who happen to feel. Emotions are guided by natural reason and are the compass that guides healthy human interactions.

5. Emotions Have Two Sources.

Emotions originate from natural reason or from parental training. The former reflects authentic reactions while the latter is learned. These sets of emotions form the base of two self-systems. The Authentic Self contains the natural emotions like joy, sadness, anger surprise, etc. that establishes what feels right and what feels wrong. The Self For Others harbors the rules of the family and the guilt and shame that occurs when there is a threat to break the rules.

6. Human Emotion Is Contagious.

Emotion is the central medium for human communication. Emotion is transmitted from one person to another using multiple senses but is often neglected by the less sensitive or untrained. Failing to accurately read this exchange can cause breakdown in human communication and relationships.

7. Healthy Relationships Require a Balance Between Care For Self and Care For Others.

Balance is implied in the Golden Rule in the word, "as": "Love thy neighbor as thyself." That spiritual truth is also a psychological truth. One must care for yourself to even understand how to care for others. It assumes that what is good for you is also good for others.

10

It's All About

Independent Relationships

Learning to Make Authentic Connections

American Psychology is different for many reasons. The core difference from other theories is the belief that about the nature of man, the purpose of human emotion and the essential role of relationships. American Psychology focuses on the relationships between people, and not the internal conflicts created by competing instincts. Human emotion is believed to stem from the imprint of relationships and the conflict between what you naturally feel and how you have been taught to feel. The belief that there is natural emotion comes from the application of the philosophy of natural reason and natural rights. The extension of these rights into relationships requires that human interactions be grounded in freedom and equality for all. In short, American Psychology is unique because it brings new terms and conditions for healthy human relationships.

You would expect unhealthy relationships to dissolve and disappear over time. That is often not the case. Many relationships that are unhealthy are maintained by obligations or need and remain in place despite the negative impact on you. Others, like work relationships, require you to do as you are told to save your job. Some choices, like the military or religious life, require you to surrender your freedom for security.

It is easy to think that all families are healthy and all family relationships are good for you. I would like to hope that is true but know from my clinical and personal experience that family interactions can be part loving and part destructive. Family relationships are one example of

187

a potentially harmful attachment that is maintained through obligation and fear. They become sustained by a survival need for human touch and connection, to be part of a loving group of people. Some family relationship cause psychological harm that may not even be recognized by any of the family members.

The Case of Mary Anne

Consider the following case of Mary Anne, a 20-year-old patient of mine whose relationship to her family is clearly unhealthy but only from the outside. To Mary Anne and her mother, things could not be better. Here is part of the dialogue from one of our sessions:

MARYANNE: "I have such a good relationship with my Mom. We go everywhere together. I don't spend much time with my Dad at all."

ME: "What does your Dad do that makes him feel so different than your mom?"

MARYANNE: "My Dad doesn't care about his children. He only cares about his work. If you interrupt anything that he is doing, he yells at you. You better never get in the way of his football. He sits in front of the TV on both Saturday and Sunday and watches every game. He has no idea what his family is doing, nor does he care."

ME: "Doesn't that bother your Mom?"

MARYANNE: "She doesn't care. She would rather go out shopping with us anyway. It's fun and we have a good time. She is a really good Mom. She's my best friend."

ME: "Does your mom say anything to your Dad when he yells at you for disturbing him?"

MARYANNE: "No. She is scared of him too."

ME: "I think your Mom has a responsibility to you to protect you from harm, even if it comes from your Dad."

MARYANNE: "What can she do? He would threaten to shut her up if she even tried."

ME: "How does Mom know what Dad would do if she doesn't say anything?"

MARYANNE: "She told us."

ME: "You are only hearing one side of the story and are caught in the middle. You see Dad through Mom's eyes. Mom may be too afraid to fight back because of the way she raised. Maybe Dad has a right to be mad about something and taking it out on her in the wrong way. As the child, you will never know but have already chosen sides. I don't think that is good for you."

MARYANNE: "My boyfriend would agree with you. He says that I protect my Mom when she should be protecting me. He tells me that I put my Mom's needs ahead of his. It causes all the fights that we have."

ME: "Do you think your boyfriend is right?"

MARYANNE: "Sometimes, but I don't know what to do. I feel so bad for my Mom. If I leave her at home, she is so unhappy being around my Dad. Somebody has to take care of her. She is really good to us. I just can't walk away from her."

Mary Anne's connection to her mother is an example of one particular type of relationship that is unhealthy but maintained through dependency. The emotional needs of the parent can cause a naturally dependent relationship to become locked into place. The parent serves their own emotional needs by using the natural dependency of a child for their own purpose. Knowingly or unknowingly, Mary Anne's mother is serving her own needs for emotional closeness by being Mary Anne's best friend and interfering with Mary Anne's growth toward independence and self-sufficiency.

Cultural Differences

Mary Anne's relationship with her mother resulted from unhealthy parent-child bonds. These unhealthy connections exist because of parental denial. Mary Anne's mother could not admit the loss of the emotional attachment to her husband and the role that her daughter played to fill this hole.

Parental denial is not the only cause of unhealthy family relationships. Cultural norms can have a dramatic effect on parent-child connections. The American culture is the melting pot of immigrants who bring different concepts of family to this country. Some of those concepts do not translate into the kind of relationships that promote the spirit of independence. They are vestiges of the culture from which they came and promote dependency that weakens the backbone of a free society.

The Case of Tom and Juanita

Consider the case of Tom and Juanita, a young couple who have been dating for two years and are considering getting married. Tom is as American as apple pie, being born and raised in New Jersey his whole life. Juanita is Latin, being born and raised in the Dominican Republic. Her parents spoke only Spanish while Juanita learned English in school. She met Tom when she came to the States for college. Her family followed her, and now the whole family lives in America.

Juanita came from the typical parent-centered family of Latin/Spanish descent. In Juanita's family, her father's needs were all that mattered. Juanita's mother catered to the father's whims without complaint and expected her daughter to do the same. In her culture, a woman served a man and the man, in turn, provided for the woman.

This demand always troubled Juanita who saw a different relationship between her American friends and their parents. Her friends were given more freedom to function on their own. She had to be home when her father came home from work, always had to check in with her parents, and had to have her father give prior approval of any boy she wanted to date. Juanita would complain to her parents, who would promptly tell her that she was being disrespectful and demand that she does what she was told.

Juanita felt stuck between two worlds. Juanita and Tom viewed each other as equals in their relationship, but Juanita was not provided that same status in her family of origin. She was raised in an Old World family that required her to care for her elders regardless of the cost to her. She was now exposed to an American culture that valued freedom, the right to dissent, and gave equal value to all members of a family. Raised in a parent-centered family, the American values of independence and freedom were a threat to the relationship of Juanita to her parents and to the overall stability of the family. What father said was law and there was no questioning his opinion.

The collision of her two worlds would occur whenever Tom did not go along with her father's wishes. She felt caught between her parents and her husband. Most importantly, she was not used to doing what she wanted, regardless of what her father or boyfriend thought. She would get overwhelmed with anxiety and feel caught in the middle.

Things only got worse when Tom approached her father to marry Juanita and asked for his blessing on their marriage. Juanita's father did not give his approval easily. He demanded that they prove their love to him by staying apart without any contact for three months. If they did as he asked, he would throw them a lavish wedding. If they did not comply, he would withhold his blessing and forbid them to marry.

Needless to say, Tom and Juanita were shocked by his request. Juanita knew that her father was demanding, but was surprised by his level of entitlement to run her life. She was terribly conflicted because she had been well trained to do as she was told. Her Self For Others was very strong, and her Authentic Self was weak. She pleaded with Tom to accept her father's demands, as she could not bear the thoughts of getting married without her father walking her down the aisle. She had dreamed of that as a little girl and did not want to have a ceremony that did not include her father. Plus,

Juanita had been raised to expect her parents to plan her wedding and did not expect to pay for it herself. If she did not do as her father wanted, her only option would be to run off and get married on her own at her expense. That thought overwhelmed her with anxiety.

On the other hand, Tom was angry and insulted by the request of Juanita's father. He felt that he did not have to prove himself to anyone. Tom felt that Juanita's love for him should be enough for the family to accept him. If he was good enough for Juanita, why wasn't he good enough for the family?

Tom and Juanita struggled through many fights to resolve this issue. Tom eventually gave in and lived apart from Juanita for the required time. They were married as promised in a huge wedding that was everything that Juanita had ever desired. Some of Tom's resentment over needing to prove his love was tempered by the joy of seeing his wife so happy. Little did either one of them know that they were sowing the seeds that would come back to haunt them later in their marriage.

Several years later, after living by Juanita's parents and working in the area, Tom was offered a new job that required them to relocate several states away. Juanita was happy for Tom as he received a big promotion and salary increase. She saw the opportunity to quit her job and start a family as they could now afford to live on Tom's salary alone. Juanita's parents were not so pleased. They expected Tom to find work close to the family and keep the family together. They let it be known to Juanita that they were not happy with this decision and wanted Tom to change his mind. Juanita tried to explain that they might get to be grandparents soon because of this move, and asked them to support her. Juanita's parents said "no." They countered that being a grandparent from a distance was no different than not being a grandparent at all.

The family continued to pressure her to change Tom's mind. For good measure, they added guilt about the father's health. They reminded her that her father had diabetes, and suggested that the move might make her father's health take a turn for the worse. Juanita now faced the same pressure to disappoint her father and family as she had about the wedding. This time, she tried to stay strong and supported Tom's right to be promoted regardless of the amount of guilt or shame that her family would heap on her.

Juanita's strength was short lived. Her family disengaged from her after the move. Neither her parents nor her brothers or sisters came to visit her in her new home. While she used to talk to her mother daily on the phone, the calls now went to voice mail and were unreturned for days at a time. Her father would talk to her, but each time the conversation would turn back to the same old question" "When are you coming home?" Juanita couldn't take it any longer. After two years of the same badgering from her parents, and still not pregnant, she asked Tom to quit his job so they could move back closer to the family.

Tom wanted no part of that decision. He was furious and accused Juanita of caring more about her own family of origin than about their own future. He felt she was being child-like and giving in to her father's whims, just like she had done all her life. Eventually, just like the wedding, Juanita wore him down, and he gave in. He found a new job in Juanita's hometown but had to take a pay cut and a demotion.

Although Tom went along with the plan, he remained resentful of Juanita and the way she handled the pressure from her family. They did find a home that he liked, but did not like the new job as much as his former job and wished that he had never left. Shortly after the move, Juanita found out that she was pregnant. This news temporarily set aside Tom's resentment. Much to her father's delight, Juanita gave birth to a baby boy, her parents first grandchild.

Juanita instantly went from scapegoat to hero and became her father's favorite. Three boys later, Juanita could do no wrong in her father's eyes. She and Tom would go over to the parent's house every Friday night with the grandchildren for a family meal. Nights at the family's house became the replacement for date nights for

Tom and Juanita. Sunday dinner was just as likely to occur on most weekends unless some unusual event would interfere. Tom barely noticed the erosion of his connection to his wife, while Juanita basked in the glory of her three boys and her family.

Twelve years into their marriage, the bad seeds that had been sown at the time of their marriage finally bore rotten fruit. A problem that had been ignored for twelve years reared its ugly face at Tom's Christmas office party. Tom came home late and glassy eyed, awakening Juanita when he came in. Juanita sensed that something was wrong and asked him to explain why he looked so different. Tom denied that anything had happened and wanted to go to sleep. Juanita was annoyed and wanted an explanation. Tom started to get belligerent and stormed off to the bedroom. Juanita followed and physically challenged him. Tom forcibly pushed her and told her to get away from him. Juanita kept coming and hit him in the chest with her fist. Tom became enraged and slapped her hard in the face, leaving a red imprint of his hand on her cheek. Juanita was stunned and ran off to sleep in the guest room and get away from her crazy husband.

The next morning, Juanita looked in the mirror and saw the bruises that had appeared around her cheek and eyes. She didn't know what to think. Her emotions ranged from feeling ashamed of herself for challenging Tom to feeling outraged at Tom for hitting her. She was also frightened that her family would explode at Tom if they saw her bruises, and wanted to avoid having to see them. When she saw Tom later that morning, there was an awkward silence between the couple. Neither one apologized to the other. They acted like nothing had happened. Her bruised face was the proverbial "elephant in the room" that was never acknowledged.

Later that day, Juanita went into the study to pay the bills. She was confused by Tom's erratic behavior the night before and wanted to make sense of what had happened. She decided to look through all the accounts and noticed that there were unexplained cash deductions made by Tom over the last few months. She brought that information to Tom and asked for an explanation. She was completely taken aback when he replied: "I've bought some coke a few times and did a few lines with some guys in the office. It's no big deal". Juanita asked him: "Did you do any coke at the Christmas party?" Tom didn't answer, walked away and refused to talk about it.

Juanita was too embarrassed about her bruises to attend her family's Sunday dinner. This was the first time that she had declined the invitation without a reasonable excuse. She told her mother that she was not feeling well, but her mother suspected that something was wrong from Juanita's evasive answers to her questions. Much to Juanita's surprise, her mother paid her an unexpected visit the next day. At first, Juanita tried to make a lame excuse for her facial bruises, but very quickly broke down into tears. She told her mother the story of Tom using cocaine and getting hostile with her after the party. Her mother couldn't believe her ears. The last thing she would ever have thought was that one of her children would end up with a drug addict spouse who beat his wife.

Juanita's mother encouraged Juanita make Tom accountable for his actions. She wanted her to call the police and file a report of spousal abuse, but Juanita was not ready to do that. She knew the cat was out of the bag. There was no way that her mother was going to keep this a secret from the family and she would have to face them. She decided to confront Tom when he came home from work that night. Tom tried to avoid her, but he relented when Juanita threatened to report the abuse. Tom came clean about the missing cash and his cocaine use. He said that he had been feeling isolated and alone in his own home. The only time he had fun was when he went out drinking with the guys in the office. He admitted to using cocaine on those occasions but didn't see the harm in it. He acknowledged that it made him more aggressive and admitted that it probably played a role in why he hit her that night. Tom apologized but did not see any problem with the occasional use of cocaine with his friends. He was not an addict and could control it. He saw no reason to promise to stop. He did not see any significant issue with getting out of control one night where he was drunk, high and exhausted from work.

The issue of dealing with the family didn't come up in the discussion. Juanita's face had healed by the following week, and they went to the regular Friday family get-together. Juanita failed to tell Tom about her mother's visit, so Tom had no idea that the family knew about the incident. After some time, Juanita's father broached the subject in front of the whole family. Tom was outraged but didn't want to make a scene. He acknowledged the issue, apologized to everyone and assured them that it would never happen again.

At home, Tom flew into a rage at Juanita. He could not believe that she would take their marital problems to the family, especially without talking to him first. He saw this as a violation of their marriage, and a continuation of the same pattern where the family came first, and he was a distant second. He blamed Juanita for his drug use. Tom told her that if she had been a better wife, he would not have needed to party so hard to survive his lonely existence.

Juanita was heartbroken and came to see me the following week. I asked her to bring Tom to the next session and here is what they had to say about the problems:

ME: "Tom, Juanita told me about your incident and the family dinner. Tell me your reactions at this point."
TOM: "This is really hard and embarrassing for me. I didn't mean for this to happen. I thought it was no big deal to party with some friends at work and do a little coke."
JUANITA: "Then why did you do it? I thought everything was fine between us. I would never have imagined you to be the kind of guy who would do drugs and keep it a secret from me."
TOM: "It was fine. I guess I didn't realize how disconnected we had become."
JUANITA: "What do you mean by disconnected?"
TOM: "Everything else in your life seemed more important than us. The boys are demanding every bit of your time, and you are

always tired. There is no effort made to find time for us or to even have sex every once in a while. On top of that, you seem more interested in spending every Friday and Sunday with your family than making time for us to go out to dinner. When's the last time we went out on a date? Saturday is the only day left, and you are too exhausted after running the boys from one sport to the other all day long."

ME: "Tom, you sound really angry and hurt. When did you first become aware that you resented Juanita so much?"

TOM: "I guess it goes all the way back to the wedding. I resented how she needed to please her father so much. I even had to give up a job that I liked so she could be back close to the family. I knew I was angry at her for those things but thought time would heal things. I thought she would be happy if we moved back closer to her family and we would be happier as a result. Guess that didn't work very well."

JUANITA: "Why didn't you tell me that when we were deciding to move back? You told me that you were ok with the move. Why did you lie to me?"

TOM: "I didn't lie to you. I expected you to be different when you came back home. Thought you would be happier and more fun. Instead, you seemed to go right back to being Daddy's little girl. I took a back seat. I didn't expect you to do that. If you had been different, I would have had no problem with the move or giving up the job."

ME: "Juanita, how do you feel about the family issue that Tom is raising?"

JUANITA: "I have always been close to my family and didn't think it was a problem for Tom. I knew the wedding was wrong but felt I had to do it or would regret it for the rest of my life. After all, my parents are old school and are first generation immigrants. They believe in the ways of the old country and see nothing wrong with how they act. I try to understand them and not take it personally when they want me to do things their way."

ME: "That is a problem for many immigrant families. They have a hard time with separation from the children and lean on them to excess to survive in the new culture. It puts a lot of pressure on you to take care of them."

JUANITA: "I feel guilty anytime I try to do something apart from the family. They give me a hard time and feel hurt and rejected anytime I miss any family event. I never realized the harm I was doing to Tom by giving into my guilt."

Juanita and Tom are a prime example of what happens when the nurturing of independence, even with an adult child is sacrificed for family togetherness. Juanita never psychologically separated from her family. Individuation was never allowed or encouraged. She never fought the guilt and shame of breaking her parent's rules about the primacy of her father's needs and remained the dependent child even as an adult. She was confused. In her mind, the natural anger at the inability to grow and develop her independence scared her. The voice of her Authentic Self was lost in the strength of the voice of guilt and shame from her Self For Others. This guilt and shame pushed her to protect her father's needs at her expense. There was little ability to listen to the weaker voice inside her, the actual voice of truth. If she was unable to protect herself from her family's demands, she was certainly not going to be able to protect her marriage or her husband from the same demands. What was good for her was going to be good for Tom too.

On the surface, Tom seemed to be different than his wife. He was able to get angry at her and openly challenge her passiveness with her family. He felt equally entitled to be angry at the unreasonable demands of her family. However, if you look more closely, you will see that Tom was very much like Juanita. Tom was unable to hold onto his anger to solve the problem. He got mad but gave it up very quickly. In the end, he was no better at solving problems than his wife. He too suppressed his anger and made whatever adjustments his wife requested. He couldn't tell the difference between an opinion and a demand, especially if the request came from Juanita. Tom would overreact and assume that he had no choice. He avoided all conflict out of the fear that he would have to surrender to avoid disappointing the other person. Tom allowed his resentment to build to the point where he was more needy and depressed than he realized.

Tom's avoidance of conflict revealed the family issues that he brought into the marriage. Tom was the good son, a devoted and loyal child who did whatever his parents wanted without complaint. He was a classic hero with an underdeveloped Authentic Self that enabled his shame to be the driving force. His obedience to authority was actually rewarded as Tom did well in school and work, receiving many honors for being compliant and devoted. He was never much of a partier, rarely drank alcohol or did drugs. His recent drug use and drinking with his office friends was totally out of character and a complete surprise to his wife.

Tom and Juanita's histories were a perfect storm. They had planted bad seeds at the start of their relationship that bore bad fruit. What started as a concession to her family at the wedding became the continuation of a life-long pattern of self-denial and failure to be an individual for Juanita. Tom never wanted to use drugs or physically abuse his wife. He thought less of men who beat their wives and could not understand how somebody could stoop to those levels. Yet, the denial of his fears about conflict sent him down the path of emotional ignorance and eventually rage. He was blind to the level of his sadness, distracted by the tasks of child rearing and work. He did not realize the depth of the depression that had come over him nor did he see that his partying and drug use was an attempt to medicate his emotions. He rationalized it away as some superficial fun with his office friends, something done all the time by other people so why not him. He did not see his own emotions or the significance of keeping secrets from his wife.

The story of Tom and Juanita is an example of the need for separation and individuation from the family to establish life on one's own terms. This need is especially true for the development of the American identity. Freedom cannot be embraced or protected if the person has no experience to understand the price of freedom. Without engaging in an adolescent rebellion and working through the conflicts created by differences, the self cannot be freed from the family obligations or family roles.

Coming from an immigrant family, this transition was particularly hard for Juanita. Being exposed to the American way of life caused many conflicts with Old World ways. Tom did not help her with this task as his fears of conflict made him unable to encourage Juanita to take on her family. In fact, he would do the opposite, getting anxious whenever Juanita would get mad and make excuses for her family. Tom had difficulty promoting American values within his own marriage. His failure to defend the right to dissent led him to indirectly support the Old-World tendencies and limit the transition of the couple into the American culture.

The Relationship Spectrum

Relationships can be categorized along an independence continuum. There are four different kinds of relationships: dysfunctional, power, dependent and independent relationships. Each of these forms of attachment serves a different purpose. Dependent connections are the norm for young children and serve the purpose of survival. As I have discussed previously, dependency is a necessary state for a child. A child must depend on significant others to have food, clothing, and shelter. They are unable to take care of themselves and need help from others to obtain these essential items.

The purpose of an independent connection is to nurture separation and individuation. While independence is your natural state, you need to encourage and nurture the growth process to achieve it. It does not come easy. It requires a parent to be very aware of the power that they have over the child on a minute-to-minute basis. If properly nurtured by the parent, there is a normal process of growth from dependency to independence.

The illustration below shows the range of these different relationships and where they stand relative to each other.

RELATIONSHIP SPECTRUM

Unhealthy   Healthy

⬅———————————————————➡

DYSFUNCTIONAL...DEPENDENCY...POWER...INDEPENDENCE

Power relationships are dependent but necessary and healthy under certain conditions. They are a different kind of human relationship designed to achieve a specific purpose. While personal relationships are based on shared experiences, power relationships are based on an exchange of goods or services for a specific purpose. Work relationships are an example of a legitimate power relationship. Employers have the right to protect the growth of their business. They hire and fire workers based on the needs of the business. While this may bring hardship to the individual who is terminated, it is part of the normal and healthy conduct of business.

The military is another example of a power relationship. There is a required submission to authority to handle the conduct of war. Commands need to be obeyed, or lives may be lost. The individual who chooses a military life accepts that fact. The dependency on authority is healthy and essential to maintain a level of discipline necessary for waging war.

Power relationships can move down the spectrum to become dysfunctional when there is an abuse of power. The differential in power by itself does not make the relationship unhealthy. The abuse of power by the employer coupled with the employee's failure to dissent is what determines the health of the power relationship. Employers don't get to harass employees emotionally, sexually or physically without legal redress. Laws define the limits of an employer's power and provide compensation for those injured by abusive bosses. The right to dissent through proper channels is defined and encouraged, with laws governing whistle blowers and retaliation protecting those who come forward. This type of relationship requires a balance of power that acts as the check and balance against abuse.

Dependent Relationships

A power relationship is one type of a healthy dependent relationship that is based on a choice made by both parties. A personal relationship is dependent for a different reason. Take the parent-child relationship as an example. That relationship is a forced choice and critical for survival. While dependency is the starting point for all human relationships, you would hope that it would not be the end point. It all depends on how the power of the parent is used. The parent can use their power to build independence or create dysfunction by promoting their own needs at the expense of the child.

I believe that the average parent wants to promote the growth of the child. However, in all families universally, the unresolved conflicts within the marriage promote fear that is resolved through dependency and family roles. The growth toward independence is impeded by the family role. Family roles are normal psychological pressures that exist within every family. All children have to face being either a Hero or Scapegoat and learn how to shed their family role. The more the parent helps the child to recognize the role and provide permission for the child to share their real reactions, the easier it becomes for the child to operate outside their role. They are freed to learn to honor their authentic self and be emotionally honest in their relationships. This process promotes the psychological growth of the child including the separation from the family to pursue their own interests.

Raising an independent child is difficult. The parent must become an expert in using the power of the parent to nurture independence rather than control behavior. The parent who wants to promote independence in their children needs to learn how to purposefully and tactfully undercut their own significance and share their power. To some people, that may sound like a formula to raise bratty children who have no respect for authority. I disagree wholeheartedly and believe it works the other way around. The child whose significance is validated becomes more secure, emotionally stable and naturally assigns respect to all others because they respect themselves. A bratty child is an angry, often neglected child who has not been taught how to organize and use their emotions. It is not a child with a character flaw. It is often a child raised in a home without limits or inconsistent limits. Children raised to believe that every person including them has some piece of the truth grow to respect themselves and others. Differences are treated as points of learning and conflicts are handled with mutual respect.

The parent who is trying to breed independence understands this task. This type of parent makes sure that they are not seen as the source of all the answers to life's problems. Even when the parent feels they know the right answer, they are careful in how they approach the subject. They need to ask the child for an opinion before they share their own. When they don't know what is the right thing to do in a given situation, or that there are multiple reasonable choices in a given situation, the parent needs to acknowledge that there is no real right or wrong in the situation. There are just different answers that carry different consequences.

If you are a parent, you will no doubt have encountered a situation with your child when you know they want to tell you something but are too afraid to bring it up. You can tell by so many signs, including avoiding looking you in the eyes, whispering rather than talking in a normal voice, a crouched body position, standing further away, and many other cues that let you know they are afraid to speak up. In that moment, the child is stuck in the fear of breaking from the family role, doing or saying what has not historically been allowed. It is not easy to speak their mind because there is a history in the family where the opinion has been met with a combination of denial, rage or shame. They have either experienced it directly or witnessed it with siblings. They believe that whatever they have to say will not be acceptable.

A healthy parent will want to resolve this situation for the benefit of the child. You can coax them, reassure them that you won't get mad, or possibly reassure them that they won't be punished for telling the truth. You hope that encourages them enough to speak up. In those moments, you are trying to break the family role and encourage freedom of expression. You are trying to build the Authentic Self and reduce the size of the Self For Others. You are trying to raise an independent child who can stare down their fears and risk being honest. Once your child tells you the truth, your reaction will either confirm their fears or validate their right to free speech. It calls for an honest and well-organized reaction from the parent. If you fly into a rage, the child's fears will grow bigger, and they won't take the chance the next time to speak up. If you give them a dose of shame and guilt, they will retreat and not speak up again and believe they have hurt your feelings.

Even if you don't react, you are reacting. Silence is frightening to a child who has just taken a risk. They will panic and might say, "What's wrong? I know there's something wrong. Talk to me." A child will automatically internalize any unexplained reaction and believe they have made a mistake. Even if you try to cover it by saying, "nothing's wrong," they read you like a book and know that you are upset. Worse, they believe they did something wrong.

In those moments with your children, you are either building their Authentic Self or adding more power to the guilt and shame in their Self For Others. Disguising your reactions, even if you think you are protecting the child from a reality that they can't handle, adds to the Self For Others. Your hidden reaction will cause them to bury their emotion that strengthens dependency, the family role and the Self For Others. On the other hand, managing those situations in an emotionally healthy way frees the child from dependency and promotes emotional honesty, the use of natural reason, and independence. In that way, the dependent child grows into an independent adult one incident at a time.

The Dysfunctional Relationship

Some unhealthy parents misuse the power of the parent and cause dependency to be encouraged. This is the dysfunctional relationship. The purpose of a dysfunctional relationship is to meet the emotional needs of the parent at the expense of the child. The parent takes advantage of the dependency of the child and uses it for their own purposes. When this occurs, it is often unintentional, rooted in deep parental denial and an abusive family history.. The fact that the parent doesn't intend to hurt the child doesn't reduce the damage done to the child. It may lessen the parent's guilt when it is realized, but the damage to the child is the same whether intended or not.

I typically use an analogy about stepping on toes to illustrate this point to my patients. There is no difference in the pain if I mean to step on your toes, or I trip and come down on them by accident. Intention does not change the level of feeling. It may change what I do about the relationship but changes nothing in the moment. The phrase, "The road to hell is paved with good intentions" applies here. Meaning well does not ensure that you are doing well.

Let's go back to the story of Mary Anne and see what happened to her. As you may recall, Mary Anne's mother was her best friend and playmate. They each would describe the mother-daughter relationship as close and loving. They loved each other's company, loved hanging out together and loved shopping together. So how could that be wrong?

The answer is that mothers and daughters can never be best friends. The bond is always irrational, with the mother having more power from the very beginning. It is not mutual. The mother defined the rules of the relationship at a very early age. The daughter grew up believing that Mom knew everything, and continues to believe that to this day. By believing this fallacy, Mary Anne's path to independence gets blocked. She cannot separate from her mother and will not believe in her own opinions without checking with Mom. She will be insecure and dependent in all her relationships until she learns how to trust her own judgment. Instead of the mother-daughter bond supporting the daughter's growth, the bond is formed to help Mom survive the loneliness of a bad marriage.

The first hint that something is terribly wrong shows up in the comment about the boyfriend. Mary Anne now faces the difficult choice of discounting her boyfriend's opinion or joining with it and challenging her mother. It feels to her like she has two bad choices. Defend my Mom and push my boyfriend away or join with my boyfriend and push my Mom away. She feels caught between her boyfriend and her Mom.

Fortunately, there is a third option. It requires Mary Anne to do what is healthy, what she knows to be the truth. Somewhere inside of her is the knowledge that parents should not lean on children to survive a bad marriage. She can ignore that fact and justify giving in to Mom or face her fears about challenging her and upsetting the relationship. But she only has to look around her at other mothers and daughters to see differences and know what a healthy relationship looks like. She knows the truth, and it is not in her boyfriend's opinion. It is in her own natural reason that happens to coincide with her boyfriend's opinion.

Separating In Anger: The Adolescent Rebellion

I have seen many examples of low-level abuses of power by well-meaning parents in my years of practice. Many caring parents overdo their need to protect their child and can't tell where caring becomes controlling. It is so easy for the parent to justify making the child do what they want because they believe that they know better than the child. In fact, they feel that they are being negligent if they don't take charge.

I have seen this reasoning used to justify bad solutions to common developmental problems. Writing the college application essay is one example. I have treated several parents where a sibling was asked by the parent to write the college acceptance essay for their child. Even worse, I have multiple cases where the parent actually wrote the essay for the child. The parent does not think they are doing anything wrong. In fact, I even had one parent who sent the essay around to her immediate family because she was proud of what she had done! The justification is that the child will not get into the college of their choice without the help and they are helping the child to accomplish their goal. They become blind to the underlying destructive message that they have no faith in the child and wonder what went wrong when the child flunks out of college after the first semester.

One of the hardest tasks of parenting involves managing the period in your child's life called the adolescent rebellion. It is a time when teens try on independence for size and rebel against parental authority. This is one of the most critical periods for fostering independence and strengthening the Authentic Self. If done properly, the teen learns to dissent respectfully without yelling, screaming, cursing or threatening. They learn to honor their anger and push back against their shame and guilt, overcoming the internal voice of the Self For Others and strengthening their Authentic Self. As Thomas Jefferson said back in 1787: "I hold that a little rebellion now and then is a good thing..."

The parent carries the burden of staying in control, reacting as calmly as possible and separating content from style. If parents take the attacks personally, they aren't doing their job. The style of the teenager is notoriously bad, but what they say typically has some truth in it. If you look to honor the truth before reacting to the bad style, the Authentic Self is validated. That often means that the parent has to expect that the teen may flood with their emotions and say angry and hurtful things that don't really mean. It is up to the parent to guide the process. Children do not separate easily, and it takes practice. They separate in anger and learn how to be reasonably angry in the interactions with their parents. In American terms, they learn to practice their right to dissent and to civil disobedience.

If they don't get angry, they can't go out on their own. You will have a "failure to launch" on your hands. Moving out of the house because "my parents are driving me nuts" is not only normal but a sign that a healthy process is alive and well. It means that you are witnessing the birth of independence, often with the same anguish and pain as the day the child was born.

Cutting The Ties That Bind

Independence has to be nurtured, or dependency will prevail. The tug between protecting your child and letting them learn for themselves is never an easy balance. Freedom needs to be taught interaction-by-interaction and problem-by-problem. Each child needs to be freed of their dependency on their parents to become independent adults. The parent must cut the ties that bind the child to the parent.

Giving the gift of freedom requires a great sacrifice by the parents. It is far easier to tell the child what to do and reinforce the idea that they need you. You can use their fears to ensure that they remain connected to you for life. If you do your job as a parent and promote independence, you raise the child to leave you. You put in all the work, time, and resources only to have them abandon you and go their own way.

So what makes a parent do the job of cutting the ties that bind when it is not in their personal best interest? It is because the child needs you to do that to grow and be a healthy human being. Dependency breeds dysfunction. The child cannot be healthy without the sacrifice of the parent's needs to feel close to the child, to protect them from harm. If you hold them too tight, they can't spread their wings and fly. They stay stuck in the nest. In human terms, they stay stuck in bad relationships that fail or careers that never take off. They aren't responsible with money or time. They don't thrive.

Parents have often asked me: "What does a child owe their parents? What is reasonable for a parent to expect from an adult child?" The answer in the Bible is to "honor your mother and father." There is a dilemma in that phrase. If honoring is interpreted to mean, "obey," then the child will never learn independence, how to think for themselves and believe in themselves. They will always have to follow the opinions of their parents and do what they are told.

There is another way to understand what that phrase means. Honesty is what a child owes a parent. The highest honor and measure of respect that you can give to another person is to be honest. When you hide your true reactions, you prevent problems from being solved. That does not mean that you have license to say whatever you want whenever you want. There is sensitivity necessary to prevent hurting the other person's feelings. However, people often justify being dishonest because they predict that the person will be hurt by what they have to say. Using untested predictions to decide what to do is often a sign of high anxiety and not healthy. It does not honor the other person or improve the relationship. You can only present what you have to say with emotional awareness. You can't predict or control the other person's reactions. This healthy process is what the child owes their parent. Honesty combined with sensitivity is the highest form of honor that a child can give their parent.

Independent Connections

So how do you know when a person is practicing independence and capable of forming an independent connection? What are the characteristics that define independent relationships? Independent people form independent connections. Independent connections are based on mutual sharing of ideas and feelings to learn from each other. Independent people use natural reason to react to situations and events and share those reactions with others. They don't regurgitate what they have been told. They critically evaluate what they are taught to form their own opinions. They can defend those opinions passionately against others who think differently without becoming upset that the other person chooses to believe an opposing view. They don't try to control the other person's thoughts or actions. They value the independence of the other as much as they do their own. The exchange enables both parties to learn from each other and broaden their knowledge of the human experience.

I have summarized below for you the ten characteristics of independent relationships:

1. Natural reason is used to form opinions.
2. Emotional dynamics are used to understand self and others.
3. Natural feelings are shared.
4. Emotional honesty is highly valued.
5. Anger is shared at its lowest level.
6. Anxiety or fear is recognized and calmed with reassurance.
7. Authentic feelings are validated.
8. Feelings and facts are given equal weight.
9. The right to dissent or have a voice is always practiced.
10. Conflict is managed with mutual respect.

Conclusions

Power and freedom are always being challenged in the daily life of a family. This is as true for a family as it is for a nation. Relationships are constantly changing within a family. People are either becoming more independent interaction by interaction or dependency is being reinforced exchange by exchange. If freedom is to be taught within American families or in families of any freedom-loving nation, each person must embrace that responsibility on a daily basis. Parents must use their power to reinforce freedom in their children. Children must learn to face their fears and listen to their authentic selves to practice independence within their families.

With that personal knowledge continuously present, people can learn to make independent connections that assign equality to all people and treat people with dignity and mutual respect. If that can be done, Americans will conquer the final frontier and succeed in giving new meaning to the phrase, "land of the free and the home of the brave." They will be psychologically free to be independent people who form independent relationships and brave enough to face their fears to be emotionally honest with themselves and others.

11

Learning To Be Genuine

Emotional Truths

To Live By . . .

The idea of being independent is as American as apple pie, but it is not guaranteed. It is earned and requires skill and training. Independent relationships take work, emotional work. You need to learn to access your natural emotions and tell them apart from your learned emotions. You have to develop the skills to manage your emotions and the emotions of others. You have to learn to respect the rights of others to their independence as much as you do your own.

Independence is based on authenticity. Authentic exchanges of emotion make independent connections. To have an authentic life on your terms, you must know yourself, your emotional dynamics, and be able to read the emotions of others.

Tenets For Managing Feelings

Listed below are ten principles to keep in mind in using your emotions to form your relationships:

1. You Are A Feeling Being Who Thinks

Emotions are more powerful than intellectual ideas. Ideas are spawned from emotional reactions. You think because you feel. Emotions trump this and spur action. Understanding your emotional world and how it intersects with others is critical to creating independent and authentic relationships.

2. You Must Recognize All Your Feelings

I n general, you are not taught to pay attention to what you are feeling or to separate authentic from learned feelings. Emotional awareness must be self-taught through introspection. You must familiarize yourself with hidden emotion and recognize how to spot the signs that your defenses are hiding your authentic feelings.

3. You Need To Learn To Recognize Whether Your Feelings Are Authentic or Learned, Rational or Irrational

Your emotional world is very confusing. Natural emotions are disproportional in your mind. Your authentic emotions are most likely hidden, while fear easily triggers your learned emotions. Anger is the central, authentic emotion that needs to be recognized to solve problems. It is most often hidden or experienced on delay. Learned emotions have a loud voice in your mind, while natural emotions sit softly. It is easy to make choices that quiet the louder voices than the softer ones.

Irrational emotions play the loudest. Irrational emotions are typically tied to the family role. They are irrational because they contain information that is relevant to your childhood, but not relevant to you as an adult. They say more about the past than the present. Authentic emotions are rational because they are based on natural reason. Learned emotions can be rational or irrational. For example, you should feel guilt if you break a rule of reason. The guilt that comes from breaking an unreasonable rule is irrational because the rule doesn't make sense.

4. You Need To Build Relationships On Authentic Emotions

The basis for genuine relationships is the exchange of authentic emotions. Real connections require an exchange of facts and a validation of emotions. When validation fails, trust is reduced, and fear causes withdrawal to occur. You become confused and doubt the emotions that you experience.

5. You Must Learn Which Emotions To Heed and Which To Ignore

Your emotions originate from two sources: your natural reason and your upbringing. The latter contain some good and some bad concepts. You are taught some rules of reason and some unreasonable rules. The rules of reason will resonate with your natural reason, and you will know it is best to follow them. You will have natural emotional reactions to reasonable rules and use them to create authentic relationships.

On the other hand, unreasonable rules evoke irrational guilt and shame and create destructive relationships. Shame exists whenever you follow unreasonable rules. You shame yourself because you will have to fight your natural reason that pulls you in another direction. You will do what you have been told to do rather than follow your heart and do what you feel is right. The relationship becomes an obligation and loses its authenticity.

6. You Must Uncover Your Emotions To Make Sense of Your Behavior

Your psychological defenses will be called into action anytime fear is present. They reduce the fear by hiding your natural emotions that pressure you to break your family role. Your defenses act to suppress or redirect your authentic reactions. Without understanding the emotional root cause, you can send mixed messages, be misunderstood, blame yourself, or unnecessarily doubt yourself.

7. You Need To Know That Emotions Often Appear Together

Emotions can come in pairs or even triads. Mad/sad is one such pair. Guilt/shame is another. Healthy reactions emerge when mad and sad pair together in your mind to guide your choices. Irrational guilt and especially shame needs to be ignored to make healthy decisions. You can also be happy and sad or angry and depressed at the same time. These "compound" emotions must be sorted through to understand how to react in a given situation.

8. You Need To Recognize When You Are Being Affected By The Emotions of Others

Emotions are contagious. Fear is especially contagious. If you are around an anxious individual, you will feel that anxiety. Joy as well can be infectious and spread to all who vicariously experience the joy of another. This contagious effect is the basis for empathy. If you can feel what another is feeling, you can put yourself in his/her place and join with their feelings. You can understand their reaction and validate how they are feeling.

9. You Need To Recognize That Emotions Can Appear In Cascades

Anger creates fear that opens the door for a rush of guilt and shame. The sequence happens so fast that it is easy to feel overwhelmed and not be able to individually experience each of these emotions. It is not unusual in these cases that the person will report that they don't know how they feel.

A similar phenomenon occurs when you flood with emotion. The emotion from the past is triggered by an event in the present, and it all mixes together. The overload is exposed in pre-judgments, assumptions, jumping to conclusions, a raised voice, tone of voice, lack of eye contact, tense facial muscles, and other physical signs. Often, you are not aware of the amount of emotion. At that moment, others see your emotions more clearly than you see your own.

10. You Need To Know that Emotions Can Be Delayed

Fear activates your defenses that hide your authentic emotions and reinforce the emotions of your Self For Others. To have authentic emotions, it is often necessary to delay your reaction to discover how you really feel about an event. It is unreasonable to expect yourself to react in the moment. Your defenses prevent the immediate experience of emotion. While "being present" is a laudable goal, it is often not biologically possible to freeze your memory and prevent the memory dump from the past.

Overriding The Fear

One of the most significant problems to use your emotions to forge independent connections is the ability to recognize fear. Fear comes in two forms, rational and irrational. Rational fear is a fear that warns you of an impending danger or threat to your well-being. It is a fear that warns you about something outside of you. This can come from a situation or a person. You will feel that fear when you don't trust a situation or a relationship.

Irrational fear is a learned behavior. There is no immediate danger. It is a fear from the inside, a fear of yourself and your own emotions. It is a warning from your Self For Others that there is a contradiction between your authentic emotions and the emotions determined by your family role. Irrational fear signals the presence of anger, one of your core natural emotions. Irrational fear is caused by your authentic emotions pushing up against your defenses, trying to get out and be experienced. To find out how you honestly feel, you need to face your fears, push through the defenses, and locate your authentic reactions.

Facing your fears is confusing. The problem is that both kinds of fear, the rational and the irrational feel the exactly the same. When you do the "right" thing according to your family role and follow the rules, you feel connected to your family, but separated from your Authentic Self. When it feels right, it is wrong. When you do the "wrong" thing, you feel separate, vulnerable, guilty, afraid, and ashamed of breaking the rules – however, you are connected to your anger. As I often tell my patients, when you feel like you are "losing it," you are actually "finding it"; it being your real reactions, your authentic reactions, and the way you really feel. When it feels wrong, it may be right.

The right thing to do, something that your natural reason tells you is right, may feel wrong. It may actually cause anxiety, guilt or shame or all of the above. If you are not prepared for this confusion, you will ignore your anger and never look for your authentic feelings in the emotional noise of the moment. You will shift into your Self For Others mode. You will lose the connection to your Authentic Self and revert to your family role.

This behavior is learned at such an early age that it feels natural. However, your authentic feelings are still underneath. Your anger may go underground and come out as rage if you are pushed. The rage may temporarily provide some internal relief from the internal chaos of the moment. It calms you down but apparently doesn't solve the problem. In fact, the rage damages the trust levels in the relationship and the problem gets worse.

Being authentic requires you to rely on natural reason and use natural reactions. Anger is the king of the authentic emotions and one of the core emotions of the Authentic Self. Irrational fear signals the presence of anger, It is your best friend, being introduced to you in a scary and confusing way. As I tell my patients as frequently as I can, "If it feels wrong, there is something wrong." You need to identify the anger to find the problem. You then must hold onto it to push back against other people's resistance to your solutions and find a compromise. Although it may cause trouble, this is your best option. There is a reason you feel the way you do. Trust that your anger is your real voice, the voice of your natural reason and that following it will give you the most authentic solution.

Ghost Of Families Past

You are usually not aware of the choices involving your emotions. You perceive, organize and categorize events at lightning speed. Your brain synthesizes all the information and warns you of impending problems through the experience of anxiety. Your mind acts like a computer that registers and predicts events. You get information that reminds you of your history, and you must decide whether history is going to repeat or not. When a present event reminds you of a past event, the fear level climbs. The higher the fear level, the more you believe that you must follow the family rules to reduce the tension.

When you believe the fear, your relationships suffer. Without pausing for critical review, fear makes it easy to jump to conclusions and pre-judge what others mean by what they said or did. You do not realize at that point that you have logged into your family role. You carry those role requirements into every encounter that you have with another human being. You anticipate and pre-judge expectations based on your family role. The rules that define that role establish the expectations for what others will expect from you and what you are supposed to do to please them. You carry around your family history and project those same expectations onto others.

You believe your fears before checking out your assumptions. In that moment, the other person does not really exist. They act like a ghost who is a surrogate that takes the place of your parents. You are relating to a figment of your imagination, a ghost who is an extension of your family who you assume has the same expectations of you as your family did.

Ghosts aren't real people and relationships based on treating people like ghosts don't work very well. Communication is brittle and falls apart quickly. People pre-judge each other and make wrong assumptions. Emotional exchanges become confusing. People fly into rages rather than listen and validate. To have healthier communication, you need to let the person appear through the ghostly mist of your assumptions. You need to give the other person a chance to explain what they mean rather than believe your own meaning. I often use a phrase with my patients that bears repeating:

"TRUST WHAT YOU SEE, BUT NOT WHAT YOU MAKE OF IT UNTIL YOU CHECK IT OUT."

Checking it out means that you place your own assumptions on pause. You can trust what you see because you don't make things up. You emotionally react for a reason. Jumping to conclusions is where the problem comes in. To avoid relating through your past, you must freeze your own conclusions. You can easily flood with emotion from the past and incorrectly interpret the other person's behavior.

In a relationship between two healthy independent people, the reaction of each person is important. It is necessary to listen to the other person's explanation to understand how your behavior affected them. You build in a pause and face the fear that keeps pressing you to do what you have been trained to do. It is important to clarify the meanings of words and actions to let the other person explain what they meant rather than provide your own meaning. You have to slow the process down to make sense of what you feel, how the other feels, and try to blend the differences. When that is done, the other person feels heard. The communication process builds trust because the emotional exchange feels honest. It feels right because the process is right.

Discernment: Learning To Trust Your Gut

You cannot control how you feel or think, but there is always a choice in your actions. You can choose to follow the path outlined by your authentic emotions, or choose to follow your fear and stay within the comfort of your family role. Sometimes that choice is confusing and sometimes it is simple. When your authentic feelings line up with your family role, things make sense. In that case, what your parents taught you passes your own test of natural reason. But what do you do when something doesn't feel quite right? How about when you get confused about whether it is right or wrong? How does one know when to listen to the fear and when to ignore it?

Many of my patients will respond to this dilemma with the phrase, "I have to trust my gut instinct." The problem is that everybody's gut is poisoned by the obligations of their family role. How do you tell when you are being true to your real self or just being run by your other self? Your initial reaction to something may feel good or bad, right or wrong. You don't want to take these initial feelings at face value. Anxiety or guilt are all signals that you need to stop and think, not react immediately. You have to make sense of what is going on inside of you. Perhaps your anxiety is now kicking in due to the power of your Self For Others. You may be giving in to your fear because you feel helpless or hopeless to impact the problem.

Using your natural reason is your answer, but you must first use your natural reason to understand yourself and the range of emotions that are going on inside of you. I call this process, discernment, a term that is used in the Quaker religion to describe a process of looking for the truth inside of you. The good news is that the answers you seek are always within you. They are just hard to find. You have to look beyond the fear to recognize any flash of anger that can be quickly hidden by your defenses. This can happen without a conscious decision because you are pre-programmed to hide your authentic emotions. You need to discern the difference between your anger and your guilt/shame. Is your anger justified? Has it risen to the level of rage by mixing with past experiences? Should you expose this anger and possibly hurt someone else's feelings? It is so confusing because of the battle in your mind in that moment. You feel guilty, and the guilt is louder than your anger. Both your anger and your guilt may feel valid, so what should you do?

The cascade of emotion happens so fast and has been going on for so long that it is difficult to slow it down. This is where emotional awareness becomes so essential. If you are blindsided by your emotions, you will inevitably get caught up in them and become confused. In that vulnerable state, your family role can look terribly appealing to reduce your anxiety. If you are aware of your family role, the patterns that you have lived throughout your life, you will not be surprised by your reactions to events. If you are caught off guard, buy time to figure yourself out. Spontaneous reactions are rarely on target. It is too hard to tell what self they come from. Discerned reactions can be trusted. You will have gone through the steps to apply your natural reason to yourself first and then to the problem. Over time and with much practice, you will be able to react faster and more in the moment. Each time that you go through the process of discerning your reactions, your Authentic Self becomes strengthened. You build up memories based on ignoring guilt and shame that you can rely on in times of doubt and fear. You live through corrective emotional experiences where you survive, and your worst fears don't come to pass. That is the process to trust as the path to independence and authenticity.

Changing What You Can And Accepting What You Can't

Change requires you to see your emotions, to tell past from present emotions, to separate rational from irrational and to know yourself more fully. This is a difficult task like asking a blind man to see. Fortunately, with your emotions, you are only temporarily blind. You can access hidden emotion but you need to know where to look. It's like reading tea leaves. There are signs all around you. You have the reactions of others to decide to trust or ignore. You have your own history in your family as a reference. You also hopefully by now know how your own defenses work and the signs that they are leaking.

Learning from the reactions of others is tricky. If you surrender to the voice of another, you may be taking the easy way out. The past to independence requires the courage to trust your natural reason. However, there are many times when those you trust see you more clearly than you see yourself. Knowing when to trust others and not yourself is a difficult task. It feels the opposite of what you are supposed to do as an independent person. You might think that independent people make their own choices regardless of the opinions of others. Standing up for yourself in the face of public opinion is often viewed as the measure of "mental toughness" – the independent man or woman who doesn't care what others say and follows his/her own heart.

This all sounds good but is overly simplistic. If you react when you are blind, even if it is temporary, you can go down the wrong path very quickly. I do know that "flying off the handle" or "going off half-cocked" under the guise of being strong is not the answer. Standing steadfastly for what is wrong is not a measure of psychological health. Denials feel like a brick wall, but that is neither strong nor healthy. That is defensiveness. Healthy people know that emotional life is confusing. You need to take many factors into account before reacting including like your history, your repeating patterns, your family role, your defenses, and your hidden authentic emotions. It is not easy to find the truth within.

Somebody Knows You Better Than You Know Yourself

Sorting through your emotions is one of the most difficult psychological tasks that you will have to do. Because of the confusion, it is nearly impossible to do on your own. You can easily fall prey to "kidding yourself" or believing that there is truth in guilt or shame. Getting the opinions of significant others about what you see or what you make of it provides a reference frame to find the truth. The truth can only be revealed when it stands the test of telling a significant other. A wife, a partner, a close friend, a sibling, a parent or a therapist are all relationships to trust for advice about whether you see yourself as clearly as you think you do.

Self-help books like this one can only provide the roadmap to emotional honesty. While you may believe you know how you feel and what you want to say, the test of the authenticity of your emotion lies in your ability to communicate the emotion. If it resonates with another in the way you intended, you can be sure that you identified authentic emotions and communicated them clearly. Trusted relationships offer protection against your blind spots. This is one of the most significant benefits to close relationships like marriage or psychotherapy. You develop a safety zone that enables you to test your reactions with those that you trust deeply.

Learning about your emotions takes courage, the courage to be honest with yourself, and admit that you need help to know yourself. It is hard work. You can get better, more authentic and independent, but not without doing the work. Change comes slowly to those who earn it.

You also have to be careful what your end game is. All my time spent with my patients has taught me a basic truth: a healthy life is different than a happy life. There is no such thing as a happy life. Happy is a momentary state of joy. It changes over time. There is nothing wrong when it ends. It is not supposed to last a lifetime. It should not be an end in and of itself, nor does it define a realistic goal for life. Hopefully, along the way, you have moments of happiness and joy that you remember for a lifetime.

Healthy is not the same as happy. A healthy life is achievable. You can learn to live your life more in balance. You can learn to understand yourself and others more fully. You can be a better human being. You can get psychologically healthier and healthier until the day you die.

I've learned something in my 65, 000 hours with my patients - there is no easy fix. Magic pills may work for children, but not adults. In fact, there is often no cure for human suffering. As a doctor, I can help people to manage problems more effectively, but cannot often fix what ails them.

217

There is no rest for the weary and no easy way out. Live involves conflicts, fighting, and sadness. None of them are medical conditions that need a cure. Sometimes the patient dies, and you can't do anything about it. The search for serenity and a life of happiness can take you on a temporary journey that ends right back where you started, staring at the same unresolved problems. Some problems are fixable. Some can be changed. Some can only be changed a little bit. Some are not fixable. In those cases, the best you can sometimes do is damage control – don't blame yourself or others, and know that circumstances will change over time.

A great example of that message was recently seen in the Disney/Pixar animated movie, Inside Out released in 2015. In this film, a variety of the core emotions are represented as figures operating inside of the minds of a family, an 11-year-old girl named Riley and her parents. Riley has to manage the experience of leaving her Minnesota home and her hockey team to relocate to San Francisco where her father has recently gotten a new job. The movie depicts how joy is afraid of sadness because it causes her to turn blue and reduces her joy. In the end, Riley learns that sadness results in stronger attachments to people as they share their sadness and form stronger bonds as a result. The meta-message is that sadness has a purpose in life, is not a mental health condition, and serves a purpose in relationships.

As an aside in case you get to see the movie, the emotions are organized differently than I organize them in this book. Joy and sadness form a bond against fear, anger, and disgust. The purpose of that arrangement is to focus on forming the bond between joy and sadness. If the movie had a sequel written by me, the purpose would be to visually present the two sides of you. They would need to add a guilt figure and a shame figure and reorganize the teams. Joy, sad and mad would be on one side. I would call them Team Authentic. Fear, disgust, guilt, and shame would be on Team Others. Life events would cause the two sides to clash and enable the *Authentics* to overcome the resistance from *Team Others*.

THE DELPHI PROCESS

There is a decision-making process to use to enable you to become more authentic and independent. I named this 4-step process, the Delphi Process, after the inscription written thousands of years ago on the Oracle of Delphi in ancient Greece: "Know thyself." This is my prescription for the work involved with building healthy human relationships. It is based on applying the traditional American concepts of natural reason and natural rights to everyday life. Its core values are freedom and equality. All men and women are treated as equals with the same basic rights. When needs conflict, these principles are used to resolve differences through negotiation, compromise and mutual respect for all concerned.

This process is not that much different than the life philosophy of an 18th-century American hero, Davey Crockett, also known as the "King of the Wild Frontier." Crockett was born in Tennessee, fought in the War of 1812, became a member of Congress, and died fighting for Texas freedom in the Alamo. Since he was accorded folk hero status because of his exploits, he was often asked about his personal approach to life. Crockett described a series of steps to making good decisions. His motto was "Always be sure you are right, then go ahead." The short version was, "think, act, and don't look back."

Crockett's idea makes sense to me, but I've added some additional steps to address the complexity of your emotions. I wish we could make it as simple as Crockett's version, but there is too much complexity and information available in modern life to be made simple. The conflicts are a natural part of your daily life. In this multi-cultural world, differences abound, and passionate conflicts are the norm rather than the exception. Husbands and wives struggle to have careers that don't interfere with family life. Children want more freedom, while parents feel more protective than ever in a threatening world. Religions conflict and offer competing solutions to life's problems. Immigrants bring old world solutions into modern American life. On a personal level, a husband wants to spend some money that his wife wants to spend another way. A teen wants to go to the shore for the weekend with his girlfriend, and his parents don't trust the family with whom he staying. The situations are endless, and the conflicts bring you face to face with your emotions.

Here's how the Delphi process works:
Step One: **STOP**

You can't smell the roses when you are running. You can see them better when you walk , but you can't really smell them until you stop. The same is true with human emotion. As you now know, real emotions take time to surface, but anxiety hits you right away. If you ignore it, it will build and stop you right in your tracks. You need to STOP when you feel your anxiety rise. You need to take stock of your initial emotions to be able to figure out what is going on and what to do about it.

In modern society, stopping is not as easy as it may sound. The demands of a busy job, the desire to achieve, the need to please parents, friends and spouse, the need to make money all make you run at a speed that requires you to suppress your emotions. Feeling makes you stop. Emotions get in the way. They are messy and confusing. They make you feel vulnerable and weak. They distract you from doing your job. They keep you up at night. They make you drink too much, smoke too much, exercise too much, or do something too much. They run you even if you don't want them to.

Time is the answer to prevent the build-up of emotion. As hard as it seems, you need to carve some time during the day to assess how the day is affecting you. You have to prevent the build-up of tension from any unresolved problems to maintain a reasonable level of tension. Keeping this chronic tension low enables you to see your emotions more clearly in the moment and avoid overload. Meditation for as little as 10 minutes per day, exercise, or massages are all methods to help to prevent the tension levels from rising to intolerable levels. These techniques need to be continuously used on a daily basis as each day presents additional problems that cause tension to rise on a daily basis.

Stopping to take the time to deal with the daily tension is only one of the issues involved in the STOP step. The second is to STOP when a conflict arises, and your anxiety starts to climb. You have to prepare yourself to override your fears to open yourself to new possibilities and new solutions to problems. You learn over time how to trust that two heads are better than one and participate in the process. This is different than surrender. I am talking about preparing to bring your thoughts and feelings to the table to define the problem and to arrive at a mutual solution that is in the best interests of all parties.

In addition to the hectic pace of modern life that makes it hard to STOP, the advances in telecommunications place a demand on people that can separate them from their emotions and create communication problems. Human emotion is hard to read. It is impossible to read if you are looking at your cell phone or a computer while you are talking. You are similarly distracted if the phone is on during conversations because you are receiving text messages. It is not humanly possible to process all the subtle information exchanged during human communication while being distracted by anything including a cell phone or laptop. I recommend to all my patients that they never bring cell phones to eat unless they are alone and to turn off their cell phones while they are talking to another person. You won't be able to STOP if you are already operating at the lightning speed of modern technology.

Step Two: **READ**

Once you have stopped, the second step is to READ, to assess the situation for yourself and the others involved. As Benjamin Franklin once said, "Observe all men, thyself first." Reading yourself first involves looking behind the fear to find the competing reactions. When you are considering multiple choices to react, you have to sort through the emotional noise in your mind. You hear self-statements that are the voices of the competing emotions and the defensive reactions that hide the authentic emotions.

In this second step, you must learn to read the internal language of your emotions to find the root cause. Many people confuse thinking with feeling. I have had several patients make the following statements to me: "I think that person is a jerk and I am entitled to my feelings." Calling somebody a jerk is a thought, an interpretation of their behavior. It is not a feeling. A feeling would sound more like, "I get anxious around that person" or even "I am really mad at that person." Fear and anger are emotions. They are not interpretations or conclusions.

To read yourself, you have to learn to look for the emotions behind the thoughts. Each person has a unique internal pattern to their emotions and their defenses. Here are some examples of the voices of some emotions and your defenses as they might sound inside your mind:

The voices of fear:

- "I can't do this. That's not me."
- "I'm going to screw this up."
- "I'm going to fail."
- "I'll never be able to do this."
- "He/she is better than me."

The voices of low-level rage (defensiveness):

- "That's your perception."
- "You're crazy."
- "I didn't say that."
- "You don't understand."
- "No, you're wrong."
- "You're the one with the problem."
- "It's all your fault."
- "You're not worth it."
- "You are such a jerk."

The voices of guilt and shame:

- "I'm going to let a lot of people down."
- "It's all my fault."
- "I feel SO bad that I did that"
- " I can only blame myself."
- "I'm such a jerk."
- "I'm selfish."
- "I'm lazy."

- "I'm self-destructive."
- "I'm a disappointment."
- "How could I even think that?"

The voices of mad/sad:

- "I'm annoyed but not sure why."
- "I'm frustrated but don't want to hurt somebody's feelings."
- "I need to have some of that but don't want to take it all."
- "You really hurt me. Explain it to me."

The objective of this step is to determine the root cause of your reactions. The goal is to separate the emotions from the two selves. Knowing your family role helps you to sort through your reactions. By finding the root cause, you can make a clear choice to follow one path or another.

Here's one example. Let's say somebody has just said something that gets you upset. If you say to yourself, "I'm not mad. I'm just hurt", you aren't clear what is going on emotionally. Fear is winning out, and you are starting to retreat into the cave to lick your wounds. Hurt is the sound of mad/sad colliding into each other. The healthiest response would be to recognize that you are mad and use it to challenge the person in a soft way that attempts to maintain the connection while you solve the problem together.

Here's a second example. If you respond to some request or situation with the self- statement, "I can't do that. It's just not me", you are now confused. While it sounds like the voice of the Authentic Self, it is actually the voice of the Self For Others. How can you say that something is "not you" unless you have considered it or tried it? It is an automatic reaction to a potential threat to act outside your family role. It is the voice of the Self For Others disguised by the reference to a self that sounds authentic.

If the Authentic Self-was really present, both selves would be present, and two different options would exist. You would have the chance to weigh the two options to make a reasoned decision. If there is only one in your mind, then the Authentic Self is being hidden, and you are operating out of the Self For Others. If it really is based on the Authentic Self, you would push the initial reaction aside and evaluate the possibilities. If you go through the discernment process and end up deciding to forego the experience, you can trust it. You have now given it due consideration and made a choice rather than be forced into a choice without any critical review.

Based on the concept of the two selves, you will always have one of two reactions to consider and multiple options to reduce the tensions of those reactions. The easiest path and the one we fall into too often is based on the knee-jerk reaction to fear. This path is the one pre-set by the autopilot of the Self For Others and activated by fear. Fear causes confusion in the mind. In that confusion, the easiest choice is the one that is compatible with the family role. Like in the military, your resort to your training when you are under fire. It is the one that will always feel the most comfortable and assumed to be the right choice. This path was created by your family and is held together by the threat to experience strong negative feelings if you make some choice that conflicts with your family role. You can stay safe and confuse the safe choice for the right choice.

The alternative path feels like it is throwing you right into the pit of guilt and shame. This path has more risk and more fear. It feels like the wrong way to go. This is the path that your authentic reactions push you to follow despite your fear. You know it is the right choice because your natural reason tells you, but there is so much noise generated by the Self For Others that you can easily become confused. Reviewing your repeating patterns and remembering your family role is important to sorting through the disorientation. The more aware you are of your family role and the irrational tugs inside of you, the easier it becomes to ignore your fears and pursue the more dangerous path.

Your partner or trusted friend/family member can act as a double check on your ability to read your emotions. Others can sometimes see your Self For Others kicking in easier than you can see it. Couples in my office will often refer to remarks they make to each other when they perceive that the family is unduly influencing their partner.

Here's what the dialogue sounds like if that is occurring:

- "You change when you are around your family."
- "You tell me one thing and then tell your family the exact opposite."
- "That is not the real you."
- "Be your real self. Be who you are."
- "You're acting just like your mother/father."

If you fly into a rage when the reference is made to your family, you are most likely hiding in your Self For Others. The apple can't fall far from the tree. You can't help but be like your family. They raised you to be like them. If you can't accept that fact, then you aren't being honest with yourself. You are believing that you are different than they are, and denying the strength of the family role. While you may be different in many ways, you also can't help but be more like them than you realize. You are merely avoiding the guilt and shame that comes from the realization that you do the same things that you are angry at them for doing.

Being authentic has nothing to do with your family. Being authentic means doing what is the healthy thing regardless of whether it is the same or different than your family. Learning to listen to your Authentic Self begins with the idea that your Self For Others is a worthy opponent. Your framework shifts. You accept that difficulty and know you operate in the autopilot setting unless you disable it. In other words, you can't help but be more like your family than you are aware. You use others to help you see when you are being like them. Rather than resist the interpretation, you look for it and use it to shift out of that mode. In those moments, your Authentic Self emerges and you have freed yourself from the ties that bind.

Some choices in life are solo decisions that only affect you. That is a rare occurrence. In most situations, another person or multiple people are affected by what you do. In those situations, you need to apply the principle of discernment to others as well as yourself. After reading yourself, you need to read others. You need to identify how a given choice will emotionally affect them and take into account their history and family role requirements. If the description of their emotions doesn't make sense to you, tell them and ask for more information.

One double check to see the right path toward authenticity involves applying the same principles to your partner's reactions as your own. Your partner's reactions contain an element of the truth similar to your own. However, like your own, each person sees only a portion of the truth. Blending the truths together ensures that the "two heads are better than one" process will result in the right answer. This agreement often requires negotiation and compromise, a process that tests the choice against the greater truth that is agreed upon by both parties.

Step Three: REACT

This step is where you make the decision. Now that you have the two paths in front you, you have to make the decision. You now decide between what you want to do, and not what others want you to do. You override the fear and stand up for yourself.

Sometimes, a person freezes at this point. They know the right choice but just can't make themselves act. They feel hopeless to act differently. This is where emotional support from trusted others comes into play. You need validation of the truth from those who know you to help you hold onto your decision and stay the course. You need to lean into others to share the confusion and your worries about how the decision will affect others. The more you process these fears and listen to the reactions of trusted friends or family, the easier it will be to make the decision.

Step Four: **RIDE THE WAVE**

One confusing way to know that you have made the right decision is that there will be a backwash of guilt and shame. Many right decisions will feel wrong, especially after you have made them. There is a period of time after you have made the decision where doubts and fears surface. You second-guess yourself. In that moment, you can't tell if your doubts are telling you that you made the right decision or the wrong decision. If you are filled with doubt and fear, doesn't that mean that you have made a bad decision? Aren't good decisions supposed to feel good?

In fact, most right decisions feel wrong for some brief period of time after you have made the decision. The Self For Others makes a last-ditch stand to flood you with the maximum fear, guilt, and shame. You get hit with an emotional wave that is hard to manage. You have rocked the boat, and now you have to ride the wave. The change you seek is on the other side of that wave.

Fortunately, the one thing about emotional reactions that you can count on is that emotions change over time. They never stay the same. They are either building or receding. You will feel different in 24 hours than you feel right after the decision. It's like riding a wave. The wave will crest at some point and back off. The body and the mind cannot tolerate that level of distress for very long. It seeks equilibrium and will return to a level of comfort in due time. Sometimes it happens very quickly. Sometimes it takes days or weeks. No matter how long it takes, riding the wave will result in the change that your choice created.

Anticipation is crucial to surviving the backlash of emotion created by listening to your Authentic Self. There is nothing you can do to lessen the wave. You can do two things to make the ride a little easier. One, don't fight it. Go for the ride. If you react with statements like, "Why is this happening?" or "I don't know what is wrong with me" or "I feel like I am losing it," you will feed the fear, and it will only get bigger. Know that the ride feels bad and commit to riding it through to the end. Second, practice damage control. Statements like "I should never have done this" make matters worse. Second guessing yourself in the middle of the storm only brings more guilt and shame and makes you want to jump off the ride.

There is no replacement for the benefit of life experience. Each time you ride an emotional wave, you get stronger inside. Your Authentic Self becomes more available. You come to know the enemy within, your family role inside your Self For Others. By facing your doubts and fears over and over again, you learn to ignore the emotions of the Self For Others. You also learn to ignore the pressures from those you love. You change despite the reactions of your parents. You change despite the reactions of siblings and friends, bosses and coworkers. Each time you do this, you strengthen your belief in the truth that comes from following your natural reason.

This ride is not an easy ride. You cannot erase the memories of your past. You flood with emotion each and every time that you try to act differently than how you were raised. I wish I could tell you that the wave gets smaller over time. The reality is that childhood emotion trumps adult emotion every time. The emotional strength of new memory traces can't compare to the strength of the emotions associated with your childhood memories. That is the reality that you need to face to change and maintain that change. The emotional reactions that arise when you consider a different direction are incredibly strong and do not diminish over time. The 60-year-old woman who must confront her 80-year-old mother is as filled with fear as when she was 20 years old and challenging her 40-year-old mother. It remains irrationally big.

If you can prepare yourself for the size of that wave, you can get better at riding it. Riding the wave tests your capacity for change. It tests the strength of your commitment to yourself. The key is to anticipate the wave. If you are surprised by the level of emotion, you can get lost in doubt and fear and resort to what feels comfortable. If you know how the ride feels and the amount of time it takes to have it rise and fall, you won't panic. You will give it the time it requires and stay the course.

Change is a process that builds over time and can go backward at any point. It is dynamic, changing in one direction or another throughout your life. But let's be clear what I am saying about change. You are not being asked to change your basic nature. Your basic personality structure, your genetic talents reflected in your temperament, your cognitive style, your defensive style, and your emotional and intellectual intelligence will not change. You can change your response to your history. You can learn to doubt the doubts. The good news is that it gets easier as you remake your personal relationships. The bad news is that the old fears never entirely go away. However, you can get better and better at facing your fears and choosing the path that is authentic rather than the one that feels easiest.

As you become more emotionally honest and independent, change begins to happen. It is subtle and soft. It is not loud and brash. It is a change that begins in your own mind, to choose to listen to a different part of yourself, your real self. You push back, and people respond differently to you. You don't give them a choice. The dependent path that enables other people's needs to matter more than yours is no longer available. The new path becomes mutual, or you choose to go it alone. When you do, others want to join with you. The change becomes contagious.

SMALL CHANGES ARE BIG CHANGES

Real change starts small. It doesn't begin in your town hall or in Washington, DC. It begins within yourself and your family. It begins by challenging your family role- learning to be different within your family before you expect yourself to be different in the world. You have to change the blueprint at home before you can bring something different to the world. If you don't change at home first, then anybody who can evoke the same childhood fears will have the same ability to control you as your parents did when you were a child. While you may physically leave your family, you take them with you. They are inside of you living in your Self For Others. If you don't know how to manage your inside world, you will not be able to stand up for yourself in the outside world. You may be able to achieve a measure of independence in business or superficial relationships, but you will remain dependent at your core, being controlled by the reactions of others in your love relationships.

The legacy of the Founding Fathers was a belief in mankind that every man, woman, and child was born with natural reason and had natural rights. Their dream is your emotional inheritance from them, needing to be reinforced every day in every relationship that you have. A freedom loving people can only be as strong as the collective experiences of thousands of people who each day embrace their freedoms, practice the right to dissent and embrace their righteous anger in every relationship that they have. Every free person needs to practice independence and equality in their closest personal relationships to practice what they preach every day and in every way. Each time you cut the ties that bind, there is a ripple effect throughout all your relationships. You build a stronger self, a more lasting marriage, a healthier family and a stronger nation. With each missed opportunity to practice the values of equality and freedom, the person gets weakened, and the opportunity to affect others gets reduced. With each opportunity that is seized, the person gets stronger, and independence for all is reinforced. It is built or destroyed one reaction at a time.

Well begun is half done ...
Aristotle

Based on 35 years of clinical experience, Dr. Stephen R. Van Schoyck introduces a novel paradigm designed to understand yourself and others in a completely new way. Up to now, mental health experts have explained human behavior in terms of good and bad, character traits and self-destructive instincts. Dr. Van Schoyck introduces a new psychology based on natural reason and survival instincts that make sense of what people do.

Essentially, you have been taught to be afraid of your emotions and lose the capacity to be who you want to be in your relationships. Without the ability to read your emotions and be your authentic self, you can't tell the difference between who you are and what you were told to be. You learn to recognize and listen to natural emotions rather than learned emotions that represent the family within. Anger becomes your best friend and the antidote to fear. Trusting your fighting spirit replaces self-doubt.

Dr. Van Schoyck introduces the Delphi Process that teaches you to make decisions despite doubt and fear. Using this method, you learn to use emotions to represent who you really are. Your reward is independent and emotionally honest relationships that support and reflect your authentic self. You become a better partner, parent, friend, and sibling.

This revolutionary approach has been developed over 65,000 hours of face-to-face contact with his patients. The concepts in the book are told through the countless stories of real life people suffering with real life problems. You will see your own emotions and recognize your real self through the eyes of their experiences and learn what they have learned to live a healthier life.

Dr. Stephen R. Van Schoyck has a private practice in Newtown, Pennsylvania. He earned his B.A. from Princeton University in 1975 and graduated from the University of Cincinnati in 1984 with a Ph.D. in Clinical Psychology. He lives in Langhorne, PA with his wife of 45 years and several dogs. They have four grown adult children and six grandchildren.

Visit Dr. Van Schoyck's website at:
https://drvanschoyck.com/

Made in the USA
Middletown, DE
24 September 2019